# Zee Bees

A Historical Memoir by
by
Robert E. Osmon

Powerful Publisher LLC
Virginia Beach, Virginia

Published by:

**P**owerful **P**ublisher, LLC

2317 Broad Bay Road, Suite 17
Virginia Beach, Virginia 23451

Web Site: powerfulpublisher.com

Library of Congress Control Number: 2007929003

International Standard Book Number (ISBN):
09769773-5-4

PRINTING HISTORY
Printed in the United States of America
First Edition, 1st Printing

Dedicated to
Coach Evan G. Ellis, Jr.
"Our Coach"

And to the
Coaches of the 1951-1954 Zee Bees,
The 1954 Zee Bee Football Team,
and their Fans.

# Forward

This book is the true story of a young boy growing up in a highly religious, football minded, small Midwestern town; how he recovered from a serious illness through his personal resolve to play football; his conflicts with a stern, unrelenting football coach with whom he had a hate/love relationship; the relationship with his best friend which forged an unbreakable bond that helped to build a championship team; and an unheralded football team that defied the odds to win its school's first championship setting a record that still stands 50 years later.

I have written this as a dynamic narrative, that is, a narrative with reconstructed conversations. These conversations are not accurate as history; but are accurate in terms of "telling the story". The story is "as I remember it"; as accurate as I can make it.

I would like to thank some people who have assisted me in the writing of this book; all the members of the 1954 ZB football team whose character and accomplishments inspired me to write this book; Coach Joe Rushforth for his continued friendship and encouragement, and for supplying me with his treasure of photos from Zion's first team back in 1941; Dru Ellis Deering, the fifth and youngest daughter of Coach Evan Ellis, for making a huge effort to dig out photos and information about her Dad's life long before he arrived at Zion Benton High School; Lonnie Bible, the present Athletic Director at ZBTHS, for his effort in locating old yearbooks and providing me with scores, Zee Bee logos, and photos of my ZBTHS as I remember it in 1954; and last but not least, Dr. Robert Powers, USNA '60, who with a firm yet gentle hand guided me to grow from an undisciplined, amateurish writer into an author capable of creating a narrative of the quality to be worthy of publishing.

Robert E. "Moose" Osmon
Author

# Acknowledgement

I am grateful for the many friends I had during my four years at Zion Benton High School. The limitations of space and the need for good story telling would not allow me to include everyone in my book who was part of my life during that period. However, I would like to recognize those classmates whom I remember as good friends and who supported me, the team, and the school making my experience there one of my fondest memories. Without them, my inspiration to tell this story would not have existed.

Jo Carolyn Anderson
Anita Beall
Pat Blagg
Jessica Bonner
Al Bricco
Leo Brown
David Buer
Marvin Cliff
Danny Crain
Porter Derrington
Pat Dreyer
Randy Dunn
Hardy Evans
Nellie Funderburk
Sally Grulke
Dorothy Heathcote
Phil Hoppe
Roger Hotham
Ralph Johnson
Al Krapf
Jack Marshall
Leona Maynard
Leroy McCormack
Mike Mintern
Earl Needles
Don Noren

Viviene Ashland
Linda Bingley
Gerry Bohn
Gerry Boyd
Gayleene Brown
Ralph Buckley
Bill Butcher
Bill Cooprider
Donna Depew
Carol Draudt
Bobby Dreyer
Don Evans
Wayne Friedel
Cece Gaydosh
Nancy Hanks
Pat Holcomb
Jean Hosken
Sandy Jacobs
Bill Kennedy
Donna Luther
Carol Maynard
Bettye McAdams
Donna McGarrahan
Maryann Neahous
Bill Nelson
Tom Oatsvall

Emily Perez
Fred Ray
Barbara Ruffalo
Caroline Sanchez
Ron Schroeder
Lynn Shumaker
Dave Suttie
Camille Taylor
Ed Townsley
Alma Jean Warren

Louis Pontillo
Delores Riggs
Patsy Russel
Gerry Satler
Eleanor Sexton
Diana Smith
Ann Taylor
Careen Taylor
Nancy Verne
Ken Wise

**********

Coach Ellis (in overcoat)
with
Assistant Coach Rushforth

# Chapter 1
# The Coach

As I walked slowly into the hospital in Highland Park, Illinois, I couldn't help but observe what a beautiful day was in the offing. It was late October 1971. The leaves were in full color now. Beautiful gold and orange! This was a time when high school football games were nearing the end of the season. The day had that crisp, clean football feel and smell. The kind that made my heart beat with renewed enthusiasm and caused my steps to be a lot more brisk than normal, even though more than a decade had passed since the last time I put on my shoulder pads. It was that kind of day!

I said to myself, "Boy, Coach Ellis would really like to get out into this weather and have at us. I can see that cocky sneer on his face, his arrogant stance, and hear his grating, irritating voice now."

"Get your butts going! What's wrong with all of you? Are we building a football team here or a bunch of old grannies?" he would bellow. And then he would see something funny in it all and let out his patented "Ho! Ho! Ho!" with his upper teeth projecting well over his lower ones in kind of a buck tooth look. A real Santa Claus laugh! "Moose, is that the fastest you can run? My God, we'll be lucky to score a touchdown the entire season."

I cringed uncontrollably at the mere thought of his voice. But then I couldn't help but laugh. All these years later I could finally see the humor in at all. I could clearly picture Coach and our team, the Zee Bees, in the school's maroon and white colors. What a great team we had! And what a price the coach made us pay to have it!

But the smile that crept slowly over my face with that thought was quickly erased. The reason I was at the hospital had nothing to do with football. The night before, Coach's wife, Dru, called me at home in Wisconsin.

"Bob," she said somberly and with obvious tears in her voice, "Evan is dying. The doctors have told me his time is imminent."

I knew Evan was very ill, but this news slammed me like a hammer.

"I....I want to see him one more time," I blurted out emotionally.

"The cancer has... totally taken over his body. If you want to see him alive one more time, you'd better come quickly." Her voice quivered and I could hear her sorrow.

"What hospital is he in right now?"

"The city hospital in Highland Park. Do you know where it is?" she asked.

"No, but we played Highland Park way back when we were sophomores. I'll find it. Be strong, Dru. I'll get there as fast as I can," I tried to assure her confidently.

## The Hospital

I had no idea at that time what imminent meant, but it sounded darkly foreboding. I immediately made reservations in a motel in Highland Park, packed up a suitcase with personal items including my old scrapbook and school yearbook, and off I went. Because of my very late arrival that night, I decided to get some sleep and make my trip to the hospital early the next morning.

The hospital had an ominous look as I stood in front of it. I had no idea what to expect. I never visited anyone dying of cancer before. "What do I say? What do I do? How do I act?" I said to myself out loud. "What does one say to a dying cancer patient that would ease his way into his transition from this earth? I have no experience in these matters. Maybe I shouldn't have come."

The moment that thought crossed my mind, I immediately chastised myself. "You wimp, Osmon. Here Coach is dying and you want to run away like a scared little kid. Get yourself together and act like a man," I told myself sternly.

So I lowered my head and prayed, "Dear Lord, I don't know what to say or do, so I ask you to guide me. Show me the reason you brought me here at this time. Help me to be a candle in Coach's life for the time he has left on this earth."

Feeling more calm and confident, I took a deep breath, and headed up the steps into the main lobby. My eyes took a quick sweep around the room looking for the Patient Information Desk so I could find the Coach's room number and be told how to get there. Suddenly I heard a voice that I couldn't have mistaken in a hundred years. I had heard it thousands of times before.

"Moose. I'm over here." The voice called out in a weakened and fragile manner, yet with a force of conviction.

The sight that awaited me almost brought me to tears right on the spot. There he was! Coach Evan Ellis! The man, who for four years screamed at me, threatened me, intimidated me, taught me, nicknamed me, encouraged me, disgusted me, and infuriated me. But he did not look like the Coach I remembered. It was the image of someone else.

Instead of the strong, vibrant, healthy and dynamic coach of my high school days, there stood a frail, sallow, cheek sunken and emaciated man. He wore one of those white hospital bed frocks that everyone wears that attaches in the back. From underneath this frock extended two skinny, fragile looking arms and two withered legs. I fought back the tears. Yet in spite of his physical condition, the twinkle in his eye was definitely there and the animation on his face looked as if he was getting ready to crack one of his gross jokes.

"You're just in time," he said to me with enthusiasm. "Dru told me this morning you'd be coming...I've been waiting." In his hands he held two small ankle weights, the kind used for physical therapy.

"Hey, Coach. You still working out?" I asked, trying to assume a cheerful manner.

"Damn right! Football season will be rolling around again before I know it, and I want to be ready. So you can help me get my workout this morning. Come here and strap these weights on for me," he ordered.

"Coach, you're always ready," I said laughingly.

Conflicting thoughts raced through my mind. "Did I miss something last night? Didn't Dru tell me Evan's demise was imminent? If so, what the hell is he doing out here in the lobby with ankle weights when he should be in bed conserving every bit of energy he has?" I asked myself. "Haven't the doctors told him the truth? Was he possibly not aware that he hadn't long to live? If so, I certainly am not going to be the one who tells him."

Numbly, without saying a word, I walked over to his chair, stooped down, and fastened the ankle weights to each of his shrunken legs. This is crazy, I thought, but what else can I do? I know Coach and if this is what he wants, no one in this hospital is going to stop him. If he chooses to work out with weights, then by God we are going to work out with weights.

"Okay, Coach. The weights are set. What now?" I asked with a concerned waiver in my voice.

"Well, now we start our workout. You look like you could use a little exercise yourself," he guffawed in the manner with which I had become so accustomed.

"Hey, I can still run the ball. Wanna see 'Moose up the Gut'?" I asked laughingly.

"We scored a lot of points on that play, didn't we?"

"We sure did, Coach."

"The nurses think I'm crazy for doing this, but what the hell do they know? They've never played football," he snorted knowing I would understand.

Evan took my arm and in a very slow, but deliberate shuffle we started down the hallway. It was a fairly long hall, and I doubted we would even make it to the end one time. But as I have learned over my 70 years of life on this planet, when there is a will, the spirit can totally dominate the body. The coach's strong will dominated his weak body. Up and down the corridor we went, slowly, carefully, but persistently. As we passed by other patients and their visitors, they turned to look at us with an awed expression. A frail coach and his former player providing physical support. I found myself wanting to scream at the other people in the hall and lobby.

14

"Do you realize this man is dying of cancer with only days left to live? Look what he is doing!! He's not wallowing in his grief! He's exulting in the life he has left. The best way he knows how! By preparing himself for the next football season," I mumbled to myself as we shuffled along.

Finally after about six trips up and down the hall, Coach said to me, "Moose, I think I'm getting a little tired. Maybe we should head for my room."

I took off the ankle weights and gently steered him toward his room. As we arrived, the nurses came to our assistance and helped place him into his bed. They fussed over him for a while as I stood back knowing this was not my venue. One of the nurses gave him a sleeping pill and a small glass of water.

Before he slipped off into a painless state of being, the Coach gave me a look of shared confidence and said, "Moose, the doctors told me I only have a few days to live. So I told them that if this was truly so, then I was going to spend my last few days the way I wanted. And I want to live these last few days as if I am going to coach one more season. How wonderful that you're here to help me prepare!"

"I'll be there to play fullback for you, Coach. We'll kick butt!"

With that he slipped down into his bed. "305 Buck. 'Moose up the Gut'!" he softly chortled.

As the pill and fatigue began to take over, he asked in a fading voice "Moose, do you remember those good old days? The days when we won Zion's first championship?"

"I do, Coach. I do," I answered as if in a trance, tears streaming to my eyes.

As I continued to stare at this man who had totally intimidated me for four years, I couldn't help but think what a role reversal this situation had become. I was now the strong person, full of health and vibrancy, experiencing the joys of life: career, family, financial success. And he was the helpless, feeble, weakened man. Weakened long before his chronological age would normally call for it.

How had it come to this? How did this relationship develop such that I would be here at this time? How had he helped me to grow as a young man so that I was now enjoying the benefits of success? I leaned back and started to let my mind slowly grasp the import of what was going on in this room at this time. How did this all start? Slowly, thoughts that long ago subsided in my mind began to surface and their emergence began to bring back memories as vivid as if they all happened yesterday.

## Eighth Grade – Central School

This story really started while I was still in eighth grade at Central Junior High School in Zion, Illinois, a small town on the banks of Lake Michigan a few miles south of the Wisconsin State Line and about 50 miles north of Chicago. When my Mother and Father divorced in 1939, my Mother and I moved to 2116 Enoch Avenue, directly across from the high school. I attended Lakeview Elementary School from grades kindergarten through seventh and was looking forward to being the big man on campus at Lakeview during eighth grade year.

But life doesn't always work the way one wishes. The Zion School System built a junior high school right in the middle of town and mandated that all Zion school children in 7th and 8th grade would attend. Lakeview students were scheduled to attend in their 8th grade year while students from Elmwood and Central Elementary Schools started at Central Junior High the year before as 7th graders. They already made close friends and were part of established groups by the time we arrived.

Because I performed well academically at Lakeview and was one of the better athletes, I brought with me my own group of friends. While I was definitely disappointed I was not going to be able to spend my last year at Lakeview, I intended to study hard, play football, basketball, and baseball, and prepare myself for high school football, my real love. So I was not too concerned about fitting in. Again, life doesn't always work the way one wishes.

On the first day of school, I immediately signed up for the school's football team. Practice started that very night. Zion was not a wealthy town, so the school did not have a very big budget with which to work. Thus, we did not play tackle football with pads and cleats, but rather played flag football in tennis shoes and jerseys issued for games only. We practiced in our street clothes on a gravel covered parking lot.

Because flag football is based primarily on speed and quickness, two traits that the good Lord saw fit not to give me, it was rather obvious that the best I could hope for was to become a lineman and probably only on offense. It was not really the position I desired, but I knew that it would be better to play as a lineman than not to play at all. So I made the best of the situation and was selected for the team as the starting right tackle on offense. I was pleased to be starting, but in my heart I knew I really wanted to be a fullback when I got to high school.

We played the first game in late September, and Central beat Waukegan Junior High School. I played very well and the coach was pleased with my effort. I came home that night and told my Mom, "We won! And I'm on the starting team."

As mothers are prone to do, she responded, "That's nice, dear. I hope you didn't get hurt! What would you like for dinner?" She prepared a juicy steak which was fine with me.

Afterwards I felt a little tired and achy. Of course, I assumed it was all from the game I had played earlier. "Mom, I don't feel too well. I think I'll hit the sack early."

"Okay, son. You can skip your studies for this one night," she agreed.

The next morning I woke up in great pain. My Mother worked at the Johns Manville manufacturing plant in Waukegan and left every morning at 5:30 AM in her car pool, so I was home alone. I was convinced it was simply sore muscles from the game the day before. I was having so much trouble moving, I decided to stay home from school. I soaked in the bath tub several times hoping that would ease the pain, but to no avail. As the day wore on, the pain got worse. I began to realize something was drastically wrong. By the time my Mother arrived home around 4 PM, I was in agony and had tears in my eyes.

"Robert, what's wrong?" my Mother asked anxiously as she came in the door.

"I don't know, Mom. But I hurt something fierce. Please do something," I begged.

My Mother immediately ran next door to a neighbor who owned a car and asked that he take us to the doctor in downtown Zion. Dr. Kalem's office was upstairs in the Bicket Building located downtown on 27th and Sheridan Road. I was in such pain that I crawled up the stairs on my hands and knees to get to his waiting room on the second floor. Dr. Kalem took one look at me and immediately called the ambulance. Before I knew it, I was headed south on Sheridan Road on my way to the Victory Memorial Hospital in Waukegan, the same hospital in which I had been born 13 years before and hadn't entered since.

After extensive tests and drawing blood from me several times, the hospital staff could finally tell me something. "Robert," the attending doctor said solemnly, "you have rheumatic fever. With a little luck we may have gotten you here in time to stop any serious damage to your heart, but you'll need to spend at least two months with us here in the hospital while we monitor your progress."

My first thoughts were about football. "So this means I'm done playing football for this season?" I asked anxiously, hoping I hadn't heard correctly.

"Not only football," he replied quietly, "but you are banned from all sports for at least a year."

"What!" I exclaimed in anguish. "No! No way! My life is sports."

Like any teen age boy whose plans to play sports are suddenly wiped out by an injury or an illness, I wondered how the Lord could do this to me. "Why me, God? This was to be my glory year and now I have nothing. How unfair! No football! No basketball! No glory! Nothing!"

"Robert," the doctor said sympathetically, "you'd better plan to get used to the idea of not playing sports. Many men afflicted with this disease end up in a wheelchair for the rest of their lives."

I was absolutely devastated. My spirits were at the bottom of the barrel.

But then out of all this discouraging tragedy came a glimmer of hope! Recently a new drug was discovered that fights rheumatic fever. It was made available to me immediately on a trial basis. After the doctor had a long discussion with my Mother making her realize there were no guarantees this new drug would work, she recognized the pain I was in and gave permission to the doctors to try it. Her decision dramatically affected the rest of my life.

Beulah Myrle and Bob Osmon

Rheumatic fever is a disease that attacks the heart and leaves the victim helpless and often gasping for air. It also can create damage to the nervous system, particularly in the extremities. But since the drug was administered to me so soon after my first attack, the doctors felt they saved the better part of my heart and with luck I would end up with only a slight murmur. Only time would tell to the extent of the nerve damage.

I was told that at the end of my two months in the hospital I would have to remain at home for the rest of the semester and then only go to school three times a week. A specialist came in from Chicago and confirmed the diagnosis. He told me that I might not ever be able to play sports again.

My immediate reaction to that terrible news was, "So why live? Am I supposed to lie around in a bed for the rest of my life? This really stinks!" I spit out nastily. I had never felt such an overwhelming sense of bleakness in my life.

"This new drug is really supposed to work well," my Mom said hopefully.

"Yeah, right, Mom! Let's all stand up and cheer," I answered sarcastically. I wanted out of the bed and back on the football field.

But my Mom stayed positive about the new drug and every day it was administered to me in hopes it could bring this disease to an end before any real damage to my heart took place.

The days in the hospital dragged on. My Mom got my homework assignments from the school which I breezed through. I read tons of books from the library, many well beyond a normal eighth grader's realm. One of the most challenging books I read was The Last Days of Pompeii. And I read that one twice. (Interestingly, many years later I was stationed in Naples, Italy and had the occasion to visit Pompeii many times. The memory of lying in that hospital bed reading this particular book came back quite vividly each time I visited.)

I also played numerous board games with the volunteer nurses: Checkers, Monopoly, and Chess. The games were great for the mind if not for the body. Finally, a few days before Christmas, it was time for me to go home. I definitely was feeling better. A few weeks before I started walking slowly up and down the halls, so my legs were starting to regain some strength. The doctors said I made an excellent recovery, probably due to my high level of fitness before the attack happened. "But," they said, "You still need to take it easy for a long time."

I stayed at home during the months of December and January. Many of my Lakeview friends came by to wish me well. They told me what was going on at Central, but frankly I really didn't care too much about it at the time. It was no fun to be on the outside looking in.

In February I was finally allowed to go back to school. Since we had no car and I was not in the school bus pick up zone, I had no choice but to walk to school, a distance of about a mile. Not a large distance under normal conditions, but since I was recovering from rheumatic fever, it was a daunting task to say the least. Again, drawing on my almost 70 years of experience, I have come to understand that what does not kill you makes you stronger. The walk to and from school each day was the beginning of my recovery. My legs and heart got stronger every day, little by little.

As I suspected, new friendships and alliances had been drawn at school. But my Lakeview friends welcomed me back enthusiastically.

Paul Jackola was my best friend at Lakeview and was an excellent athlete. He was a strong, well built blonde haired boy with a ready smile and a heavy Northern Wisconsin type accent. The two of us played sports together since the fourth grade when Paul first came to Lakeview. He never had a lot to say, but when he did, it was worth listening to.

Paul worked with cars and cycles from the time we first met. He owned a bright red Cushman motor scooter that was the envy of everyone in school. Riding around town on the back of that scooter was always a big treat for me. He sought me out on my first day back and said, "Bob, we sure have missed you. Sorry you didn't get to play football and basketball with us. Maybe next year."

"I hope so, but right now the doc is not saying one way or another. And this year even baseball is out for me," I replied forlornly.

"Hey, don't give up hope. We're going to need you on our freshmen football team next year." With that comment he punched me in the shoulder and gave me a big smile.

Finally, in May near the end of the second semester, Dr. Kalem gave me news that set my spirits flying. "Robert," he said with a small smile in his voice, "your body has handled this disease so well that I am going to allow you to start exercising. No basketball, football, or running, but you can start in with exercises. Don't expect to see miracles. Go slowly, but, yes, you can start. I need to monitor your heart very closely. If there is any sign of a murmur or deterioration, I will tell you to stop."

Of course, I never heard the last part. The very next day after school I was in the gym doing sit-ups, pull ups, pushups, and trying to climb the rope hanging from the ceiling. Anything to make myself stronger. While Dr. Kalem said nothing about playing football next year, my imagination heard him say it might be possible. That was all the incentive I needed.

After several weeks of doing these exercises each afternoon after school with a determined and dogged discipline, a slim, handsome young man walked up to me, introduced himself, and asked why I was doing all these exercises. I explained that I was ill all year long and therefore not able to play any sports. I added that I wanted to play football for Zion Benton High School next year, so I knew I had a long way to go to get ready by next fall.

He told me, "I wanna play football for Zion next year too. How's about us working out together? Then maybe next fall we'll end up as teammates. Waddya think?"

"Hey, that'd be great. It's boring doing these exercises every afternoon by myself," I answered excitedly. I knew this young man to be one of the more popular boys in school and was surprised that he would want to work out with me. Little did I know then, but this interested and caring classmate would become my best friend and inseparable companion during all four of my years in high school.

## Loren Stried

My new friend and I were the only ones left in the gym at Central as most students already left for home.

"Thanks for working out with me," I said to this young man who had offered his time in a welcomed display of friendship. "My name is Bob Osmon."

"I'm Loren Stried," he replied with a friendly smile and offered his hand to me.

From the moment I shook his hand, I knew we would be good friends. What good fortune it turned out to be for me!

Loren was then and still is one of those down to earth, solid citizens. An honorable, loyal, and friendly individual who makes the world a better place in which to live. He was slender in build, athletic, and handsome in looks. He was popular with everyone, especially the girls. (I always figured that would be good for me if girls were always hanging around him.) He had a pleasant way that exuded warmth and kindness. He ran mink lines in the marshy area between Lake Michigan and the bluffs of Zion and sold the pelts to earn spending money. He also hunted pheasants for food and shot crows for their bounty.

Loren's Mom and Dad were members of the Christian Catholic Church, the church which was established by Dr. John Alexander Dowie. Dr. Dowie was an immigrant from Australia who served God as a divine healer, making sure that everyone knew that his power came from God and not himself. He had a huge following in Chicago and in 1901 made the move from Chicago to northeast Illinois, buying up large tracts of land and naming his city Zion, the Beautiful City of God. He also brought with him a number of industries which included the Zion Lace Factory from England and a cookie factory which became famous for its Zion Fig Bars and Zion Chocolate Chip Cookies. These industries provided the income for church members who came to Zion to earn a living. In addition, farming abounded all around.

The Seals of Zion

The church was officially named The Zion Christian Catholic Church which had nothing to do with the Roman Catholic Church. The term Catholic in this case meant universal. They had very strong beliefs. No alcohol, no smoking, no eating of pork. They also didn't believe in doctors or drugs. I hoped the differences between our two religions would not become an issue between Loren and me. After what I recently went through, I strongly believed in both drugs and the doctors who administer them.

My parents were Methodists. My Grandmother came to Zion in 1917 as a member of the Christian Catholic Church and remained so for all her life. My Mother grew up in the church, but when my Mom and Dad married, my Mother switched to the Methodist Church...probably to appease my Dad.

Dad was an honorable man and a highly respected businessman among the citizens of Zion. But he was not particularly religious. My Mother was a strong and pious woman with an outgoing personality that knew no strangers. She was deeply religious in her personal beliefs and insisted I be brought up with a strong respect for God. Neither my Mother nor Father drank alcohol, but my Dad liked to occasionally smoke cigars. Guess our differences could be a lot worse than this, I thought.

"So what position do you want to play next year?" I asked curiously.

Loren replied enthusiastically, "I want to be the quarterback. I think it's exciting to call the plays and make decisions on who should carry the ball. How about you?"

"Fullback. I've always wanted to play in the backfield. My older brother Carl was a fullback for Zion and I want to be just like him."

"You look big enough to be a fullback."

"Yeah... I wasn't fast enough to play in the backfield in flag football, but maybe I can make it in tackle football," I responded hopefully.

"I think you can... if you work out enough."

"Waddya say we keep working out together... maybe we can both get to play the positions we want next year?"

"Let's do it," replied Loren confidently.

Once again we shook each other's hand in a firm and knowing manner. The friendship had begun.

We continued to work out religiously every single afternoon after school until we were all dismissed for summer vacation in the middle of June. Several nights a week Paul joined in with us when he wasn't working on cars at home. Paul and Loren played on both the football and basketball teams together, so they already knew each other rather well.

"I want to play for Zion next year too," stated Paul firmly. "I'll probably be a tackle."

"Next week is Orientation Day at the high school," I told them both. "We'll have a chance to sign up for football then."

"Good! Let's all do it together," Paul proposed.

On the day of orientation after all the endless presentations regarding majors and minors, it was finally announced that those desiring to play football next year should meet with Head Coach Joe Rushforth in the boy's gym. The three of us grabbed a seat in the front row of the bleachers so we wouldn't miss anything.

Joe Rushforth looked like a military man... neat, trim and strong. He was not a huge man... but he was well built. Veins bulged from his muscled arms. He had the reputation of being a "nice guy"... but we also heard that he was demanding and tough as nails. So, we were in awe of the man as we gathered to listen to him.

"Boys, we here at Zion look forward to having you as part of our program next year," Coach Rushforth began with encouragement in his voice. "Zion has been building its program slowly and we think we will have some very good teams over the next few years. Hopefully some of you will help us in that effort."

After a few more comments, he asked each of us to stand up and introduce ourselves. When it came to me, I stood and said, "Bob Osmon."

"Oh, Bob, I know who you are. Your brother Carl played on the same team with me in 1940, Zion's first," acknowledged Coach Rushforth with a smile. "If you're half as good as he was, we'll be very happy to have you on our teams."

I gulped. I hadn't expected this. I didn't want to tell him about my illness and that I may not even be able to play come fall because of it. So I mumbled, "Yes, sir." And sat down.

"So, you've got an in with the Head Coach," teased Paul as the three of us walked out of the gym together. "Must be nice."

"Come on Guys, my Brother was great... I'm not looking to be a star. I just want to make the team."

As the three of us parted at the end of the school year, we all agreed to keep up our workouts all summer long. Little did we know then, but this promise between the three of us was the start of a pact that would grow to include others and have results which we could never envision at the time.

## The Dream Begins

I was standing outside on my front lawn smelling the purple lilac tree in our yard that bloomed each spring and emitted a delectable aroma that permeated our house. I was contemplating what I had to do to prepare myself for the coming fall season.

My legs were still not back to normal when summer vacation began. Walking to school and back was good for my legs to slowly strengthen them, but I knew that during the summer I had to get them back into shape for running. The distance from my home to the Lake Michigan waterfront was exactly one mile. So I made my goal to build myself up to the point where I could run down to the waterfront and back to my house without stopping by the end of summer.

Two miles of daily running shouldn't be too tough, I thought naively. That should get me ready for my first tackle football season.

The day after school let out for the summer I decided it was time to start. I rolled out of bed, put on my tennies, and charged outside. A nice balmy, sunny Illinois day was breaking and the flowers were in full bloom. The smell of the lilacs in our front yard buoyed my spirits.

"What a great day to start," I said to myself in a state of confidence. "This shouldn't be too hard."

I took off running north along Enoch Avenue in a modest loping stride. By the time I reached the corner of Highway 173, exactly one block away, I was gasping for air. I plodded to a stop and thought, whoa!! This isn't going to be as easy as I imagined. I'll never make it to the lakefront this way. How in heck am I going to do this?

After giving it much thought, I decided I would run as far as I could in spite of the pain in my legs and lungs and then walk until I got my breath back. Somehow I made it down to Sheridan Road using this method, a distance of about four blocks. I had to walk all the way back home. There was no way I could run any more.

My body hurt all over. My lungs, my legs, and my head all pounded. I took a long, hot bath and plopped back into the sack, sleeping half the day away. When I awoke, everything ached. How terribly discouraging! I decided I needed some kind of inspiration, or I would never get out of bed and put myself through this pain again the next morning. So as I lay there I gave some deep thought as to why I wanted to play football for Zion Benton so much .

First of all, my older brother Carl was an outstanding football player on Zion's very first team in 1940. The only schools in Zion up to then were run by the Christian Catholic Church and they did not have a football program. Many of the high school age boys, including my two older brothers, and girls went to Waukegan High School in Waukegan, Illinois about ten miles south toward Chicago. Over the years Waukegan developed many outstanding football teams and players. An example of the latter was Otto Graham, an All American quarterback at Northwestern and later an All Star Pro with the Cleveland Browns.

My elder brother Orval played the center position for Otto Graham when they both played for the Waukegan Bulldogs. He often held me in rapt attention as he regaled me with the stories of the great teams he played on at Waukegan. He also told me how proud he would be of me if I played football someday.

When a public high school in Zion was established in 1939, it included the Township of Benton which bordered Zion on three sides. Thus the school was officially named Zion-Benton Township High School, ZBTHS. From these initials came the unique name for our mascot, Zee Bees. There is no other mascot like it in Illinois, the nation or maybe even the world. The shouts of "Zee Bees! Zee Bees! Sting'em! Sting'em" became such a well known cheer throughout the State of Illinois that it clearly identified us as being from Zion Benton everywhere we played. I was proud of our school...and its cheer.

In the first year of football competition, using some players that played at Waukegan and some who never played before in their lives, Zion beat many good teams posting a 5-2 record. They lost to Lake Forest, the Lake County Champion, by only one touchdown.

Zion' First Team - 1940
Second Row; Paul, T. Ray Miller, Carl Osmon, Neal, St. Germain, Erickson, Joe Rushforth, Sattler, Chapman, La Belle, Liddle, Gallaugher.
First Row; Gallaugher, Ken Johnson, Turner, Ballegooyen, McCarrel, Owen, Wright, Owen

My brother Carl played both offensive and defensive end on this first team and for years afterwards I heard often what a wonderful a player he was.

"Robert, your Brother played with the ferociousness of a lion and was as tough as nails. As a defensive end on Zion's first team, he crushed runners in their tracks," friends of the family would tell me. "He played fullback on the team the following year. He could pound into the line like a bull dozer."

So over the years I developed a strong desire to be like my older brothers. I wanted them to be very proud that I followed in their footsteps as outstanding football players.

Additionally, one of my cousins, Leland Noll, was valedictorian of Zion's first graduating class in 1940. He also wrote the school song. It was an original score and the words reflected a special loyalty and sense of patriotism that permeated most high schools throughout the Midwest at that time. The words of the school song are still prominently displayed at the new Horizon

Campus Zion High School on the wall of the school cafeteria. It goes like this:

*"Hoorah for Zion!*
*We know you're trying!*
*To bring us all to victory!*
*We know you're loyal, through all your toil!*
*To good old ZBT! Rah! Rah! Rah!*
*Throughout the ages!*
*We'll sing your praises!*
*As you fight on for your name!*
*We've got a rooter, in every village!*
*To bring us All American, All American, All American*
*fame!!!!"*

So early on my family made a significant impression on the history of Zion Benton High School and I felt strongly that somehow I too wanted to add my mark.

But secondly and even more so from an emotional point of view, I grew up right across the street from the high school. From kindergarten through seventh grade I walked past the high school every single day on the way to Lakeview. And I lived or died with the fortunes of the Zee Bee football team.

Whenever Zion had a Friday night game, my neighborhood pals Ronnie, Donnie, and David Myrum and I watched the first half through the fence of the football field. The gates opened after the end of the first half and we scampered in free.

We played a game of touch football in the end zone trying to emulate our heroes while the teams had their halftime break. When the teams came back on the field for the second half, we went up in the stands and screamed our lungs out for the Maroon and White.

Zion had many good teams over the years and numerous outstanding players, but somehow none of them brought home a championship. As a young boy sitting in those stands listening to the cheering crowds and the enthusiastic singing of "Hurrah for Zion", I knew that I desperately wanted to play football for the Zee Bees someday.

"How great it would be if I could make the team and be able to wear a Zee Bee uniform. Even more exciting, how wonderful it would be if somehow I could play on a team that wins the championship. Wouldn't that make my Brothers proud? It would be an accomplishment I could cherish all my life," I cried out loudly in my wild daydream.

Suddenly I realized I had my inspiration. All I had to do was to keep remembering I came from a family of football players and that I too wanted to make my mark on the history of Zion Benton High School football. That would be enough to inspire me each day.

The next morning I was at the running again and every morning all week long. Each time I made it only one block before stopping. But I began to notice that my recovery time was becoming less and less. I could start to run again with a shorter time to recuperate. By Monday of the following week I made it two blocks before stopping. By the end of the month I ran all the way to Sheridan Road, about four blocks from home before I needed a rest.

By the end of July, I ran all the way to the lakefront without a single stop. Finally about the middle of August, my legs were much stronger, and my lungs were able to intake oxygen at the rate I needed. One day it finally happened. I ran the entire distance to the waterfront and back to my home without stopping. My sense of elation was unbounded! I did it!

Keeping in mind my Brothers and how proud they would be of me and how proud I would be to wear the Maroon and White did the trick. Any man can conquer his biggest weaknesses with the right motivation. And just in time. Fall football practice started in one more week.

## Medical Exam

I was sitting in our kitchen thinking about how I would do in football in the fall when my Mom arrived home from her job at Johns Manville.

"Robert, you know you have to see Dr. Kalem before I will allow you to play football this year," she said with a serious look on her face. "So I made an appointment for you tomorrow evening. Please be here when I get home so we can go together."

Oh, Oh, I thought. These were words I was dreading to hear. What if Dr. Kalem says absolutely not? I couldn't bear the thought.

"Okay, Mom. I'll be here." My heart was definitely not reflected by my words.

The next evening after work the two of us walked to Dr. Kalem's office in downtown Zion. As I bounded up the stairs without any effort, I realized how much I improved since my Mom brought me here almost a year ago.

Dr. Kalem ran a number of tests on my legs and listened to my heart at great length. "Robert," he said with a degree of astonishment, "this is amazing. Your pulse is strong and steady, and I cannot detect the slightest hint of a heart murmur."

I let out hoot of joy!

"It appears the medicine worked and your running all summer has strengthened your heart to the degree that I can authorize you to play football," he concluded.

"That's great, Doc!"

"However it does appear there is some nerve damage to your legs. You may not be able to run as fast as you could in the past."

The entire way home I was ecstatic. I completely ignored his last admonition.

"Mom, I can play! I can play!" I exulted to her.

"All right, but remember each year we'll need to go back to do this again. I don't want you playing if you are at risk," she warned concernedly.

"Yeah, I know," I answered less enthusiastically.

I reluctantly accepted that I would always have the threat of the effects of rheumatic fever hanging over my head.

## Methodist Youth Fellowship and Football

About a dozen teen age boys and girls piled out of cars in front of the Winthrop Harbor Methodist Church one beautiful, bright Illinois Sunday afternoon. We were all members of the Methodist Youth Fellowship, briefly known as the MYF.

In Zion, every church had an active youth program. It was a way to keep teenagers focused on God while at the same time allowing them to have social interaction with supervision. My church, the Memorial Methodist Church, had a particularly active program. I joined the moment I turned 14 in February of my 8th grade year and spent every Sunday evening for the next four years at the church in some kind of MYF activity.

One Sunday in the middle of the summer, our minister arranged for us to spend a day with the MYF teenagers in Winthrop Harbor, a small village to the north of Zion located on the Wisconsin state line. I never met anyone from Winthrop Harbor before, so I thought it would be fun to go and find out who some of my classmates would be in the following year.

The moment I walked into the church, two young men walked directly up to me and introduced themselves.

The first was a fairly tall, very slender but wiry fellow with a twinkle in his eye. He spoke with great confidence.

"Hi. I'm Phil Anen," he said with a smile. "You look like a football player. You planning to go out next year?"

"Yeah, I'm planning on it. I guess you are too," I replied. "And by the way, my name is Bob Osmon."

The second boy was heavier built, handsome in looks, and obviously a little more reticent than the first one. But his manner was very friendly.

"Hi. My name is Dick Bogue. I'm planning to go out also," he affirmed. "My older brother Don played for the Zee Bees last year."

"Good to meet you, Dick. So, did you guys play flag or tackle football in grade school?" I asked innocently.

"Are you kidding me?" Phil replied sarcastically. "We couldn't even afford the flags here in this town. I think there is one football in the whole school. Can't wait to get to Zion and put on some real equipment."

"Are there any other boys from here who you think will play football?" I asked.

Again Phil jumped in with the answer.

"Yeh, there are two other guys who I think will be good players. Leon Hallgren is a tough nut even though he isn't real big. But he's not afraid of anyone."

Dick quietly added, "And the other is Bob Lee. Bob is solidly built and strong as an ox. Weighs about 160. He'll be a darn good player."

"I look forward to being on the freshmen team with you both next fall," I said enthusiastically. "I have two good friends, Loren Stried and Paul Jackola, who'll be coming out also. I think they too will be excellent players."

"I can't wait!" exclaimed Phil.

"Hopefully we'll have a good team," I said crossing my fingers.

The services were about to start, so we broke off our conversation for the moment. But before I left for home we all shook hands once again. As I walked out the door I murmured to myself, "I think I'm going to like both of these guys. Things are shaping up for our team."

**First Comes the Equipment**

About 50 boys ranging from seniors to freshmen were milling around the boy's gym in August getting their equipment issued to them. To the untrained eye, it appeared to be nothing but chaos. But to the managers running the show, they knew exactly what they were doing.

My childhood buddy, Donnie Myrum, the assistant manager, barked out his instructions. "Pick up your pants there. Your thigh and knee pads over there. Then try to find a helmet that fits. Freshmen, you hold back until the seniors get all their stuff."

He's done this before, I realized.

"If the shoes are too big, wear extra socks," shouted Don.

I spotted Loren across the gym and headed his way.

"Hi, Bob. How was your summer? Glad to see you again. Did you keep up the workouts?" Loren asked me with obvious interest.

"Darn right, pal. Every day. How about you?" I responded enthusiastically.

"Almost every day. Some days I was running my trap lines and other days I was hunting all day. So I didn't always do planned exercise, but I kept my legs in good shape," Loren answered positively.

Loren looked around the gymnasium as the gear issue continued. "Let's give it our best shot."

We shook hands firmly. The look we both gave each other was one of determination and resolve.

"You got that right," I replied quickly. "Let's get our equipment."

Paul strode up and clapped us both on the back. "I've been working on cars all summer to earn money for the family. Didn't do much running, so I'll probably die out here the first few days. But, hey, I'm ready to go."

As I mentioned earlier, Zion was not a wealthy town, so our equipment was not exactly the top of the line. I doubt if I could say it was the middle of the line. In fact, it was pretty bad stuff. Being freshmen, we were issued equipment that was old, used, dilapidated, and torn. Shoes that didn't fit, pads too big or too small, helmets that looked like Knute Rockne's teams played in them, etc. But it was football equipment and that was good enough for the three of us at the time. However, since none of us ever played tackle football before, we didn't even know for sure how to dress properly.

"How do you put these darn things on anyhow?" I groused as I struggled with the shoulder pads trying to figure out which side was the front or back.

Loren looked at me with a look as confused as mine. "I'll be darned if I know."

Paul put down his shoulder pads and picked up some hard, curved pads. "So what are these for?"

"I think these are thigh pads," Loren answered as he experimented sliding them into pockets inside the football pants we were issued. "Yeah, this seems to work."

I followed suit and went back to the shoulder pads. I surmised that the laces were probably in front for ease of lacing them up, so I put them on that way. I hoped I was right.

"Looks good to me," Paul observed and put his on the same way.

Next came the jerseys. They were so old that the numbers were only on one side. I had no idea which side the numbers went on. I pulled the jersey over my head and the smell of years of use twitched my nose. It was a smell with which I became very familiar.

"I'm not sure the numbers go on the back. I think they go on the front," Loren offered.

"Numbers on the back, the back," I responded impatiently, not wanting to show my own doubts.

"Okay, if you say so."

"I think they go on the back so the ref can see them," Paul offered tentatively.

"Now that makes sense," both Loren and I chimed in.

The helmets weren't much more than solid leather which wrapped around our heads. No suspension, no face mask, no protection at all. There was only one way to put on the helmet, but it sure as heck didn't feel right.

Donnie Myrum came over to us looking amused. "You guys need a little help?" he asked with a smile.

"Yeah, my friend," I replied with relief in my voice. "Please show us how some of this stuff goes on."

He patiently took the time to explain how everything was supposed to fit together. I still love him for giving us that courtesy. Finally we were all reasonably clad for battle and headed out to the practice field.

Along the way, Phil and Dick came up to us along with two other young men.

"Hi, Bob. Here are the two guys I was telling you about at church last summer...Leon Hallgren and Bob

Lee," Phil said as he introduced us.

I in turn introduced Loren and Paul. We all shook hands firmly and with a look of determination in our eyes.

"Hey, any good looking gals coming in from Central School?" asked Leon immediately. "I'm ready for some new blood."

"Leon," Bob said with a bit of disgust in his voice. "We're here to play football, not chase women."

"That's why I'm playing football," replied Leon with a big smile. "So women will chase me!"

We all laughed and turned our thoughts back to football.

"Wonder what our coach will be like?" I asked philosophically.

"I hope he knows a lot about football because we sure don't," Loren observed.

"I don't know about that. I read a lot of books about football this summer," I said with too much pride in my voice. "So I have a good idea how this game should be played."

In retrospect, we knew so little about football that we didn't even know what we didn't know. And God couldn't have picked a more appropriate man to teach us exactly what we did need to know.

I rate Evan Ellis as one of the most brilliant minds I have ever experienced when it came to coaching football. He was a student of the game and knew every nuance and formation of every team in the country. He could cite plays and defenses that made a major difference in historic games throughout the annals of football history. He often held me in awe with his depth of knowledge of offenses and defenses, and the personalities of different coaches who advocated various styles of play. But he also had a side which we all came to dread. We all paid a high price to learn from the Master.

**\*\*\*\*\*\*\*\*\***

Coach Evan Ellis in College Days

A Marine

A Brilliant Football Mind
A Student of the Game

The Zee Bees paid a high price
to learn from the Master

# Chapter 2
# We Meet the Coach

There will always be two things I particularly remember about the endless days of drills and running plays on the Zee Bee practice field; the aroma of freshly baked cookies coming from the Zion Cookie Factory when the wind was blowing off Lake Michigan and the acerbic voice of Coach Evan Ellis yelling at us from the moment we walked on the field until we walked off.

The former is always a pleasant memory. It reminds me of the days after practice when my teammates and I went to the cookie factory, and for a quarter bought a big bag of broken chocolate chips. These luscious cookies, along with a quart of milk, made as delicious a treat as one could ever enjoy after a grueling practice. Sitting on the Lake Michigan beach eating those cookies and drinking milk with Loren, Paul, and my other football buddies was an experience I will always fondly remember.

The latter still makes me cringe even 50 years later. Coach Ellis had a bark in his voice that penetrated your very senses, got under your skin, grated on your nerves and made you wish that somehow you had decided to play tennis instead of football. He seemed to see everything. Dog it for one moment, and he was on your butt like a drill sergeant.

"Is that the hardest you can hit? You can't run any faster than that? Tackle like you really want to hurt somebody. If twenty pushups are all you can do, we are in trouble. You block like an old lady," the Coach sneered and flailed us all like Marine recruits. "This is not tiddlywinks out here, gentlemen. This is football. If you want to play for me, you better suck it up and get with the program."

These were but a few of the biting remarks that were thrown at all of us on a daily basis. No one was immune from his sarcasm and scathing remarks. Everyone felt his sting at one time or another. But I felt like much of his criticism was being directed straight at me. His barbs pricked me at every single practice. I knew everyone was getting his fair share, but I in particular was incensed about it. It grated on me personally to the point I began to hate his voice and his attitude after several weeks of practice.

"What's with this guy? Is he a sadist or what? Have I done one thing right for him out here yet?" I complained as we all plodded back to the locker room.

"I don't like his attitude either," Loren reassured me. "But I think he's getting us prepared for the real thing."

"I'm ready for the real thing... right now."

"Our time will come."

If I thought running two miles at a jog was preparation for playing football for Evan Ellis, I was sadly mistaken. The first two weeks' schedule included two a day practices in the worst of the August heat. I was still exhausted from the first one when I dragged myself out to the practice field for the second torture of the day. To make matters worse in those days coaches didn't believe in supplying water.

"Water! You want water? Football players don't drink water. Only wimps drink water. If you feel weak, take a salt pill," Coach barked at us in a nasty, condescending voice.

It's a miracle that none of us had heat stroke out there. As soon as we hit the locker room, many of us would walk into the shower, put our mouths right up to the nozzle, and turn on the cold water full blast to hydrate our bodies once again. Playing for Coach Ellis was not going to be fun.

After tackling practice, blocking drills, running sprints, and doing exercises twice a day for two hours each, my body ached all over. I went home absolutely exhausted, ate dinner, and collapsed on the couch not moving until I went to bed. In the morning every single muscle in my body screamed with pain. My Mother was of no help.

"Well, I can't see why you would want to do that to yourself anyhow. Working on your studies would be a much smarter thing to be doing," she advised knowingly showing her motherly concern.

Under my breath I answered sarcastically, "Gee, thanks, Mom. That really helps."

But each day we all showed up for another round. And each day would be more of the same. Blocking and tackling – tackling and blocking. Wind sprints and drills – drills and wind sprints.

"When in hell are we going to stop all this blocking and tackling crap and start learning football?" I groused to Loren as we headed out to the practice field one afternoon. "I've about had enough of this."

"Those tackling drills yesterday really tore me up," said Loren wearily. "But I do think this coach knows what the heck he's doing."

"Maybe so… but I can't see it."

"I think I tackled a lot better this morning. So did you! So quit complaining and hang in there like the rest of us."

Always the man with the cool hand, I learned over my four seasons of high school football to listen to Loren. He had a steady, calm way of looking at every situation. Nothing much perturbed him. But I couldn't help wondering as we jogged out to the field, our cleats clicking on the sidewalk, making that special sound as they do, what kind of man is this Coach Ellis?

"Is this slave driver a man I want to play for?" I asked myself out loud as I was stretching before practice. "And what does he know about football? All we've done until now is bang heads with each other. He had better show me something soon."

The difference between a teenage boy and a 30 year old man is light years, especially in those days. In the early 50s in Zion, Illinois few of us traveled outside our little town. If we did, it was to go to the Wisconsin State Fair in Milwaukee or the Wisconsin Dells for vacation. I went to Boy Scout Camp in Oconomowoc, Wisconsin for several years, and my Dad took me to Cubs games in Chicago, but that was about it for travel. Television was in very few households at that time and I seldom read the paper except to see how the Cubs and Bears fared the previous day. Thus my view of the world was very limited.

Football became a continuous daily battle: a personal battle between a coach who was unrelenting in his personal diatribe and sarcasm towards me (at least in my eyes) and a young boy who did not understand why the coach couldn't see how much he wanted to play football for Zion Benton High School. In my world, I gave him my best. In his world, I was hardly worthy to wear a football uniform, let alone be on a team he coached. What was it about this coach that made him this way?

If, in those callow days of youth, I knew of the world of experience Coach Ellis had under his belt before he ever came to Zion, I would have had a totally different outlook towards the way he acted. Our life's experiences shape us all and make us what we are. His experiences clearly made him what he was at that time. It's just that none of us knew anything about him.

## Young Evan Ellis

Evan G. Ellis Jr. was born November 24, 1920 in Hiteman, Iowa. His Dad was a miner who later bought a small farm in Cheriton, Iowa. He had one sister, Dee, who was about five years older. They lived in a little farmhouse with no heat except for a coal burning stove. Evan used to go out to the railroad tracks and throw rocks at the train as it went by. The engineers got irritated and threw chunks of coal back at him. He collected the coal and took it home to be burned. I guess that is where he developed his strong throwing arm.

Evan played basketball and baseball in high school and boxed on the side locally. He was graduated from Cheriton High School in May, 1938. After high school, his Dad got him a job in the coal mines, but he hated it and eventually quit. His Dad felt he was a punk and needed to be straightened out. But Evan had other ideas. He went to a baseball camp in Michigan for several months and returned to play semi professional ball in an Iowa league as a catcher. But World War II came along and as it did with many young man's plans at that time, it altered his life completely.

Evan Ellis, Catcher in Semi-Professional Baseball

Evan enlisted in the United States Marine Corps in June 1942 and was immediately sent for basic training to San Diego, California. He came out of basic as a Sergeant and was shipped to the South Pacific for duty. During the period January 1943 to August 1944, he fought in the battles of Guadalcanal, Tarawa, Saipan, and Tinian. For readers who may not recognize those names, they included some of the most bloody and deadly fighting the Marine Corps experienced during WWII. Although he was never wounded, he did experience five different bouts of malaria, a nasty tropical disease carried by a tropical mosquito that makes its victim break out in a terrible sweat and gasp for air.

After his fifth malaria attack, Evan was transferred to the Reserves for the rest of the war and was discharged in October, 1945. Upon arrival back in Iowa, he wasted no time using his GI Bill of Rights, a program designed to help veterans go to college. He enrolled in Simpson

College in Indianola, Iowa. It was there he met Drusilla (Dru) Nemecek, a pretty and vivacious young lady from Illinois. By the time Dru decided to leave Simpson to go to Colorado State University in Greeley, Colorado to get her teaching certificate, Evan was smitten and meekly followed.

One event that happened in Greeley is worthy of telling here. Evan became the first string catcher on the Colorado State Bears baseball squad. He was an excellent catcher and one of the leading batters on a very successful team. When the playoffs for the NCAA championship came along, CSU swept everybody until they finally reached the championship game in the Far West Sectional against Southern California. Win this one and the Bears would go to the Final Four in baseball.

The night before the championship game, malaria attacked Evan's body once again. While he lay in a hospital bed in a heavy sweat, the team took the field without him. The second string catcher started in his place, but was spiked in the sixth inning and had to leave the game. An infielder who never played catcher before came in to catch. In the seventh inning with the score tied, Southern Cal put a man on first. Knowing that the third string catcher was behind the plate, the runner took off on the first pitch. The infielder's throw to second sailed high over the second baseman's head into right field and the runner kept on coming to home for the score. Game over!! How ironic that the bite of an anonymous mosquito somewhere in the South Pacific during World War II would affect a championship baseball game in Los Angeles years later. I'm sure Evan's disappointment was crushing.

Dru graduated in June 1949. Evan and she were married August 12, 1949 in Riverside, Illinois. Dru stayed with her parents in Riverside and worked as a special education teacher while Evan returned to CSU to earn his Bachelor's Degree, graduating in March 1950. He returned to Riverside and worked in the trucking business for Dru's Dad as he looked for a coaching and teaching assignment somewhere in Northern Illinois. He received a job offer to teach and coach at Zion Benton Township High School.

In August Evan moved to Zion with Dru. He taught history and coached the freshmen boy's football, basketball, and baseball teams. He came to Zion at age 30 with a number of lifetimes already under his belt. The following year, 1951, Loren, Paul, and I, along with our few hopeful teammates, enrolled in high school and signed up to play football. Fate cast us all together. The series of events that led to my writing this book had begun.

## The Coaching Begins

Nineteen of us in a motley collection of uniforms and equipment were kneeling on one leg on the Zee Bee practice field as Coach Ellis began his talk. He drove us hard in tackling and blocking, but none of us felt like we really learned anything about football yet. Maybe today would be the start.

"Boys, this is a football. Please note that the ball is tapered at both ends. There is a reason for that. The men who created football designed the ball this way because they wanted to create the most exciting game in sports. Football is that today because of this shape. Let me demonstrate," Coach Ellis explained somberly as he faced all of us after our warm up sprints and calisthenics.

The Coach was wearing what we all came to know as his standard dress: football pants, a Zion jersey, a whistle around his neck, and a Colorado State baseball cap. I admitted to myself that he at least looked like a football coach. He went on.

"When you throw a basketball down on the ground, what happens? It bounces straight back up to you. When you throw a baseball down on the ground, what happens? It bounces straight back up to you. But look what happens when I throw this football down!" he continued in a deadpan serious voice.

With that the Coach threw the football in his hands down on the ground with a quick snap. The football bounced crazily away from him and off to the side in a herky-jerky motion. With that he let out a big "Ho! Ho! Ho!" as if this was the funniest joke that had ever been told. All of the team including me could not help but laugh at this simple explanation.

Although I couldn't keep from cracking a smile at this buffoonery, at the same time I said to myself, "This is going to be our football coach? We want a coach who really knows his football and instead we get a comedian." (As a matter of fact, many years later when I coached my own high school football teams, I used exactly the same line. Not surprisingly, I got the same laughs.)

Ellis went on. "Football consists of two actions: blocking and tackling. Everything else is secondary. If you tackle well, it doesn't matter what defense you use. If you block well, it doesn't matter what offense you use. That is why we have concentrated on these two things so much to date and why we'll continue to do these same drills every day."

That remark elicited a groan from everybody. Our aching bodies were vivid reminders of those drills.

The coach went on unfazed. "Now it is time for you to start learning to run an offense. Most college and pro teams are now running the Magic Tee. (The T-Formation. Always said with a decided sneer and a curl to his lip as if it were unworthy of mentioning.) But I still believe in the Single Wing, an old time offense that gives many advantages to the team that uses it well. New Trier High School in Winnetka, Illinois uses the Single Wing and is competing against much bigger schools because of it. Minnesota has a player named Paul Giel who is a terrific tailback and the Gophers use the Single Wing competitively in the Big Ten. Princeton has a tailback named Dick Kazamier and they dominate in the Ivy League. So that is what we're going to run. The Single Wing. Now let's get some of you up here and I'll show you what it looks like."

"First the backfield," he said as he looked us all over skeptically. "Who are my backfield candidates?" About eight of us stood up and walked forward. He looked us all over and turned to me saying, "You want to play in the backfield? You look more like a tackle to me."

I answered loudly and clearly. "Yes, sir. I want to play fullback."

"Well," replied the Coach with a bit of a sneer on his lip. "We'll see. This offense might be able to use a hard hitting fullback. And what about you?" he asked Loren.

Loren too was forceful in his answer. "I want to be your quarterback, Coach," he quickly responded.

"You look a little small to be the quarterback in this formation," Coach snorted. "I need somebody who is tough and can block, not a fancy, dancy ball handler."

Loren again quickly responded. "Coach, I can be anything you need me to be." With that, Loren became the first player on our team to earn Coach's respect. We all learned that this definitely was not an easy thing to do.

Coach Ellis turned to the rest of the team and yelled, "Did you hear that? This man is ready to do whatever is needed for this team. When you all feel that way, that's when we'll have a real team."

"What do we have for linemen?" he called out sarcastically. "Does anyone here know anything about playing in the line?"

Phil stepped right up to Ellis and said, "I want to be an end, Coach."

"An end? You look so skinny a big breeze could blow you away. What's your name anyway?"

"Phil Anen, sir... from Winthrop Harbor. And no one is going to blow me away."

"Well, Phil Anen from Winthrop Harbor. I like your attitude," Coach grinned. "From now on you are Philibuck. You got any objections to that?"

"No, Coach. That's fine with me," Phil answered with a nod of his head. So Philibuck it was from then on.

"And who are you?" he asked of Dick Bogue. "You don't look like a football player either."

"My name is Dick Bogue and I'm trying out for center."

"Center?" Coach sneered. "In the Single Wing that's a position that takes a tough man to play. He needs to make a clean snap to the backs and then block a man over his head as well. What makes you think you can be our center?"

"Well, sir," Dick began in a respectful voice, "my older brother Don Bogue is the center on the Varsity and I want to follow in his steps."

"Bogie is your older brother? Well, if you are half as good as he is, you might make a decent center. And from now on, you'll be called Bogie too."

Coach Ellis proceeded to line us up in a Single Wing formation. For those readers who are not familiar with the single wing, I can well understand. It went out of existence at least 40 years ago. Zion and New Trier were the last gasping vestiges of this old offense in the State of Illinois. So I will explain its premise.

In the single wing, two backs, a tailback and a fullback, line up about four yards and three yards directly behind the center. The ball is snapped to one of these two to initiate the play. The quarterback is set behind the right tackle and is used primarily for blocking, although he does occasionally handle the ball on trick plays. The wingback is set outside the offensive right end and again is primarily a blocker, but is used for reverses and to receive passes. The line is formed in an unbalanced alignment to the right. The left tackle moves to the right side so there are four linemen to the right of the center, but only two to the left. The right side in this alignment is called the strong side and the left side the weak side. (The left guard and left end were always quick to point out that the weak side meant weak only in the sense that they had one fewer man on that side. Not that there was any degradation of power on that side.)

The beauty of it all was that the tailback could run or pass, the fullback could run or block, the wing back could run reverses, the line could get double team blocks on the biggest man on the defense, and the left guard could pull to make trap blocks on an unsuspecting right tackle. It was designed not to make spectacular plays, but to gain three or four yards at a time and thereby control the ball and the clock as the team slowly worked its way down the field. Frankly, I liked the entire concept. It suited my personality and my skills. Plodding, but persistent.

## The Team Takes Shape

"Okay, girls," Coach said sarcastically. "Line up in your assigned slots and let's run a few plays."

We stumbled to our assigned positions.

"Our first game is coming up soon and I'd like to think we could at least line up correctly."

During the ensuing weeks the selection process for first team positions took place. The offense began to look like something that could work. Loren was set as the quarterback and I was selected for the fullback spot. The tailback was Bobby Young, a compact, solid runner, with quick moves and acceleration. He wasn't easy to bring down.

The wingback was Arvid Detienne. Arvid had excellent speed and was a good blocker, so he was ideal for that slot. He was a steady, reliable kind of guy and he became a close friend.

Paul was a shoo in for the right tackle position. He was big, strong, tough, and a good leader. He was my close friend for many years... I was glad to have him as our anchor at tackle.

Bill Hosken was the fastest member of our team. He was bright and became a rugged blocker. He came to Zion from North Prairie School. Bill alternated between playing the line and the backfield.

Bobby Middleton was another candidate for tailback. We called him "Middy". He had a short blonde crew cut and was somewhat of a "loner". While at Lakeview Elementary, Paul, Middy and I were considered the three best athletes in our class in the school. He wasn't as compact as Bobby Young, but had quick moves and good speed. Middy stuck mostly to himself and was a bit too arrogant for Paul and me. I grew up with him and tried to understand him, but it was hard.

And then there were the Harbor Boys.

Winthrop Harbor, (known in teenage slang as Windy Harbor) had the reputation of a tough town and was not so influenced by the mores of the Zion Christian Catholic Church. While the Harbor Boys didn't ride motor cycles and carry packs of cigarettes in their rolled up tee shirts, they did gave the impression that it could be that way if they decided to do so and no one would challenge them. Out of this little village of less than a thousand came a disproportionately high number of players for our team.

Leon became the starting left guard. He was a cocky, tough little lineman of 135 pounds who willingly took on players much bigger than himself. He could have been the lovable and super cool Danny Zuko character from the movie "Grease" very easily... slick hair, handsome, popular with the girls. He fit the mold perfectly.

Bogie, quiet and unassuming, became our center, a position critical in the successful operation of the Single Wing. Philibuck was a wiry, enthusiastic member of the team who from time to time would crack us all up with his humorous comments in tense moments. It was good to have someone like him on the team. He became the starter at left end.

Probably the best overall player on our entire team was Bob Lee; a solid, tough, hard hitting, quick, and decisive player. If we all had Bob's skills, I think we would have been unbeatable. He was installed as the right guard on offense and was our nose guard on defense.

In all, there were only 19 players on the freshman team, not even enough to scrimmage against each other during practice. This was a problem that plagued us throughout our four years in high school. There was no real tradition of championship football at Zion at the time and the grade schools did not start playing tackle football until years later. So football was not a sport that all the boys at ZB High School wanted to play.

At that very early time in our development, Coach Ellis made a most prescient observation that would hold true four years later. "Boys, I guess you all will have to learn to be iron men. You are by necessity going to play both offense and defense, so you had better prepare

50

yourselves for it. No two platoon system for the Zion-Benton Zee Bees."

For clarification, the two platoon system has one team of 11 players who only played offense and another 11 who only played defense.

I had no way of knowing it at that point in time, but only seven of us from that original freshman team would stay together through all four years. Those were Phil Anen, Dick Bogue, Leon Hallgren, Paul Jackola, Bill Hosken, Loren Stried, and I. Particularly gratifying to me is the fact that all these years later I still consider each of them very good friends and always look forward to seeing all of them whenever I return home for a reunion. The bonds of shared adversity, formed at such an early age, are indeed difficult to break.

**Moose up the Gut!**

"We have two basics plays and if we run these properly, we can beat anyone," Coach Ellis emphasized. "The first is the end sweep by the tailback with the fullback leading. It's called the 409 sweep; the four back (tailback) going through the 9 hole (between the right tackle and the right end). The second is called the 305 Buck, the fullback (3 back) going straight ahead through the five hole between the two tackles. We'll use the left guard to trap the defensive left tackle when possible. We can run these left or right depending on the way we line up."

It didn't make a lot of sense to us then... but it soon would.

"We'll also use a buck lateral where the fullback hands off to the quarterback as he goes through the line and the quarterback will pitch to the tailback going wide," the Coach explained in a knowledgeable manner. "It's a trick play we can use occasionally if the defense keys on our fullback. And the reverse will be the tailback handing off to the wingback going around the opposite end. This keeps the other team honest."

We listened in rapt attention. Finally, we were learning some football.

"I'm sure some of you are wondering about our passing attack. Well, let me tell you how I feel about passing. When you throw a pass two bad things can happen and only one good thing. The ball could be dropped for no gain which isn't good. Even worse it could be intercepted so we lose the ball. Again, not good!"

Coach looked at us all as if expecting a challenge to his theory. There was none.

"The only good thing that could happen is somehow we catch the ball. But most ends fall down after the catch anyhow. I don't like the odds, so we are going to run, run, run, and run some more. Any questions?" asked Coach Ellis with eyebrows uplifted.

We all knew better than to question anything he said. That would be like asking for a major butt chewing. Besides all that running sounded good to me.

"So let's give some of these a try," he ordered. "And let's try to look like a football team. Okay, girls?"

It looked so simple when he demonstrated it, but actually running the plays seemed awkward and difficult. Coordinating the actions of all eleven men to do the proper movements all at the right time was chaotic. We ran the same plays over and over and over again until we were all dragging. Throughout this entire effort, Coach was haranguing us unmercifully.

"This is the most pathetic effort I've ever seen. We look like a bunch of old ladies out here. Get the lead out! Are you here to play football or tiddlywinks? If I don't see some improvement you all are going to be running laps."

"What the hell does this guy expect from us?" I often complained to Loren. "We're busting our butts and all he can do is yell at us. We're all freshmen trying to learn to play football. He's nothing but an egotistical tyrant. I don't know if I want to keep playing for this guy or not."

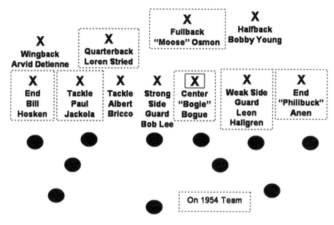

# Single Wing 1951

Our practice field was no more than a big open field located on the Shiloh Park grounds near the school. Between the high school and the practice field was a swamp that we had to skirt around. It was finally filled in years later. No lined practice football field for us. Not even a goal post. But there was plenty of space to run and tackle.

The Varsity practiced on the same field, so none of us complained. Additionally, there were no lights. However, some nights the Coach made us stay out on the practice field so late that it was too dark to even see the ball. He let us go only when one of the other coaches reminded him that the school buses had to leave. Every day we ran the same plays over and over again.

About a week before our first game, Coach Ellis made an announcement which caught me totally by surprise.

"Every football team should have a player named Moose," observed the Coach. "I have given it deep thought as to whom to give this prestigious and honorific name."

He paused for a moment while a little snicker crept across his face.

## Moose Up The Gut

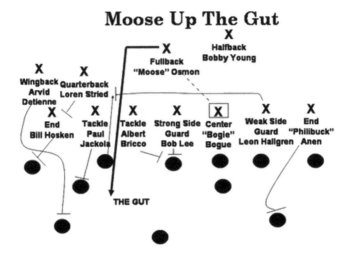

"From this day forward, Osmon, you will be our Moose. A fullback is just a center with his brains kicked out anyhow, so you'll do perfectly," he cackled.

He let out one of his big guffaws with the buck teeth projected over his lower ones. "Ho! Ho! Ho! Now we got us a Moose."On the one hand I was honored that he would select me for a special name, but didn't know for sure that Moose was an especially endearing nickname. I thought maybe something else might be more appropriate. But from that moment everyone started calling me Moose and to this day when I return to Zion, my teammates call me Moose, not Bob.

"Furthermore," the coach continued on a roll, "since the 305 Buck has Moose running straight up the middle, the play will now be called 'Moose up the Gut'!"

And "Moose up the Gut" it was. At times Loren called that play so many times that Coach Ellis asked him if he had forgotten the other plays. But, fortunately, it worked most of the time, especially for getting first downs in short yardage situations. It was our bread and butter play that brought me some of my best and worst moments in playing football at Zion Benton High School. But it was always at the heart of our offense.

The Freshman Football Team

Front Row: Dick Bogue, A. Bricco, Bob Lee, M. Mintern,
G. Miller
Second Row: W. Buckley, R. Fout, Leon Hallgren,
L. Pontillo, Bill Hosken
Third Row; Phil Anen, Paul Jackola, C. Handyside,
Loren Stried, Bob Osmon, Coach Ellis
Fourth Row: Bobby Middleton, J. Davis, Arvid Detienne,
A. Krapf

**********

# Chapter 3
# The Season Begins

The old yellow Zion school bus slowly moved out of the parking lot behind the boy's gym. Loren and I shared a seat together.

"This is great," I said enthusiastically. "We get to wear new uniforms, we get out of school for the afternoon, and we get a fun ride to Lake Forest."

"It'll be fun if we win," said Loren with a worried look.

"I can't wait until we get a chance to try out our team against the Scouts," I continued enthusiastically. "I wonder how much we'll beat them by."

Loren and I were ready to test our team against a real opponent. Coach Ellis drove us unmercifully during the prior two weeks and I was sure we were ready. Loren was a little more reserved about it than I.

"I dunno, Moose. Those guys from Lake Forest have been playing tackle football since sixth grade."

"Aw... so what!"

"They have better equipment and training facilities than we do."

"We can beat 'em... I feel it!"

"I don't think they are going to be pushovers by any means," Loren countered hesitatingly.

Lake Forest was a very wealthy town with moneyed families like the Armours, the Wrigleys, and the owners of the Chicago Tribune who lived there. Many of the homes were in truth estates, not houses.

"Yeah, I know," I said not to be discouraged by his caution. "But we're Zee Bees and that should make up for a lot."

Ah, the naiveté of untested youth. From the time of kickoff until the final second, the game was one disaster after another. We were off sides, we moved too soon in the backfield, we fumbled the ball, and we even ran the wrong way on some plays. The skills displayed by the Lake Forest Scouts clearly demonstrated which was the superior team. There was no doubt they played together for several years. Their experience was evident.

During halftime Coach screamed and pummeled us verbally about letting them do that to us. "You guys play like you're scared to death of Lake Forest. They put on their pants one leg at a time like we do. Have you all forgotten how to block and tackle? By God, we'll do more of that next week!"

It was to no avail. We took the field in the second half determined to make a better showing, but we were overmatched. We lost the game 33-0 and never came close to scoring until the 4th quarter when the offense finally started to click.

But there were some good things about the game. Loren did a good job calling plays. I thought his selection and sequence of plays were excellent, even though their defense was too good for us. I learned that I really enjoyed running the ball and that "Moose up the Gut" actually was a consistent ground gainer for us. The combination of the blocking up front, my size, and the drive in my legs showed that this play would work for us. But beyond that, not much worked on offense.

In spite of the score, I thought our defense played reasonably well. Had it not been for a few untimely penalties, we might have held them to two TDs. Paul and Bob both made quite a few tackles at the line of scrimmage. I saw all of us make some very good tackles at various times throughout the game. We simply didn't do it very consistently. Frankly, we played like anyone might expect a freshmen team to play in its first game ever.

But the one thing that stood out in my mind and became a trait of our team throughout the four years was that we never quit, no matter what the score. Everyone on the team was still playing his heart out when the final whistle blew. After the game the locker room was rather upbeat in a defiant way instead of everyone hanging his head in remorse.

"I told that pot licker over me that I'd push his butt all over the field the next time we play," Leon announced to us all.

Phil ranted on and on about the referees. "I think those refs were actually the assistant coaches for the Scouts. They screwed us a dozen times. It'll be different when they play us on our field."

Even Bogie who was normally rather quiet commented, "Can't wait to go at them again. We finally started to move the ball in the fourth quarter."

In spite of a sound beating, I felt this team could play well and do some damage to opposing teams in the future. We needed to hang together as a team and begin to improve.

On the way home, Coach Ellis stood at the front of the bus and gave us a little pep talk which further buoyed our spirits. He said, "Boys, we were up against a superior team today. They are better trained and far more experienced than we are. But I want you to know that I'm very proud that none of you quit in spite of the score. If you continue to exhibit that kind of attitude, we'll win a few games this season." That made us all feel a lot better.

He then got a little twinkle in his eye and asked, "Do you know the real reason why the Lake Forest kids are such good athletes?"

Well, of course, none of us had any idea.

He said, "Because when the school bus drops off the boys at the gate of their estate, they still have to run several miles to get up to the front door of their home. So they stay in great shape all year round."

Then he let out one of his big "Ho Ho Hos" and thought he just told the funniest joke anyone heard in years. It was the perfect thing to do. We were already disappointed about this loss and for Coach Ellis to alleviate the tension like that was just the right touch. Even I laughed a little at the joke. But the sting of defeat still hurt.

"We're going to get these guys someday," I said determinedly.

"We'll sure have the chances," said Loren philosophically.

"I don't like getting beat like this," I muttered angrily.

"In due time, Moose. In due time."

## The Bears

The following Monday Loren and I were getting dressed in the boy's locker room. We had a grueling practice, but now that it was over and we showered, our spirits were coming back strongly.

"The Bears highlights are on the tube tonight," said Loren. "Why don'tcha come on over and watch them with me?"

"That'd be great. Thanks," I replied enthusiastically.

"Maybe we can learn something from George Halas," offered Loren.

Loren's Dad was one of the few people in town who had a television set in the early days of the 1950s. On Monday evenings, WGN Chicago aired the highlights of the Sunday Chicago Bears games from 7 – 8 PM. The playback was from a film taken the day before and was in black and white. We were told the scores of the other games, but there were no highlights of other teams.

In those days the Bears were coached by the legendary George Halas. Johnny Lujack was their quarterback, but it was their defense that earned them the title "The Monsters of the Midway". The team was absolutely brutal on defense with players like Bulldog Turner, Bill George, Ed Neal, and Eddie Sprinkle. I liked to imagine that the Zee Bees could someday be the Chicago Bears of the North Suburban Conference.

Loren's parents always welcomed me warmly for the Monday Night Highlights. His Mom in particular would make sure that I sat down at the dinner table with them each time I made a Monday night appearance. This became routine for Loren and me after several weeks. In later years I often remarked that next to my own Mom, Loren's Mom fed me more than anyone else in the world.

Kayo Dottley was a big, booming fullback for the Bears and it was with awe that I would watch him run over the defenses in the NFL. "Loren, I'd love to be able to play exactly like Kayo someday. Boy, is he good," I said with respect in my voice.

Loren laughed at my comment. "Problem is, Moose, they only play the Magic T in the pros. No one uses the Single Wing."

I never came close to the kind of ability that was needed to play in the professional leagues, but it was good to have hero worship in those times. Kayo Dottley gave me the image of a hard charging fullback that I tried to emulate.

After carefully watching the film highlights, Loren and I discussed in great detail how we would have played the game, the plays he would have called, and the defenses I would have used. It was as if now that we had one game under our belts, we had more football smarts than George Halas.

"I would've run Dottley off tackle when it was third and three," Loren stated firmly. "The defense was looking for the sweep."

"I would've moved into an eight man line when the Lions had 4th and two," I added with authority. "Halas should have known the Lions would never pass in that situation."

It may have been a little cocky for two young freshmen in high school to think they knew more about football than the great George Halas, but our analysis of each game laid the groundwork which would pay off for us in the future. Loren's Dad was a big football fan also, so he did not mind our tying up his television for one hour every Monday night. But I'm sure he often chuckled listening to the two of us critique Coach Halas.

## Waukegan B Team

The next game was an away game against Waukegan's reserve players. There were so many boys out for the team in Waukegan that they had fourth and fifth freshmen teams. This was powerhouse Waukegan and I did not know what to expect. After the pounding we received from Lake Forest, my cockiness had been shaken a bit. But the entire team bounced back from the loss and played rather well. Our blocking and tackling were definitely crisper. Bobby Young made good yardage on end sweeps and I made some good gains with "Moose up the Gut". I scored a touchdown in the first half and it was an amazing feeling of elation. My first touchdown in a Zee Bee uniform. I was absolutely thrilled.

On one series around the 15 yard line, Loren called for a buck lateral. It required me to receive the ball, head into the line so that it looked like a "Moose up the Gut", but instead hand off to Loren who spun around to receive the ball. As I was hitting the line, I saw the Waukegan players all converge on me. Loren pitched it out to Bobby and he ran untouched into the end zone.

"Good call," I yelled to Loren. "Worked perfectly."

He smiled happily. "Thanks. Feels great to score!"

Throughout most of the game our defense kept Waukegan from getting very close to our goal line. Paul and Bob again were superb on defense. Phil, Loren, Leon, and I all got a good share of the tackles as well.

We won the game 13-6. It was as if we won a championship. The bus was ten times noisier on the way home than it had been the week before.

"Hey, these guys weren't so tough," Leon snorted. "Big, bad Waukegan. Big deal."

"At least the refs were half way decent this game," Phil concluded. "We only had to play against eleven guys today."

"Boys, now you have tasted victory," yelled the Coach. "It makes all the sweat, aches and pains worth every minute. It is so much sweeter than defeat. Now let's keep the ball rolling."

Monday night football highlights were a joyous occasion that week. We let Mr. Stried know that since we now won our first game, we understood the game of football far more precisely than the week before. We told him we probably would not lose another game all season. While he was very happy for us, he gently reminded us that it was a B team we had beaten, after all. But that couldn't douse our enthusiasm in any manner that evening. Kayo scored on a 30 yard run and the Bears won big time. That just added to our excitement.

If any of us thought Coach might let up on us a little because of this victory, he was sadly mistaken. Ellis pushed us harder than ever. I thought I played reasonably well, but Coach seemed to focus on me after that game.

"Moose, you've got to hit the line faster," yelled Ellis at the top of his lungs. He stood akimbo glaring at me. "And don't stand up so straight when you run with the ball. Someone is going to rip your head off someday."

I knew whose head I wanted to rip off. I could never understand how he couldn't see I was giving him my all. But I was far too intimidated by this man to ever say something like that. So I bore down even harder and did my best as the week dragged on in preparation for the Crystal Lake Tigers.

## Crystal Lake

The boys from Crystal Lake were big and strong farm boys. Without question the worst games I played in my four years were all against Crystal Lake. They always seemed to have my number. They loaded the defensive line on our right side and since we had no real passing attack, it was very effective. "Moose up the Gut" went nowhere. They out muscled us. We lost 20-0. Another shutout against us.

Monday night football highlights were much more subdued. Kayo Dottley didn't score that Sunday either. And the Bears lost. Gloom on gloom. Fortunately Mrs. Stried's meal was wonderful.

## Betty Rae Birky and Joyce McEwen

It was around this same time that Loren and I both began to show a growing interest in the girls of our class. He always had a good rapport with most of the girls, but for me to spend much time talking to them was a new phenomenon. The female members of our class in those days liked to wear poodle skirts, black and white saddle shoes, and fuzzy tight sweaters with big heavy medallions on a chain around their necks. If strategically placed, the heavy medallion lying exactly in the middle of their chests would definitely emphasize the curvature of their breasts.

While I am sure that none of our gals ever wore those medallions for that specific purpose, it did have an effect on most of the guys in my class. Not only was it difficult to pay attention to the teacher, but we had to learn not to ogle as well. But it was a challenge we never wanted to go away.

Loren began dating a striking, vivacious redhead … Betty Rae Birky. Betty Rae lived in Russell, a very small town located on the Wisconsin border, west of Windy Harbor. In fact, there may not have been more than ten families there at the time. She was full of spunk and personality. We all called her, "The Perky Miss Birky". It wasn't long until she captured Loren's heart. They became a steady couple soon after they started dating and continued their relationship throughout the four years of high school.

Because she was Loren's steady and I was Loren's best friend, this gave me special privileges. This meant I could talk to her any time I wanted without anyone suspecting a romance was brewing. It was like having immunity from teenage gossip. We had numerous classes together and slowly got to know each other like brother and sister. As a result, Betty Rae and I became fast friends. This strong friendship continues even until today.

My first venture into romance didn't progress nearly as well. Joyce McEwen was the cutest girl I had ever seen in my life. She had a cute little button nose, a winning smile, a vivacious personality, a tight little figure, and a cute haircut. I was smitten. Because I was now a football player, I knew I reached a certain status that I did not enjoy the year before, but this seemed to have no effect on the object of my desire.

Joyce sat in front of me in Miss Wise's Latin Class 101 and distracted me to no end. I passed her notes on a routine basis talking about any subject that I thought would interest her. While she was as polite to me as I could ever hope for, there was no indication of mutual interest in a relationship. When a young freshman girl was as cute as Joyce, there were too many upper classmen who had the same idea of dating her that I had. They were so much more mature than I that I wondered how I could ever compete.

There was one glimmer of hope however. A freshmen hay ride was planned and only freshmen could attend. It was supposed to be about a two hour ride around town ending up at one girl's home for hot chocolate and cookies. It was to be for couples only. Aha!! A chance!

I strategically placed myself near her locker at the end of classes for the day. With a deep breath and much trepidation, I asked with a waver in my voice, "Joyce, uhm… can uhm… would you like to go with me to the freshmen hay ride?"

She smiled that cute smile of hers and answered, "I'd love to go. It should be fun."

I was in heaven. Even practice wasn't so bad that week. When Saturday evening came, I walked to her house, rang the doorbell, came in and met her Mom and Dad. The two of us headed to the park to meet up with Loren and Betty Rae. We staked out a spot on the hay wagon and settled in with a warm blanket. It was a chilly October night, but having Joyce warm up against me was enough to make my spirits soar.

Loren immediately put his arm around Betty Rae, but I dared not make that move yet. It was our first date and in public, so I didn't think I should push it. But the conversation, school song, cheers, and the hot chocolate and cookies were good old plain fun. How I often wish I could recapture those moments again.

After the party broke up, I walked Joyce to her home. As we stood on the front porch, I decided it was time to make a move. I took her by the shoulders and tried to plant a kiss on her cute lips.

"No. Don't do that," she said curtly as she turned her head away. "I don't know you well enough."

"How well do you have to know me before you'll kiss me?" I quickly retorted with irritation in my voice. "We've been friends for two months."

"A lot longer than I know you now. Thank you for a nice evening." With that she spun and went in the house.

I was crushed. The big tough football player had been spurned by the cutest girl in the class. I was embarrassed that I had been rejected, so I stomped home in a huff.

As I came in the front door, my Mother was waiting up for me (something she continued to do even when I was 35 years old and had traveled around the world several times). I slammed the door as I walked in, demonstrating clearly that not all was well with me.

"What is the matter, dear?" my Mother asked sweetly. "Did something bad happen at the hay ride?"

"I tried to kiss Joyce McEwen good night and she wouldn't let me," I responded irritably.

This was something I really didn't want to discuss with my Mother. But I let the cat out of the bag. I was doomed.

Hearing my comments brought my Mother's strong religious convictions and her small town Midwestern outlook on life to a boil in a hurry. In no uncertain terms she clearly explained to me why Joyce acted that way.

"Well, Robert, if Joyce let you kiss her on the very first date, then you would probably expect her to let you touch her breasts on the second date. What kind of girl would she be then? And if she did that, you certainly wouldn't want to date her a third time, now would you?" my Mother snapped at me.

I thought about that for a minute or so before answering. Actually that scenario didn't sound too bad to me. But this was Zion, after all, and I clearly understood her point.

"Yeah, you're right, Mom. I really shouldn't be upset. She did the right thing. She hardly knows me."

So I went on to bed feeling somewhat mollified. Little did I suspect at that time it wouldn't be long before I inadvertently took that second step.

## Clipboards and Model A Fords

The next game was against Kenosha High School at their home field. Kenosha is located in Wisconsin about 5 miles north of the border with Illinois. The school was huge. The football team was particularly well known for having produced a powerful fullback, Alan Ameche, who became a Heisman Trophy winner at Wisconsin and an All Pro Fullback for the Baltimore Colts.

The Kenosha freshmen team had a short, stubby kid, well built and reasonably fast. He played fullback and looked like Alan Ameche to us. He carried the ball three out of every four times and we could not stop him. I hit him well several times, but also missed him several times trying to make an arm tackle. This lackluster effort resulted in one of the most enduring stories I have about Coach Ellis.

Because of the short distance from Zion to Kenosha, Coach Ellis, several of the dads, and Paul drove their cars to the game that afternoon. We changed in our own locker room first, so we were all in full pads and uniforms when we arrived.

At halftime the score was 6-0 in favor of Kenosha. I thought we were playing rather well as a team. Bobby made some good runs. Middy spelled him and did well I thought. Bobby was a hard man to bring down... Middy was a hard man to catch. But we all missed tackles that infuriated the Coach.

"What's the matter with all of you? This kid is not that good," he screamed waving his hands wildly in complete frustration. "Hit him low and you can drop him in his tracks. Show some aggressiveness out there. You all act like he's Alan Ameche. What are you? A bunch of wimps?"

I wanted to say, "Oh yeah! Well, if you think he's that easy to bring down, you get your butt get out here and tackle him."

I glanced at Middy. He sat sullenly, staring at the ground, a look of concealed anger on his face. Coach glared at Middy.

"Middleton!" shouted the Coach ferociously. "Are you afraid to stick your head in there and make a tackle?"

Middy continued to stare at the ground. Coach next looked straight at me with fire flashing in his eyes.

"Moose, you couldn't tackle my Grandmother if she were running down the field carrying a ten pound sack of potatoes."

With that he cocked his arm and threw his clipboard directly at my head. Fortunately I ducked and it bounced harmlessly off my shoulder pads. He spun around, stomped over to his car, got in, and drove away. He left us all standing there with our mouths hanging open.

"Do you realize he left us?" Phil asked astonished. "I didn't think we were playing that bad."

Now what do we do? Do we keep playing? Who starts the second half? Questions flew from everybody.

At this point Paul demonstrated his exceptional leadership ability. "We keep playing. Loren knows what plays to call and Moose knows what defense to call."

Everyone grunted their approval to this plan.

"Let's get back in there and do our best," shouted Paul. "We can still win this thing."

With or without the Coach, we were going to give it our best. I decided I too needed to step in with some guidance.

"Whoever started the game in the first half, go in as the starters for the second half," I told everyone with authority. I'd be darned if was going to let the childish behavior of our coach bring down my team.

We played reasonably well in the second half and I thought as a team we showed some real grit. I don't know if it was because what Coach said to us or rather it was because he wasn't there to bug us. We lost the game 12-6, but at least we were competitive throughout the game. Against Kenosha that was a major accomplishment. I still thought we were improving. That doesn't mean much when you lose, but improvement was better than not improving. But a moral victory was not very satisfying.

After the game ended and we were picking up all our gear, we suddenly realized that the four of us who rode up in Coach's car had no ride home. Coach hadn't returned, so now we were one car short. Fortunately, Paul had his Model A Ford. Because he took his Mom to work every day before he came to school, he received his driver's license while he was 14 years of age, the only one of us to have done so. He drove five of the players up to Kenosha in his car.

Fortunately the old Model A had a wide running board on each side, so two of us stood hanging on each side as we headed home. The car performed admirably. Henry Ford would have been proud of his creation. Possibly we were the first football team to use it for this purpose.

A total of nine of us were either jammed inside or hanging off either side of the old Model A. There was a dirt road which Paul knew about which would take us to the state line, but once we got there, we had to come out on to Sheridan Road.

At that time Sheridan Road was still one of the main thoroughfares from Chicago to Milwaukee. I'm sure we must have been a most unusual sight to the other drivers on the road. Nine boys, all in full football uniforms, packed in or on one Model A Ford, and cruising down Sheridan Road as all the local factories were letting out.

Fortunately no one fell off. We all got home safely. Can you imagine the screaming that would take place by parents if this happened in today's world? If Coach ever had any remorse about his actions that day, he never mentioned it or showed it.

## A Setback

On Monday morning we all noticed that Middy was not in uniform. None of were sure what the problem was. We soon found out.

"Boys, Middy informed me today that he was quitting football," Coach said in an agitated state. "Says he wasn't playing enough, so he's decided to work on... roundball."

We all were a little surprised. This didn't seem like Middy. He was a tough competitor. I decided to talk to him the next day. I sought him out at his locker first thing in the morning.

"What gives? Ellis says you quit because you weren't playing enough," I demanded to know.

Middy shrugged.

"Bobby may be getting more offensive time, but you play a lot on defense."

"Frankly, I don't like Ellis," he snapped back at me. "He's always yelling at everyone... including me and I don't appreciate it."

"Well, neither do I, but I'm not quitting."

"I'm not quitting anything!" exclaimed Middy defensively, fire in his eyes. "I'm not gonna play football for Ellis."

"Come on, Middy... we need you," I said. "We'll only have him for our coach this year, so stick it out with us. We're starting to improve."

"No way! I'm done with football for this year."

"Darn it, Middy... the rest of us put up with Coach!"

"Mind your own business, Moose."

When Middy made up his mind, he stuck to it.

"Okay," I replied with resignation, "but at least think about coming out next year."

"We'll see!" With that he turned and walked away from me.

Well, I tried, I thought. The confrontation left me with some bitterness with respect to Middy. Maybe next year he'd play... and I would feel differently.

## Mom and Mud

Finally it was time for our first home game. This was a rematch with the Waukegan reserves. We were all in an anxious state...for the first time we were going to play before the home crowd. We wanted to look good for our parents, friends, and classmates who would come out that evening to watch us perform after school. What was really exciting was the fact we got to play on the Varsity field with bleachers, lights, and real goalposts.

"Hey, Moose," Loren hailed me as we headed to our locker room to change into our game uniforms of maroon and white. "Are your parents coming to this game? My Dad'll be there."

"I don't think so," I replied with resignation in my voice. "My Dad thinks playing football is dumb."

"Really?"

"He thinks I should be learning a trade after school so I'll be able to take care of my family someday."

"Our parents had to go through the Depression… so I guess I can see how he feels."

"Maybe… but it bothers me sometimes. My Mom knows nothing about football, so I doubt seriously if she'll show."

I paused a moment to reflect on the attitude toward football of both my parents. Neither would stop me from playing, but neither was wild about the idea either.

"Joyce will be one of our cheerleaders tonight," I said as a brighter image flashed across my mind. "Can't wait to see her in a cheerleader outfit."

"Keep your mind on the game," Loren replied laughingly.

"Joyce'll be as cute as can be… I'll bet."

"Betty Rae told me she'd stay after school and be there too."

"Lots of our classmates said they'd be there," I observed.

"So…we've got to play well tonight," said Loren rubbing his hands together tensely.

Play well we did. Unfortunately for everyone, fans and players, we had a heavy downpour which didn't help matters. In spite of the steady rain which made the field muddy and slippery, we controlled the ball throughout the game with a steady, balanced offense and a rock solid defense. I scored one touchdown on a "Moose up the Gut", Bobby scored one on an end sweep with Loren and me as the lead blockers, and Arvid scored one on a reverse.

Bill, Leon, Phil, Paul, and Bob all played good hard nosed defensive football. Everyone picked it up a notch for the home crowd.

Coach had little to say to us at halftime and after the game was almost pleasant. "Boys, when we block and tackle like we did tonight, good things are going to happen. Learn from this victory."

Many years later Coach Ellis told me of an incident that happened during the game which if I knew about it at the time would have embarrassed me beyond belief.

As I mentioned previously, I lived right across the street from the high school, so it was a short walk from our home to the football field. My Mother worked at Johns Manville on the production line and normally got home about 4:30 PM. So she was not around when the game started at 4:00. Much to my surprise, she came to the game in spite of the rain and tried to make sense of it all. By then our uniforms were covered with mud and it was impossible to tell who was who from the stands. In the middle of the third quarter, Coach Ellis felt a tap on his shoulder and looked around to see a soaking wet, bedraggled little lady standing there.

He asked politely, "Yes, ma'am. May I help you?"

The lady asked, "Yes. Which one is Robert?"

Now at this point Coach Ellis could have told this lady to get the hell off his football field. Couldn't she see a game was going on? But, no, he was as gracious as he could be under the circumstances.

"Well, ma'am, there are a number of Roberts on the team," he replied courteously. "Robert who?"

With that the lady looked at him like he was a man from another planet. In a voice full of exasperation, she said, "Well, Robert Osmon, my son." As if to say, "You're the coach and you don't even know who my son is?"

Coach said, "Oh, Mrs. Osmon. Well, let's see. That is Robert right out there," pointing to a figure that was now totally covered in mud and indiscernible from any of the other players on the field.

My Mother looked through the rain at the field which was now a morass of mud. "Is he all right?" she asked.

Again Coach responded as politely as he could under the circumstances. "Yes, Mrs. Osmon. Robert is fine. In fact, he is playing very well this afternoon."

My Mother smiled and said sweetly, "Oh, thank you. I just wanted to be sure he was okay." With that my Mother went back into the stands and took her seat.

When I arrived home, Mom told me she attended the game, but never mentioned that she came on the field and talked to the coach. If she had, I would have been mortified. Since I don't recall anyone needling me about it the next day, I must assume no one else even noticed the event. In a small town like Zion, mothers are expected to look after their sons, even in the rain at a muddy football game.

**Lynn Reinier**

Class Party at Lynn Reinier's Home in 1951
In back; Betty Rae Birky, Lynn Reinier, Phil Anen,
Leon Hallgren.
Behind Muggs; Bob Osmon.
In front; Dick Bogue.

Nat "King" Cole's smooth, melodious voice came wafting out the car radio as Loren, Paul, and I approached the Reinier residence just off Wadsworth Road near Lewis Avenue on the outskirts of Zion.

*"They tried to tell us we're too young,*
*Too young to really fall in love,*
*They say that love's a word,*
*A word we've only heard,*
*And can't begin to know the meaning of."*

"So, Betty Rae and you seem to be hitting it off very well. How does it feel to be in love?" I asked Loren half way kidding.

"It's great! My parents think I'm a little young to be going steady, but they really like Betty Rae, so they didn't try to stop it," he answered thoughtfully.

"Well, you were lucky to find her so quickly. I don't see myself going steady for a long time," I stated somewhat obstinately.

"Yeah? What about Joyce?" Paul needled.

"I don't think I'm the type to go steady," I said, embarrassed that Joyce had not responded to my amateurish advances.

We turned into the Reinier's driveway, a tree lined, very private road. It led to their home and the parking area.

"Wow! Nice place, huh?" I asked Loren quickly changing the subject.

"It's beautiful!" Loren responded enthusiastically over the crunch of the gravel. "You should ask Lynn out. She's a wonderful girl."

"I agree with you there... but she's going with Tom Douglas right now."

"Because Tom's a junior and a starting tackle on the Varsity... a cool guy... handsome..." joked Loren.

"There's no way I could compete with him," I admitted, not ready to admit also that Lynn intimidated me somewhat.

"You never know... unless you try," Paul counseled.

Lynn was a beautiful girl, both inside and out. She had long flowing hair, always carefully in place. She had a sweet personality, and a killer smile. She was gracious, kind, and someone with whom a boy could be a good friend. She exuded class. On top of all that she was very intelligent, artistic, and knowledgeable in the field of classical music. She also attended my church at Memorial Methodist. My Mom thought she was absolutely terrific.

The Reinier's were one of the very few families in town to own a swimming pool, so Lynn graciously had a gang of guys and gals over to her home for parties several times a year. It was her first party of the year for many of us in the freshmen class. Loren and I were both looking forward to sharing the day with new friends and classmates.

Because most of our classmates didn't go steady, we enjoyed many social events as one big group. Loren, Leon, Philibuck, Paul, Arvid, Bogie, Bill and I were usually among those invited. Joyce, Betty Rae, and Lynn always seemed to be the prime organizers of all our functions and were always present along with a number of the other gals from our class. We would normally number about 20-30 depending on whose home we were in and how much room was available.

Although no one really set the guidance, it was an unspoken rule that those classmates who were dating upper classmen would not bring them to our class parties. As a result, over the four years we were in school, it gave us the wonderful opportunity to become truly close friends with our own classmates, both guys and gals.

"Bob. Loren. Paul. How nice you all could come," Lynn cooed softly as we entered her lovely home.

"Thanks...thanks, Lynn," I stuttered.

Her voice could melt butter. "Please make yourselves at home and have some chips and Coke."

"Okay," said Loren looking around for Betty Rae.

"You all really looked good in the game against Waukegan," said Lynn with a flip of her long hair.

"Well, thank you, Lynn," I responded. "But we have a tough one coming up next week against Lake Forest. They creamed us last time."

"I'm sure you'll do better this time," she encouraged sweetly.

Lynn always had something positive to say. It was one of the reasons she was so appreciated by so many of our classmates.

"We'll all be there to root you on," said Lynn pumping her hand up and down like a cheerleader.

All the girls chimed in with encouragement. "We'll be in the stands next week... watching you guys. But let's hope it doesn't rain again."

"We need all the help we can get," responded Loren.

We knew we would need this support and more if we were to even make a game out of it against the Scouts... they were that good.

The party started and we all had a great evening sharing time together. In those days everything was strictly good clean fun. No alcohol, no drugs, no rap music. Doris Day, Theresa Brewer and Frank Sinatra. We danced, ate, had soft drinks, swam in the pool, and simply enjoyed each other's company.

**Rematch**

The rematch against Lake Forest was our second home game. True to their word, all the girls were out to support us. I heard them screaming for us the entire game. Joyce was again one of the cheerleaders. She sure looks cute in that outfit, I thought. I wonder what I could do to make her interested in me. The thought engulfed me. I reluctantly shook it off and tried to focus on the game.

I was certain that we would do much better against Lake Forest this time, but, alas, again we were overmatched. Nothing went well at all. Playing against a superior team naturally creates misplays, fumbles, and off sides penalties. We did all those things and more. They had too much speed and skill for us, although I thought we played much better than the first game, especially on defense. Our tackling was definitely improving.

On one particular fifteen yard penalty against us, Phil decided to give the referee some unsolicited advice. "Hey, Ref! Why in hell are you only giving penalties to us?"

The Referee glared at Phil and then tried to ignore him by walking away.

But Phil stayed right at his side. "We're on our home field now. You should be giving them the damn penalties like they did to us at Lake Forest," he yelled.

The referee happened to be a member of the Christian Catholic Church, so when Phil used words like hell and damn, it did not set well with him. He kept right on walking for another fifteen yards after he marked off the first fifteen. No cussing at the ref. This was, after all, Zion.

At halftime, the Coach unloaded on us all again. "Well, boys, you've made about every mistake in the book on offense. The defense is actually starting to look like you mean business, but there are still too many mistakes on offense."

Coach paced up and down the locker room, glaring at each of us individually.

"About everything that could happen to us has happened...except for the air going out of the ball. I wouldn't be surprised if that happened too!"

Honest to God, this is a true story. On the ensuing kickoff by Lake Forest, the ball deflated in the air as it was coming down and plopped on the field. We all looked at each other not knowing what to do. Finally Loren ran over to it, picked it up with one hand as you might grip a bean bag, and took off running.

It was so comical to see this happen that I totally forgot to block for him on the play and he got tackled hard by a couple of Lake Forest players.

"Man, those two guys nailed me and knocked me back ten yards," Loren gasped in amazement as he came into the huddle.

"Can you believe Ellis called that one?" I asked in disbelief.

"He must have extra special perception when it comes to football," Paul laughed. "No mortal coach could have predicted that happening."

Later in the half, we forced Lake Forest to punt and the ball slowly rolled to a stop around our ten yard line. There were about five Lake Forest players standing around waiting for the ball to stop moving so they could down it. All of a sudden, Bill sidled up the sideline, stooped down, picked up the ball and started sprinting down the sideline. His legs moved so fast they were a blur.

"Go, Bill! Go!" I screamed at the top of my lungs. I was jumping up and down like a little kid.

After a moment of hesitation, the Lake Forest players realized what was happening and took off after him. By then it was much too late. With Bill's speed, they never came close to him. A 90 yard touchdown!

It was absolutely incredible to watch. Everyone on both teams was stunned to see it happen. I screamed the entire time. We all raced downfield to pound Bill on the back.

"Great run!" shouted Loren.

"You really showed them!" said Paul proudly.

"Way to kick their butt!" I shouted.

More accolades came from everyone on the team. Finally, we scored on Lake Forest. We lost 27-7. But, by God, we scored! And we cut our deficit to only 20 points. There was hope for the future.

## Woodstock

The last game of our freshman year was against the Woodstock Blue Streaks at Woodstock. Although he continued to push us hard, Coach Ellis actually said a few good things about the team. During the last practice of the year, he called us all together.

"Boys, you all have come a long way since we started practice last August," he began with a note of pride in his voice. "The offense is showing signs of being able to score, the defense has really tightened up, the tackling is much more precise, and the blocking is crisper."

He paused for a moment as if to collect his thoughts so he could say what he wanted to say. Then he continued.

"I think you have the makings of a good team here. Your skills aren't quite what they should be yet, but you have a wonderful team spirit. If you all stick together and keep improving each year, I think you might be good enough to beat Lake Forest and Crystal Lake by the time you are seniors."

My heart swelled with pride. The coach who harangued us and berated us all season long actually said something good about us. In spite of our losing season, I was very proud of the fact that I was part of a team that represented my school. I was also pleased as punch to learn that our Coach who we sometimes reviled, but always respected, thought we were getting better.

"Now let's end out the season with a victory. But either way, I want you to know that I am proud of all of you who have stuck it out this season through all the bad times. Keep playing your hearts out and the good times will come," stated Coach Ellis with assurance.

Those words meant more to me than he would ever know. I began to think maybe this guy wasn't so bad after all. But I wasn't about to start singing his praises yet.

The next day, 2 November, 1951, as we were boarding the bus, Fred Stanton, who was at that time the Zion Benton Athletic Director, came on board the bus and made a surprising announcement.

"Coach Ellis is not going with you to the game. Earlier today Coach Ellis' wife Dru had their first child, a little girl named Betty Dee Sivyer Ellis. He's at the hospital with her now," he explained.

"A baby girl?" I groused irritably to Loren and Paul. "He's not allowed to have a baby at this time."

"Football coaches don't have babies during the football season!" Paul protested.

"We need Coach for the last game," I said, looking at Loren for encouragement.

"You're right," said Loren, still shocked at the announcement.

Suddenly I realized what I just said. For the first time since I started practice in August, I actually wanted Coach Ellis to be with us. Up until then, I would have been happy if he never came to any of our games.

"Does this mean I'm starting to like this man?" I asked myself. "Or do I simply realize he is a genius at football and his presence will help us win this game." I didn't know for sure, but I didn't like the idea of his not being there.

"I know this is the first time you have been without Coach Ellis at any of your games," said Mr. Stanton, "but he told me he had complete confidence that you can carry out his game plan without him on the side lines."

I saw everyone nod appreciatively with his comment. We all knew we were well schooled in the right things to do.

"I will be going with you and serve as your coach," he further explained. "Loren will call the offensive plays... Moose will call the defense, and Paul will make all the decisions regarding penalties on the field."

Mr. Stanton looked at us with an encouraging look. "Let's have fun and play well. Any questions?"

There were none...only looks of surprise and concern.

"Looks like Coach put everything in our hands," Loren said to me as the bus headed out Highway 173 on a long two hour ride.

"I hope we don't disappoint him," I said hopefully.

"We can only play our best," Paul stated. "We're as prepared as we can be."

"You're right," I agreed. "But I don't like not having him on the sidelines in any case."

It was a frigid, bitingly cold night. The weather was bitter all week long and as we got off the bus, it seemed even colder in Woodstock, a small town about 55 miles west of Zion. We all dressed in silence and walked onto the field. It was absolutely frozen solid.

Great! I thought. Our coach isn't here and the field is frozen. This should be lots of fun.

But Loren put things in the right perspective. "Come on, guys. Forget about the cold," he said enthusiastically.

"Let's win this one for Coach Ellis and his new daughter."

I was freezing, but I knew Loren had the right attitude. I shook off my skeptic attitude and ran onto the field for the kickoff with the same optimism I had for all our games.

It soon became obvious that everyone on the team was ready for a big game. Everything we did that night clicked perfectly. The blocking and tackling by the entire team was superb. Paul, Leon, Bill, Bob, and Phil opened big holes for me all night.

"Great blocking, guys," I yelled after my first touchdown.

"Keep coming over me, Moose," Leon said in the huddle. "I'm knocking my guy straight backwards on every play."

"Your snaps are perfect, Bogie," I said, clenching my fists in front of me. "I was afraid the cold might make me fumble."

"Okay. Here we go again," Loren directed. "On one. 'Moose up the Gut' on one!"

That night I scored five touchdowns with "Moose up the Gut", gained over 100 yards rushing, and made a dozen tackles. There were so few penalties against us that even Phil couldn't bitch about the refereeing. Everything Coach taught us jelled in one game. The final score was 45-7.

I was in a state of euphoria. I was like the man who shoots 17 holes of miserable golf, but gets a birdie on the 18th and can't wait to play again the next day. I was ready to start the next season tomorrow.

"Coach Ellis is right," I said to Loren on the way home in the bus. "Winning is a helluva lot more fun than losing."

"You've got that right," Loren agreed. "We have to make sure we can pick up next year playing like we did tonight."

The entire team shouted its agreement.

# The Pledge

The next week we all walked on air. Dan Loblaw, a Zion man who was the Sports Editor for the Waukegan News Sun that serviced all of Lake County and surrounding areas, wrote about our freshman season.

*"Zee Bee freshmen finish off their season with a huge win at Woodstock. Bob Osmon, the younger brother of Carl Osmon, a former star player at Zion, scored five touchdowns leading his team to victory. If the team can maintain this momentum next year, it could bode well for the Zee Bees in the future."*

I remember how proud I was to send this clipping to my Brother Carl who was then a petty officer in the US Coast Guard stationed in Bermuda and to my Brother Orval who was now living in Chicago. But I knew this was only one game and I was a freshman. I knew I had a long way to go before I could be as good as they were.

The following Monday night after we watched the Bears beat up on the Rams, I knew I wanted to say something to Loren that had been on my mind.

"You know, with the exception of Lake Forest and Crystal Lake, we didn't play too badly this year."

"I agree."

"We were in every game. And after the way we beat Woodstock, I think we can win a lot of games."

"We really improved in the last couple of weeks," Loren responded as he leaned forward earnestly.

"I have a proposal," I stated with a serious look on my face. "Let's make a pledge between the two of us. Let's agree to do everything we can to be ready to play some real ball next year."

"I'm for that," said Loren enthusiastically.

"Let's also set a goal of winning the North Suburban Conference championship. Maybe we'll be good enough by the time we're seniors. Waddya think?"

Loren nodded thoughtfully in agreement. "But we'll need more than the two of us to win a championship. We need to get everyone else on board as well."

"I know Paul will support us and the guys from the Harbor are really enthusiastic, so I think they will too," I replied acknowledging his foresight. "But we need to take the lead."

"Let's call everyone together and see how they feel."

"I'll call a meeting this week," I responded resolutely.

I paused a moment while I got my thoughts together. Loren knew I had more to say.

"But we still need a special pact between us... to make it happen," I said. "Let's set an additional goal for the two of us... to become All Conference players."

"Now, Moose, that's a wild dream. We're only freshmen. Do you realize what you are proposing?"

"Yeah, I do," I answered firmly. "I know it might sound crazy for us to be talking about this as freshmen, but let's try anyhow. What do we have to lose? Are you with me? I think we should give it a shot!"

Loren grasped my hand in a strong, affirming handshake. "We can try. Moose, you are amazing! I don't know where you get these ideas."

"I read somewhere it is better to shoot for the moon because if you fall short, you still end up in the stars."

"Then the moon it is."

With that Loren turned to his Father who was listening to this conversation of two young boys with dreams in their hearts.

"Dad, we want you to be a witness to our agreement. Moose and I are pledging to each other to do everything we can to try to win the conference championship for our team... and for us both to be All Conference as seniors."

Loren's Dad slowly shook his head as if in disbelief.

"When you two decide to do something, you don't set your goals low, do you?" he observed.

No, I thought. I guess we don't.

**Playing With the Big Boys**

The season wasn't quite over for the Varsity. They had a good season that year, losing only to Lake Forest and

Crystal Lake, the two teams that continued to be Zion's nemesis. It was obvious that these two schools were the ones to beat at all levels of competition.

Coach Rushforth brought Paul Jackola and me up to the Varsity for the last week. I knew Paul deserved this chance. He played well all season and gave every indication he would be a strong leader in the future. I would have liked to think it was for my skill, but in my heart I knew it was probably because of the coach knowing my Brother so well. I recalled that first day at the football meeting when Coach Rushforth singled me out as "Carl's brother"… and the teasing I took from my friends as a result.

We were not much more than cannon fodder during practice, but it was a thrill on game night to dress with the Varsity and sit on the bench with those older players. Our Varsity rolled over Horlick and late in the game Coach Rushforth put both Paul and me in the game on defense. I felt fear… not of playing with the bigger guys… but at the thought of letting Coach Rushforth and my Brothers down.

"C'mon, Moose," shouted Paul. "Let's show the Varsity what some freshmen can do."

We raced onto the field. A thrill that is difficult to describe ran through me. Paul made several good tackles which clearly showed his potential for stardom in the future. I was as nervous as could be and could hardly think straight.

But on one particular play, I observed the opposing quarterback drop back to pass, saw out of the corner of my eye the left end coming towards me from across the field, and knew instinctively what to do. I dropped my shoulder, barreled straight at the end, and hit him as the ball reached his hands. He flew high up and over me, and dropped the ball.

I felt like a man mountain. Having the Varsity players congratulate me for that tackle was very gratifying. I said to myself, "Hey! I can play at this level. Let me at 'em." I glanced at Coach Rushforth. He gave me a brief nod of approval… and I felt terrific.

# Expanding the Pledge

About 12 freshmen players gathered together in a circle in the girl's gym. The season was now over for both the Varsity and us. I called for the meeting of the freshmen team and to my great pleasure almost everyone showed up.

"Guys, in spite of some of the scores, Loren and I think we had a pretty good year," I began. "Remember, Coach Ellis told us that if we stuck together, we could have a good team by the time we're seniors."

I could see that I had everyone's attention. Loren motioned me to go on.

"So I'd like to see all of us pledge to each other do our best over the next three years to keep our grades up, stay active in sports, and do everything possible to have winning teams each year...and especially prepare ourselves to have an outstanding team as seniors...to win the North Suburban  championship! Waddya think?"

Phil was the first one to speak up. "Great idea, Moose."

"We'll have to keep ourselves in really good shape," I said.

"I'm gonna work in gymnastics this winter... and run track in the spring," said Phil with enthusiasm.

"Bob and I are going out for wrestling this winter," Bill pitched in. "And I'll run track in the spring."

"I'm going to play basketball this winter," said Paul. "I'll be helping my Dad with car work come spring... that keeps me in pretty good shape."

"How many guys are going out for basketball?" asked Arvid.

"Uh Oh...it'll be interesting to see what Middy does. Ellis is the freshman basketball coach," I reminded everyone.

We all laughed self consciously. No one forgot how Middy left the team. It disappointed all of us.

Arvid, Loren, and Leon raised their hands. Then everyone looked at me. Leon put his hands on his hips and kind of snorted. "So what are you going to do, Moose?"

"I don't know yet, but I'll do something to stay in shape...I promise."

Paul took a step forward and asked, "Hey, how about Middy? Do you think we could get him to come out for football next year?"

"Yeah," said Leon shaking his head. "He's hard to take sometimes...but he's a darn good player."

"I talked to Middy about that after he quit," I said. "He told me he wasn't ever gonna play football for Coach Ellis...didn't like the way Ellis talked to him."

"Hell... none of us like the way he talks to us," said Phil.

"It wouldn't hurt for us to talk it up with him before next fall," said Arvid.

"Arvid is right," said Loren. "We've gotta keep together and stay in shape... but we've gotta make sure we have the best guys."

"Maybe he'll be okay under a new coach," I offered hopefully.

We all wondered what it might be like under a new coach for next year. I ended the meeting with a quick wrap up.

"Okay, guys. We all agreed we'll do our best to stay in shape...to build winning teams while we are at Zion...and to set a goal of nothing less than a championship when we are seniors."

"Let's all shake on it," said Loren enthusiastically.

With that idea firmly planted in our hearts, we all gathered around in a circle and put our hands on top of each other.

"Zee Bees! Zee Bees! Sting'em! Sting'em!"

The pledge to each other and the team was now a solemn pact between us.

### Skating at Shiloh Lagoon

Twenty or so freshmen boys and girls met one evening at the Shiloh Park Lagoon in the center of Zion for a fun skating party. The lagoon froze over early that year and we couldn't wait to try out our skates and become better acquainted with new classmates.

One of wonderful things about growing up in Zion was that it was a protected, safe, and recreation oriented city. It was imbued with an atmosphere of peace and tranquility. The Zion Park District and its employees did a superb job of providing safe and supervised recreational activities, so parents had no qualms about allowing their children to go to any group events in town.

Many of the guys and gals in my class became exceptionally close friends because of this atmosphere. We partied together, studied together, supported each other in our after school activities, and experienced high school in a way not many high school students outside of Zion ever did.

The gals were the primary organizers. They arranged hay rides, beach parties, dances, and scavenger hunts. During the winter months when the pond was frozen, we went ice skating as a group once or twice a month.

Shiloh Park was a beautiful park located exactly in the middle of Zion. It was part of the master plan laid out by Dr. Dowie and served as the recreation center for many of us. It was filled with baseball fields, tennis courts, basketball courts, swings and slides, and picnic benches. Fourth of July celebrations were always held in Shiloh Park. Each year after the pond in the middle of town froze over, the Zion Park District erected a modest sized wooden cabin, complete with benches used to change one's skates and a pot bellied stove to warm everyone up after several hours of skating.

In late November that year, a cold snap came in and the girls announced that our first class skating party of the year would be held one evening during the week. All of the boys were hot to go. So there we were, racing each other up and down the pond, horsing around as boys are prone to do, and showing off to all the girls. Joyce McEwen, looking as cute as ever, was there which put me in great spirits.

After about 30 minutes of clowning around, Leon yelled out, "How about a game of 'Crack the Whip'. The ice is perfect for it."

Phil snickered. "The way we skate it will probably be our heads that get cracked."

"Crack the Whip" was a game that required about ten boys and girls joining hands in a straight line. We all started skating as fast as possible toward the other end of the pond. Normally one boy was designated as the pivot. He suddenly stopped short and began to pull on the person next to him to stop. As this pulling action moved down the line, each subsequent skater picked up speed. As this force was extended out to the last person in the tandem, that person ended up rocketing across the ice. This produced many shrieks of delight and a great high. Everyone took turns being the last person on the line.

Because of my size, I was normally designated as the pivot. On one particular occasion, Joyce was on the far end when we started skating. As I stopped short and pulled on the person next to me, who then pulled on the person next to her and so on down the line, I saw Joyce pick up a lot of speed, break loose from the person who was holding her hand at the end of the line, and sprawl head first onto the ice.

"Oh, no!" I shouted out loud.

I skated over to her hurriedly. She appeared to be a little stunned by her fall.

"Are you okay?" I asked very concerned.

"Yes, I think I am," she answered somewhat hesitatingly. "But I think I'm a little shaken up."

Trying to act the gentleman as my Mother always insisted I do, I went behind Joyce to help her up. I put my hands around her from behind and lifted her. Suddenly I experienced a new, but absolutely pleasant feeling.

"My God," I mumbled to myself. "I think my hand is on her left breast. I've never felt one before, but I think that's what it is. Full and soft, yet firm. Wow!!"

I realized what I was feeling was undoubtedly through a bra, a blouse, a heavy ski sweater, and a big down parka, but nonetheless, it was a breast.

"Thank you for helping me, Bob," Joyce said sweetly as she brushed herself off. "I think I'm okay now!"

I really didn't want to let go, but I knew if I held on much longer, everyone would begin to get suspicious, especially Joyce. So reluctantly I stepped back.

"You need to be careful. Maybe you shouldn't be on the end of the whip."

She smiled. "Maybe!"

For a young man entering the beginning stages of female/male relationships, this was a giant step forward. From that day on, I hoped beyond hope that the opportunity to pick her up again would occur. But we don't always get our wishes. As much as I hovered around Joyce every time we all went back to Shiloh Park lagoon for skating, I don't think she ever fell again for the next four years. Darn it all anyway! I shouldn't have told her to be so careful.

## Class Officers

As a class we were together for about two months when it was announced that class officer elections would take place early in November. A group of our classmates came to me and asked if I would consider running for president. I was flattered and amazed. What a turnaround from last year. I told them I would be glad to run.

This group also asked Arvid to be our vice president, Loren to be our treasurer, and Beverly McElmurry, to be our secretary. Beverly was a friendly girl with short cropped hair. She was one of the Majorettes for the band. She was a popular choice.

There was no opposition, so we were all elected unanimously. Noting that three of us from the football team were now class officers made me realize some of the benefits of being a football player. My goal at Zion was no more than to wear the Maroon and White uniform with pride and be part of the team. But I intended to enjoy my new found status as long as it lasted.

**********

# Chapter 4
# Now What?

Loren and I were sitting on the bleachers in the boy's gym in early November trying to decide what our next sport would be. Since we made our pact to do everything we could to stay in shape, this was a major issue for us to discuss.

"Okay, football season is over, so what do you think we should do this winter?" Loren asked.

"Well, Joe Rushforth coaches wrestling so that would put us in good stead with him," I replied. "I know Bill and Bob will be on the wrestling team. It would get us in good shape."

"True, but basketball is a lot more fun and we could use the running to keep our legs strong. Besides, girls come to basketball games. Nobody watches wrestling," he countered.

Hmm, I thought. Good points. "What about doing calisthenics and lifting weights like we did last year in eighth grade?"

"C'mon, Moose. It was great exercise... but it wasn't much fun," he countered. "I want to be on a team."

Being on a team with friends is very important when you're a teenager. So that left basketball.

But in my eyes there was one major reason why I didn't want to play basketball. The coach was Evan Ellis!

"I had enough of Coach Ellis in football... I don't need his demeaning attitude again in basketball," I groused. "Besides I know I'm not that good anyhow."

"But remember our pledge to each other. I think all the running we'd do would be good training for football too," he countered with more than a little exasperation.

We did a quick poll of our football teammates and found out that Leon, Paul, Arvid, and Bobby would all be going out for basketball. That sounded good to me.

"Our entire backfield will be together again. Should help with our teamwork, I guess," I mumbled to myself. "But Coach Ellis again?"

Leon closed the deal for me. "C'mon, Moose. All the girls like seeing guys in basketball shorts. Maybe we can meet some good looking gals on our away trips."

That did it! Leon convinced me! So I made my decision. Basketball it was. I have no doubt that many life decisions were made on reasoning no more valid than this one.

## Roundball

10 players gathered around Coach Ellis in the girl's gym on the day we held our first practice. I couldn't help but wonder if he would be as harsh and demanding in basketball as he was in football.

Middy was the best player on our team. He was an excellent ball handler and the most consistent shooter by far. But after dropping out of football because he did not like the harangue from Coach Ellis, we all wondered how he would take the discipline and criticism from him in basketball.

Paul was the next best player.... a solid force at the center position. He was an excellent rebounder and played great defense.

After that, the rest of us were mediocre at best. Including Loren and me, we had two full teams so we could actually scrimmage each other. That was more than we could do during football season.

Coach wasn't quite as fanatic about basketball as he was football, but he still drove us all incessantly. With him, everything had to be all out all the time. Fortunately he carried his sense of humor with him into basketball.

"Boys," he said as he gathered us all together for the first day of basketball practice. "This is a basketball. Please notice it is round. So from now on when we speak of this ball, we will call it a round ball and we will play roundball, not basketball. When you throw it down on the court, it will bounce directly back up to you. That is why basketball isn't nearly as exciting as football. Roundball is only good for one thing. It is an excellent way to stay in shape between football and baseball. So that is what we are going to do. Work hard and stay in shape for football and baseball."

I watched for Middy's reaction. He gritted his teeth and took it all in. Middy was the star of the basketball team. I guess even he could put up with Coach Ellis to be the star.

It soon became evident to everyone that I was a not a very good basketball player. But I did have an excellent shot from around the key and could hit a high percentage of free throws. This was the result of the high school building a parking lot with about a dozen hoops on it when I was in fifth grade. All summer long the Myrums and I shot buckets until I could make shots almost blindfolded.

My specialty was free throws. I could knock in ten in a row with no sweat. But basketball, oops, 'scuse me, roundball, requires constant sprinting up and down the court from one end to another. My heavy legs and chunky build couldn't handle it. By the time I got in position to shoot, I was gasping for air and that threw off my shot.

I also worried about the rheumatic fever and wondered if it had "taken my wind" for roundball. I tried to erase that thought from my mind as it sounded like no more than a lame excuse to me.

Loren was a much better player and made the starting team along with Arvid, Paul, and Middy. Frankly I was content to sit the bench. I never got yelled at that way.

Our team wasn't too bad and we cruised along with about a .500 record. Paul and Middy were the heart of the team. They played basketball together since sixth grade at Lakeview. Paul played center while Bobby was the point guard. Between them, they scored about 80% of the points for the team.

Coach Ellis shouted at us all, as usual. He didn't shout much at Middy... he was so good at roundball that even Coach Ellis was pleased...that is until we played Woodstock. Something was wrong with Middy that afternoon... he didn't sprint down the court... he didn't play aggressive defense like he usually did. I could see

Coach Ellis' temper building... and I waited for the explosion.

Finally, Coach took Middy out of the game. "What are you doing out there, Middy? You look like an ice cream man dinging up and down the court in a slow truck!"

"We're beating 'em, Coach" retorted Middy. "Aren't we?"

Coach pointed to the bench and stalked away from Middy. The man couldn't tolerate anything less than full speed... even from his star.

## Roundball and Lake Forest Academy

One early Saturday morning we played Lake Forest Academy at Zion. Neither Paul nor Middy showed up. Coach was absolutely furious. It wasn't as if we had a lot of depth. I was put in at center for Paul and Leon filled in for Bobby. Our ineptness was only exceeded by the ineptness of the players of Lake Forest Academy. I scored six points, but as a team we scored only 25.

The amazing thing was that their team scored only two points. They missed every single shot from the floor they took and only scored on two free throws. Coach said that was the most amazing basketball game he had ever seen. But we all knew he was an angry man.

On Monday he called us all together before practice.

"Boys, Paul and Middy have admitted to me that they didn't come Saturday morning because they simply didn't feel like playing. Obviously they didn't want to represent their school or team," he told us in an angry voice. "I think they let all of you down, but I'm going to leave it up to you whether or not they should stay on the team."

"What?" I screamed to myself. "I don't want to vote on this. Paul and Middy are our only stars and if we lose them, we'll be crushed in every game. Besides Paul has been my lifelong friend. I don't want to vote him off the team."

I couldn't understand why anyone would not want to play for his school. I felt honored to wear the maroon and white uniform, even if I was not a starter. I really wanted to talk to Loren to get his read on this, but there was no time. I also wanted a chance to talk to Paul. I knew he was a hard worker and maybe he had duties that needed to be done at home that Saturday morning. But none of us were given that chance.

I knew if I voted against Paul and Middy it would appear the reason was because I wanted to get to play. But I knew that wasn't the truth. I was quite content to sit the bench. This was one time I fully agreed with Coach. Roundball was no more than a way to stay in shape as far as I was concerned.

Coach passed out slips of paper and asked us to write yes or no. I really agonized over what to do, but finally decided there was a principle here that needed to be upheld. I decided, quite frankly, if a player is selected to play on a school team and becomes a representative of that school, then, by God, he needs to act like he appreciates that privilege. So I voted to have them dismissed from the team. I felt terribly about doing so, but had to follow my conscience.

Obviously I wasn't the only one because when the votes were counted, it was near unanimous. I felt badly for both Paul and Middy, but it was their choice not to show up. It was the first time in my life I was put to a test to make a difficult decision.... one that affected my friends and my team.

I found that over the years more than once I was put in an awkward position defending a principle. But then I also feel I am a better man for having done the right thing when forced to take a position. In any regard, Coach Ellis taught me my first lesson in responsibility to a team requiring the full support of every player on that team. It was a lesson that brought great dividends to us in ensuing years.

At the first opportunity I had the next day I went directly to Paul to talk about it. I could see by his eyes he wasn't happy with me.

"Paul, you know you are one of my best friends," I started slowly and carefully. "We've done tons of things together since fourth grade and know each other like brothers."

"So?" asked Paul, a bit of hostility in his voice.

"Coach Ellis asked us to vote on whether or not to keep you on the team... I want you to know I voted 'no'."

"I would expect you to vote that way."

"I don't understand why you didn't show up last Saturday."

Paul's eyes softened a bit.

"I screwed up, that's all. It makes me sick that so soon after we took the pledge that I did this dumb thing."

"Please don't be mad at me," I asked in a sincere voice. "But I had to vote my conscience."

"I'm madder at myself than I am at you," said Paul. "Let's leave it at that...I won't ever let anything like this happen again, I assure you."

I realized then and there that Paul was indeed a man of character and honesty. While I was sad that he would no longer be on our freshmen basketball team, I was proud to know he was my friend and that this episode would not diminish our friendship in any way. I breathed a sigh of relief.

"My friend," I said in total sincerity, "You're an important guy to me. We're gonna need you next fall."

"I'll be ready. Count on it."

With that we shook hands and parted as good friends again. I also needed to clear the air with Middy. I finally tracked him down in the girl's gym shooting baskets.

"Well, Moose, I guess you're happy now because you'll get to play every game," Middy shot at me as I approached him.

"You know damn well I didn't vote Paul and you off the team because I wanted to play more. Why didn't you show up last Saturday?" I pressured him for an answer.

"I don't like the way Ellis chewed us all out in football... and I don't like the way he coaches basketball."

"You played for Coach okay for awhile..."

"I know...I told myself I could play roundball for the man...but he really made me mad."

"Because of the Woodstock game the other day?"

"That was part of it…I just don't like his whole attitude toward all of us."

"I can understand that," I said sympathetically.

"I don't really care whether I play or not," he openly admitted. "The rest of you can finish out the season playing for Ellis if you want, but I'm not gonna do it."

That ended the discussion. I could see that the only reason he might go out for football next fall was the fact that we would have a new JV coach. But Middy was also a great baseball player and Ellis coached freshmen baseball. So something had to give somewhere. I knew this situation was out of my control, so I put it behind me and got ready to be the center on the basketball team.

I worried about the inner conflict I had with Coach Ellis. I could see in Middy the same feelings I had. But I couldn't see myself quitting for any reason. It made me resolve to play ball whatever the Coach said… or did.

## Mumps

I was no sooner installed at the starting center position when I suddenly came down with a huge swelling in my throat. Turns out it was mumps.

My Mom and I were standing in Dr. Kalem's examining room when he broke the news to me. "You have the mumps and it is my professional opinion that you should have your tonsils removed as soon as possible," he told me as my Mom listened quietly.

"Why? Why now?" I complained. Immediately my mind envisioned sitting around doing nothing for several weeks and having to fight to get back into shape once again. "Can't it wait until after the basketball season?"

"We can't take the chance of the infection causing the rheumatic fever to recur," said the Doctor.

Fear shot through me. I didn't want to hurt my chances to play football… or to do anything else. I had already been through that!

Sternly the Doctor told me, "Bob, if you go back to basketball before you have these tonsils out and are over the mumps, not only could you have a reoccurrence of the rheumatic fever, but your testicles could swell up and you could be sterile for the rest of your life."

"Whoa, Nellie," I replied quickly. "That's got my attention. Let's get'em outta there."

So my basketball playing days were over for that year, but I came to every game to cheer on Loren, Arvid, and my other teammates. Except for the game I missed while my tonsils were being taken out.

## Hitting the Books

One evening in the locker room after one of the freshmen basketball games, Loren came up to me with a bit of a worried look on his face.

"Moose, I need some help on my studies. I'm having trouble in Science and Social Studies. If I fail I might not be eligible to play football next fall."

"Hey, no problem. How about I come to your house tomorrow night and we'll get started?"

Getting good grades was never an issue with me. Because I was always such an extensive reader, I seemed to have the ability to take tests and do far better than I would normally expect to. I could quickly analyze the question and reason out the answer. It is now common knowledge that some people are natural test takers and some are not. Loren was in this latter category.

To prepare him for these tests, I pretended I was the teacher and put together a series of 100 questions in each subject that I would ask the class if I were the teacher. For a week before the exams almost every night I went over and over these questions with Loren at his home. I also told him of ways the question may be slightly rephrased to sound like a different question. By the end of the week, he was knocking out the answers perfectly.

"I appreciate your help this week," he stammered nervously, "but I'm still very concerned about these exams."

"Man, you know these subjects cold," I replied positively. "Give it your best shot and you'll do fine.

Pretend its fourth and two on the goal in the fourth quarter. You can handle the pressure."

One week later Loren ran up to me with a big smile on his face. "I passed everything. You made the difference," he said happily as he slapped me on the back.

"No sweat, pal. I never had a doubt you could do it."

"Thanks, Moose!"

## Latin 101

I was standing at the front door of my home with my hands jammed into my pockets dreading the confrontation which was about to take place. I knew my Mom was going to be one unhappy person when she saw my report card.

Grades for the first semester came out and I was given a D in Latin 101. All my other grades were As and Bs, but a D in Latin? I knew I hadn't given it much attention. Between football, basketball, being class president, parties, skating, and generally doing everything but study, I hadn't really burrowed into Amo, Amas, and Amat.

In the other classes I could get by because I paid attention during the class periods and picked up everything I needed for the tests. But Latin actually required some work. However the biggest factor in this crisis was that Joyce McEwen sat right in front of me. Her presence distracted me more than anything else for the entire period. I spent my time trying to dream up ways to get her attention.

I hated to show this report to my Mother, but in those days a signature was required on the report card to prove that a parent saw it. I wasn't devious enough to initial it myself. So I faced the music. When my Mom read it she exploded.

"Robert, what is this? You had nothing but straight As during all eight years in elementary school and now in the first semester of your first year of high school you bring home a D! How do you explain this?" she demanded irately.

"Well, uh, you see," I stammered looking for words. "First of all I don't think Miss Wise likes boys. She clearly favors the girls in our class. And secondly there are only two of us boys in the class. And thirdly I don't know why I have to take Latin anyhow."

I hoped this would alleviate the situation somewhat. These excuses didn't slow down my Mother one iota.

"I won't stand for this. I will tell you what is going to happen," she continued red faced.

Secretly I hoped she was going to call Mr. Pearce, our school principal, and demand that he have the D up graded to at least a C. But, no, I totally misjudged my Mom.

"If you don't get at least a B+ in Latin by the end of the second semester, you will not play football next fall," she stated loudly and clearly.

Gulp! That isn't what I wanted to hear. How would my teammates react if they found out I couldn't keep my pledge because I didn't get high enough grades in Latin? I knew my Mom well enough that once she set her mind to something, she wasn't about to change it. Since she really didn't want me to play football anyhow, it would be no big deal to her to keep me off the team.

"Gosh, Mom! Why are you so adamant about this? You know I'm going to graduate from high school. It'll be no sweat."

I did my best to get her to back off, but to no avail. At the time I felt my Mother was being unreasonable about one lousy grade, but deep in my heart I knew exactly why she felt so strongly about my making top marks.

## Beulah Osmon

My Mom was born Beulah Myrle Ohneth on the Fourth of July in 1900 in Chicago, Illinois, a few blocks from Wrigley Field. My grandparents came to Chicago from Canada to be part of Dr. Dowie's Christian Catholic Church. My Grandfather had a job with the Chicago and Northwestern railroad in Evanston, so they didn't make the move to Zion in 1901 when a lot of Dr. Dowie's followers made the move. My Mom was the oldest of six in the family and was two years from graduating from high school when my Grandfather was killed by a train. Apparently one train came through an intersection, but he didn't know one was coming the other way. He was struck by the second train as he crossed the tracks. In the early 1900s there were no warning signals on the crosswalks.

Grandma Ohneth was pregnant with my Aunt Becky at the time, so there was no choice but for my Mom to quit school and go to work. So at age sixteen she took on the responsibility of the entire household.

After a year of struggle in Chicago, the family applied to the Christian Catholic Church for assistance. The members came through in a very positive manner. They brought my Mom's family to Zion in 1917, provided them with a tent to live in, food to get started, and the supplies necessary to build a home.

My two uncles, themselves only teenagers at the time, built a family home at 2116 Enoch Avenue. My Mother took a job in the Zion Lace Factory to pay for food for the family during the winter. The house was finished in the spring of 1918 and remained our family home until my Mother died in 1983.

My Mother continued to work for the family until everyone graduated from high school. My Aunt Bernice told me of my Mom paying her bus fare to ride to Waukegan and back every day as well as giving her lunch money. Aunt Bernice said she always admired my Mother for being so generous to her when my Mom could have insisted on her going to work at age 16.

In 1935 my Mom and Dad married and for four years lived at 1917 Elim Avenue. I was born February 13, 1937, just days before the huge tabernacle erected by the Christian Catholic Church burned down. It was where Dr. Dowie held many of his healing services. My Mother often talked about how she wrapped me up in blankets and took me to the fire.

Unfortunately my parent's marriage didn't last, and in 1939 my Mom moved back to 2116 Enoch to live with my

Grandmother. She eventually bought out her siblings so she became the sole owner of the family home. I lived there until the day I graduated from the Naval Academy in 1960.

When World War II broke out, Johns Manville needed workers to keep up the wartime effort. My Mom began work at the Waukegan plant which required her to leave the house every day at 5 AM. She was one of the famous "Rosie the Riveter" women who worked in production plants to help the war effort replacing men who were on the front line. She continued to work there after the war as the wages were higher than she could earn in Zion.

When I was in third grade in 1947, my Mom was working on a punch press making gaskets. Her job was to put a sheet of asbestos into a press and the man she worked with would hit a button to bring the press down and cut out the gaskets. One day there was a mix up in the operation and the man hit the button before my Mom got her arm back out. Her left arm was crushed almost to the elbow and had to be amputated.

By the time my Aunt Bernice took me out of school and brought me to the Victory Memorial Hospital, my Mom was out of surgery and chatting merrily with the nurses around her as if nothing had ever happened. I have always tried to remember my Mother's bravery when adversity has seemed overwhelming. She could have easily wallowed in self pity, but that was not her way. What a role model she was!

Mom had a prosthetic arm made and learned to carry a purse, but in actuality she did everything with her right hand. In today's world she would have received millions of dollars and retired for life, but back then the factory gave her only $7000. She wisely invested it. She bought the empty lot next door and converted our garage into a small home. She received rent on it for the rest of her life. She continued to work at Johns Manville until she retired in 1962 at the age of 62.

Thus when I came home with a D after having straight As in grade school, it was obvious why she felt so strongly about my grades. She never received a high school diploma, worked in factories all her life, and never had the chance for higher education. Now she saw her son who obviously had the brains to accomplish bigger and better things wasting his chance to do so by not taking studies seriously. She was furious about it and I felt the sting from my laxity for months to come.

To add to my disgrace, Miss Wise realized the same thing. She also saw I was wasting my talent. So at the beginning of the second semester she reorganized the seating arrangement in the room. Joyce McEwen was now located on the complete opposite side of the room from me.

I was crushed. I incurred the wrath of my Mom and no longer sat behind the cutest girl in our class. This was a devastating blow at the time. But as teenagers, high and lows move in and out of our lives quickly. I believe to survive those days required resiliency and a certain doggedness. Fortunately I had both.

Actually, these two events turned out to be a boon to me, although I didn't realize it at the time. First of all Latin and I became really good friends. I started studying at least one hour a night in total concentration on Latin. Once I caught on how to conjugate verbs, it became fun doing my homework.

I likened the study of Latin to developing a mathematical formula, one that once it was mastered, would mostly fall into the same pattern time after time. And I made up little trick phrases to help me memorize words. "Imperatur", meaning emperor, became "I'm for Otto". "Pulchra puella", meaning pretty girl, became "Pretty Polly". Silly maybe, but it worked. I received an A at the end of the second semester and all was well with my Mom.

It also turned out that this effort in Latin lead me to a lifetime interest in languages. I studied Spanish for two years at the Naval Academy and became fluent through additional study and usage while stationed in Panama for two years. The Navy sent me to one year of Turkish language training in Monterey, California and I became fluent after spending two years in Turkey as an advisor to the Turkish Navy. On my own I learned Italian,

Japanese, and Russian, not fluently, but enough to carry on a conversation and ask directions.

This talent put me in good stead with the natives of each of these countries when I visited. So I guess I need to be very grateful to Miss Wise for giving me a D in Latin early on in my academic training. But I'll never forgive her for moving Joyce McEwen away from me.

## Hebron and Crystal Lake

Near the end of the basketball season, Loren and I followed closely the fortunes of Hebron High School, a small 84 student school about 50 miles west of us in McHenry country. Even though they were a very small school, smaller even than Zion, they were beating many of the bigger schools in the Chicago area. A number of sportswriters were rating them as number one in the state. The strongest basketball team in our conference was Crystal Lake.

"Loren," I said one day as we were eating lunch in the cafeteria. "Dan Loblaw has an article about Hebron in the Waukegan News Sun. They are going to play Crystal Lake at Crystal Lake. I'd really like to see that game. Would you like to go?"

"If we can find a father to drive, I'd love to see'm play," he replied enthusiastically.

I talked it up a bit and several of us went to the game, having convinced one father to drive us out there. Crystal Lake's basketball court was on a raised platform like a stage and the spectators sat in the crowd as in a theater. No bleachers. This always intimidated the opposing team, and it did Hebron on this night. The Green Giants lost their only game of the year to the Tigers that evening, but it was terrific game. Hebron's Judson twins and Bill Schulz were the best high school basketball players I ever saw.

Later the following month Hebron played Quincy for the title game in Champaign Urbana at Huff Field House. It was the first time a high school basketball game was televised in the State of Illinois, but alas not in Zion.

Several of my teammates met at my home. My Mom served sandwiches and chips to everyone while we huddled around the radio listening to WKRS out of Waukegan. That night Hebron beat Quincy in overtime for the state championship. Loren and I both realized the impact of that event.

"If a small school like Hebron can win a state championship in basketball, then a small school like Zion can win the North Suburban Conference championship. Don't you agree?" I asked.

"You're darn right, Moose. We can do it too. We'll have to work our butts off, but if Hebron can do it, so can we."

Coincidentally, a number of years later after he become an All American at the University of Illinois, Phil Judson, one of the twins on Hebron's championship team, became the head basketball coach at Zion. It was a thrill to shake his hand after all these years and tell him how we listened to him beat Quincy so many years before.

"Coach Judson, in 1952 your Hebron basketball team became the inspiration that my friend Loren and I kept in our minds for the Zee Bee football team. We were convinced that if Hebron could pull off this tremendous feat, then certainly the Zee Bees could pull off a small miracle also," I told him with great respect.

Coach Judson replied modestly. "If we inspired you to bigger and better things, then it was our honor."

How ironic to meet him all those years later and at Zion-Benton High School. Life does unfold in strange ways.

## Betty Rae's Barn

"Come on in boys," Betty Rae's Mother said to Phil, Leon, Loren, and me as we stood on their front porch in Russell. "Betty Rae and the other girls are out in the barn waiting for you."

"Thank you, Ma'am," said Loren.

"I hope you have a good time tonight. Remember to keep the lights on."

We all chuckled a bit at this small admonition. Betty Rae's Mom was an enthusiastic host and always believed it was better to have a party at her house than somewhere else. That way she could keep an eye on things. We all thought she was great! She affectionately called our gang of guys and gals "The Almighty Crowd".

As we walked through the house on the way to the barn in back, we could hear Doris Day's bouncy voice coming from the record player.

*"I walked down the street like a good girl should,*
*He followed me down the street like I knew he would,*
*Because a guy is a guy wherever he may be,*
*So listen while I tell you what this fella did to me."*

Betty Rae's Dad had a car repair shop on the bottom level of their big barn. Many wealthy customers from Chicago hired him to customize their vehicles. He was quite well known for his work for many years.

When Betty Rae became a freshman in high school, he converted the second floor of their barn into a dance floor and rec room. It was perfect for a party. All the girls were excellent dancers, so it was a great chance for the boys to learn the new steps and hold these lovely ladies in our arms. Betty Rae, Joyce, and Lynn greeted us all with smiles.

"C'mon in, guys. Sandwiches are made and cokes are in the cooler. We're ready to teach you some new moves," Betty Rae offered enthusiastically. Perky as always.

We had a wonderful evening. We spent the hours in deep discussions over classes, teachers, latest hit songs, who's dating whom and what sports we all would be playing in the spring. It was an easy and comfortable atmosphere, one in which we all felt like we belonged.

To impress the girls in my class, I always had some bit of trivia that I threw out from time to time. It didn't always work, but I kept trying.

"Did you know that George Halas started the Chicago Bears way back in 1919 when they were called the

Decatur Staleys? And he's been their coach ever since," I told everyone seated around my table.

While the guys were interested in my knowledge, none of the girls were impressed in the least bit.

"Do you go around memorizing stuff like that?" Betty Rae asked me in amazement.

"No," I answered. "I keep it all up here," pointing to my head. "Then I pull it out when I need it."

"That is what psychologists call an eclectic mind," Lynn laughed. "I've always suspected you had one. You come up with the darndest things sometime."

"Hey, guys! Guess what? I got an eclectic mind. Anybody want to touch it?"

"Oh, sure, Moose," Leon said sarcastically. "Will that make me any smarter?"

"Absolutely. Give it a try. Here," I said as I bowed my head before him.

"No, thanks," he retorted. "If I'm going to put my hands in anyone's hair, I want it to be a cute chick's."

Everyone got a big laugh out of that comment.

"Hey, Betty Rae, I've got a question for you," I said slyly. "As we came in, your Mom told us to keep the light on up here. What would she do if we turned them off? After all, we are guys and guys are guys wherever we may be."

Leon was quick to react to this idea.

"Let's find out."

Leon walked to the wall and flicked off the light switch. Betty Rae almost jumped out of her skin.

"Oh, no. My Mom will be here in no time flat. Watch!"

It took Betty Rae's Mom exactly 42 seconds to arrive on the scene. But she was so clever about it that we all could do nothing but laugh. She burst in the door with another basket of sandwiches. She clicked the light back on again.

"I thought you all might be out of food, so I brought you some more. Are you all having a good time?"

Phil immediately stepped forward and with a mischievous grin said, "Sorry about the lights, Mrs. Birky.

I think Moose bumped into the light switch while he was dancing."

Yeah, right, Phil, I thought. She'll sure buy into that story.

We all assured her it was a great party as we chuckled to ourselves.

"The food is wonderful, Mrs. Birky. Thank you for making all the sandwiches for us," we chorused.

"No problem, boys. Glad I could do it," she said smilingly as she headed out the door. Then she turned and looked right at me.

"And by the way, Moose, try not to bump into the light switch anymore." She smiled knowingly.

Suddenly she was gone, but we all knew from then on that Mrs. Birky meant what she said when she told us to keep the lights on.

## Baseball or Track?

Loren and I were jogging around the track at the end of PE class in late March when I decided to approach him about what to do in the spring. It was a subject that had consumed a lot of thought on my part recently.

"So what are we going to do this spring? Ellis is now the freshmen baseball coach. I can't seem to get away from this guy."

Loren countered, "I really love baseball. I don't care how tough Coach Ellis is. I'm playing."

"I know I'm a good hitter and have a good eye for the outfield, but I don't want to put up with his garbage any more this year."

"I'm going to play baseball," Loren reiterated determinedly.

"I think Coach Ellis is a fanatic about baseball like he was about football," I told Loren emphatically.

"You do what you want, Moose," said Loren. "But I'd really like to have you on the team with me. Can't you overlook Coach's attitude for just the rest of the year?"

I really enjoyed baseball and wanted to be on the same team with my best friend. But the thought of having

Coach Ellis scream at me for another season was not a pleasant one. I decided not to make the decision on my own. First I talked to T. Ray Miller, the former football coach for the first ZB football team. He coached both Joe Rushforth and my Brother, so I felt he would be good authority. I asked him what he thought.

"Baseball is a fun sport," he said. "But if you are really sincere about becoming a good football player, running track would be much better for you. Build up your speed and legs."

Then I talked to John Timmerman, who was the assistant football coach and head track coach. Zion had only one coach for the entire track team. He was one of the nicest men you would ever want to meet.

"I agree with T. Ray, Moose," said Coach Timmerman. "You need more speed and running track would help you."

"I do need more speed... that's for sure."

"Come on out for track and we'll see what events we can get you into."

I told Loren, "What a great change this is going to be. A coach who actually encourages each of us to do his best. He doesn't just yell at everyone for how badly you're doing."

In a way, I rejected Coach Ellis as Middy had done... but I convinced myself it was a good move. Track made sense to me, and since Timmerman was also the assistant football coach, I thought it would put me in good stead for next year. Phil, Dick, and Bill all committed to run track, so I knew I would have friends from the football team out there with me. I made my decision. Track it would be.

Unfortunately I didn't do as much running as I had planned. It soon became obvious my forte was not in the sprints or long distance running. After trying out for several running events with little success, I resigned myself to becoming a shot putter and a discus thrower. The running part of my development for football would have to be done on an individual basis.

I played intramural softball during my time in the Navy until well into my fifties, so the skills I would have learned in playing baseball would have been more beneficial in the long run. It causes me chagrin even unto today that I made the decision not to play baseball because I wanted to stay away from Coach Ellis instead of going with my friend and my heart. But then, couldn't we all do better in making important life decisions if we had the ability to look back and have a second chance?

## John Timmerman

John Timmerman was one of those dedicated coaches that deeply cared about his boys. He talked to each and every one of us at great length trying to determine what we wanted to do and where our skills could best be used. He was a man for whom we all wanted to perform our very best.

He was born in Rising City, Nebraska, but graduated from high school in Lima, Illinois. He served as an Air Cadet in WWII in the U.S. Navy, but the war ended before he saw any action. After the war he attended Carthage College in Carthage, Illinois graduating with a PE degree in 1949. He coached and taught at Leaf River, Illinois for two years while he finished up his Master's Degree with the University of Illinois, also in PE. At that point he came to Zion as the assistant football coach under Joe Rushforth and as the head track coach.

I always appreciated Coach Timmerman's caring and guidance. He consistently encouraged me to do bigger and better things. When it became painfully obvious I would never be a competitive runner, he guided me into the shot and discus events. I was very competitive with the discus throwers from other schools in the conference and actually held the Zion school discus record for several years. Due to his mentoring and encouragement during the four years we were in school, the Zee Bees almost won the conference track championship when we were seniors. We fell short by three points only when a referee disqualified our winning relay team for stepping out of a lane.

John Timmerman and I became lifelong friends. At the age of 80 years, John spent an evening in my home in

Williamsburg and the next day attended the Navy/Tulane football game with me in Annapolis. It was an honor for me to introduce him as my former coach to my friends and classmates.

Dick Bogue's older brother, Don, became my mentor in both the shot and discus. He was a big man and quite a good football player, so I looked up to him with admiration and respect. He also was one of the top performers in both the discus and shot in the North Suburban Conference. I paid close attention to his instruction as he explained the different techniques to be used. Fortunately, all along my life's way, I have been blessed with good mentoring, and I often thank God for it. So although baseball may have been a more satisfying sport for me to play in the long run, having John Timmerman and Don Bogue in my life as mentors was a blessing. Also, unbeknownst to me at the time, Don was not to be the last member of the Bogue family to enter my life.

The election committee for our class decided it would be good for the same officers to stay in those positions for another year. Since we really didn't have a full year serving as class officers due to the elections not taking place until the previous October, it seemed practical to do so. All the officers agreed to serve again, so I ended up being the class president for the second year.

The second semester came to an end. In reflection, freshman year had been quite an up and down year for Bob "Moose" Osmon. I excitedly looked to the future with great anticipation. What would life hold in store? More than I could ever imagine at the time.

**********

John Timmerman
Assistant FootballCoach
Head Track Coach
Mathematics Instructor

# Chapter 5
# Sophomore Year - 1952

The hospital was quiet except for the occasional sound of a cart being rolled down the hall. I was shaken out of my thoughts by the sound of Coach Ellis' voice.

"Moose, tell the nurse I'm hungry. I'm ready to eat," he growled at me.

I scurried away to take care of that task without the slightest irritation that he was giving orders again. After I watched him hungrily scarf down his hospital food, I told him I had been thinking back to our freshman year.

"Honestly, Coach. Did you ever think we would be any good?" I asked curiously. "We were killed by Lake Forest and Crystal Lake. It must have been discouraging as a coach to see us lose so badly."

I saw the twinkle in his eye and the start of a smile on the edge of his lips. "Actually, I always thought your team had potential. You all never played together before, hadn't even worn pads before, and you looked like a bunch of Keystone Kops out there on the field half the time," he recalled with a chuckle.

He paused for a moment as he thought back almost 20 years. "But you all had a certain spirit which isn't often seen in a lot of teams. None of you ever gave up no matter the score. It's something a coach can't teach a team. It comes from within and either the team has it or not."

He paused for a moment as I saw his mind reaching back to 1951. Then he continued. "Yes, the defeats were hard to take, but I saw continued improvement in every game we played. So in answer to your question... yes, Moose, I did think your team could be good someday," he answered me in an openly honest manner.

I wanted to ask him right then why in hell did he give us all so much crap, especially me? But it was such a special moment I couldn't bring myself to do it.

He took several deep breaths and went on. "In addition you all provided with me some of the funniest things that ever happened during my coaching career on a football field. Do you remember the time when the ball deflated on kickoff and old Stride picked it up in one hand and ran with it?" he guffawed.

"Stride" was a nickname Coach gave Loren Stried during our senior year. He was big on nicknames.

"I remember. I thought it was so funny at the time I didn't even try to block for Loren… and he got killed by two Lake Forest guys," I laughed.

"How about when Hosken picked up that football after it rolled dead on that punt and took off for a 90 yard touchdown? Those Lake Forest players never knew what happened," he said very animatedly.

"I stood there and screamed 'Go! Go!' from the time Bill picked it up until he crossed the goal line," I shouted in a loud voice. "Somehow after his run I knew we would beat Lake Forest one day. I don't know why. I just knew."

"Did I ever tell you about the time your Mother came down on the field in the rain during the Waukegan game?" he asked me inquisitively, with one eyebrow cocked up at me.

"Oh, my God, no! What in the world did my Mother do?" I replied with trepidation.

As I listened to him tell the story of my Mother coming down on the field and asking him "Which one is Robert?" I could barely hold back the tears. How could somebody who is going to die in a few days or less be telling football stories and talking to me as if there was absolutely nothing more important in the world than reminiscing about our old football team. I was overwhelmed with emotion. He went on for about an hour, guffawing and reminiscing with great relish.

"Gosh, it is great to see him in such high spirits," I said to myself. "I wish all the other members of our team could be here to hear this."

Finally, the Coach started to slow down, coughed deeply several times, and settled back with a sigh. The nurses came in and gave him his medicine. As he slowly dozed off he came up with one more "Moose up the Gut" followed by a low chuckle.

"Sleep well," I whispered.

Dru was in and out all day long checking on us. The time was about 8 PM and I had been there since early morning. The intense emotion of it all was wearing on me also.

She said, "Bob, there's no more you can do today and all the family is here now, so why don't you get some rest."

I nodded in agreement and went back to the motel. I showered and lay down in the bed, but my mind wouldn't shut off. I kept going back; back to Zion, back to football, and back to Coach Ellis. These three memories were etched in my mind and heart and would never, ever be removed. Not then. Not now. Not ever.

## Building Blocks and Relationships

The summer between my freshman and sophomore year my Father decided to build a motel along Sheridan Road near the Dunes Theatre. During one of our trips to see the Cubs play (and lose), he told me how the tavern business was too grueling and that he realized Zion needed a good, clean low cost motel for folks visiting from Chicago and the area. He was going to do most of the work himself, but needed help on the grunt duties. That is where I came in.

"Son, one day you are going to have to make a living for yourself and take care of your family. So this summer will be the start of your learning a trade. I want you to help me build this motel," he told me in an authoritarian voice. "But I need to warn you. It'll be hard work. I'll lay the blocks, but I expect you to mix the mortar. You'll need to keep me supplied with both mortar and blocks as I work down the line. Do you think you can do it?"

"Dad, you've got to be kidding me. I'm a football player and played sports all year long. I think I can keep up with you," I replied indignantly.

After all, I thought, my Dad is 56 years old, practically an ancient old man. I realized he was still pretty strong, but my keep up with him? Hah!!

Ahh, the arrogance of young boys! It is a rite of passage for all sons to think they can outdo their old man. I knew I could outdo mine!

Dad dug out the basement with a backhoe and laid the foundation with a big cement truck the week before I got out of school. When I arrived early on the first Monday morning after school let out, he was ready to go to work. To get there I rode my bike from the north side of Zion where I lived to the south side outside the city limits where the motel was to be built… a distance of maybe four miles. I didn't even break a sweat.

My Dad began in a kindly, instructive voice. "Son, you must meticulously use the exact proportions of cement, sand, and water to prepare my mortar. Too much water and it is sloppy. Too little water and it is too hard. Too much sand and it is grainy. Too little sand and it won't adhere to the blocks."

"Okay, Dad."

"Now take this hoe and I'll show you the correct stroke to use while mixing."

First of all he showed me how to mix the sand and powdered cement. Then he taught me to put the water at one end of the mortar tub so the mixture could gradually be combined so as to get exactly the right consistency he wanted. And once it was mixed, it had to be brought to him instantly before the water started to evaporate and the mixture began to harden.

"Any questions?" he asked with a slight smile on his face.

It didn't seem too hard to me… cement, water, sand. What's the big deal? "Nope, I'm ready to kick butt!" I answered with exaggerated confidence.

My Father showed me the huge pile of Laninstone blocks which was delivered the week before. "You also must keep me supplied with blocks. If I have to wait for you, the mortar consistency will harden and you'll have to make a new batch. I'll take my time at first so you can get used to it."

"Yeah! Yeah! Okay, Dad," I cockily replied with a slight sneer on my face. "Let's have at it."

Four hours later I was drenched with sweat, aching all over, and my Dad was waiting for both blocks and mortar. "Sonny boy, you are going to have to do better than this or we will never get this motel done by the end of summer," he said in a kindly, yet stern manner.

I got the distinct impression my Dad was teaching me a very valuable lesson, but somehow it was lost on me at the time. What I wanted was water and rest. Fortunately he saw I needed both, so we took a short break.

"This is how I started in this business," he stated with a hint of nostalgia in his voice. "Work was hard to find when I was a young man right out of the Navy, so I took what was available."

"It's darn hard work!"

"Yes... it is. Since then I turned my building skills into a very profitable way of taking care of my family."

For the first time in my life, I began to wonder how my Dad became such a good builder. What led him to this profession? How did he happen to be in Zion in the first place? I realized I knew very little about him. I thought this might be a great time to ask him about his life. I reasoned that the more he talked the more rest I could get. He was much too wise for that ploy.

"I'll tell you some things about my early life from time to time, but for now, back to work," he directed firmly.

Over the summer we took breaks and ate lunch together. He slowly unveiled what had been unknown to me before. And what an interesting story it was.

## Carl Van Osmon Sr.

Carl Van Osmon was born in Bald Knob, Arkansas on December 8, 1896. My Grandfather John William Osmon and his brother Jabez moved from Southern Indiana to Arkansas several years before in hopes of finding better farm land and more prosperity. They found neither. My Dad, my Aunt Opal, and my Uncle Fred all grew up on a flat bottom boat on one of the rivers nearby. Life was hard and they had to scramble for food and clothing. Both my Grandfather and Grandmother, Mary Susannah

Vandermark Osmon, died from the harsh way of living early in life. Their children moved into the home of my Grandfather's brother Elijah. No one went to school. They all worked the fields and hunted to stay alive. My Father felt an obligation to repay his Uncle and stayed in Arkansas until he was 18, but the day he turned 18 he enlisted in the U. S. Navy. This was 1914. World War I had begun.

Dad went through boot camp at Great Lakes and was sent to the USS Mercury, a troop transport out of Norfolk, Virginia. He became a fireman. He told me that when he reported on board, the petty officer in charge directed, "There is the coal, there is the furnace, and here is a shovel. Any questions?"

My Dad was a big, strapping guy and he thought this was fairly easy work compared to what he did in Arkansas… and the food was a lot better. He made 12 voyages across the Atlantic ferrying troops over and bringing wounded home. He told me that on every trip there was at least one ship sunk by German U-Boats. He worked in the bowels of the ship and knew he would never survive if a German sub torpedoed his ship.

Dad told me that on Navy ships during WWI, a seaman never talked to an officer and if an officer was walking down the passageway, the seamen would flatten themselves against the bulkhead to make way. Thus he didn't have much positive to say about officers. (How amusing it must have been to him years later when his own son became a Naval Officer).

Dad made it through the war unharmed, came out as a fireman first class, and was discharged at Great Lakes in 1918. His cousins, Mary Ellen, Amanda, and Lucy Vandermark from his Mother's side of the family, moved to Zion a few years earlier. They offered Dad a place to stay until he got his feet on the ground, so he chose to live with them for almost a year.

A short time later he got a job as a laborer in a building crew. After the war, people were demanding homes and there was a shortage of skilled workers. Dad was so proficient in this area he soon was elevated to foreman. Over the years he probably built 100 homes around Zion.

My father married one of his cousin's friends, Libby Reese, and had two sons, Orval and Carl. My Dad was a great Cubs fan and his favorite Cub's pitcher was Orval Overall, so when my older brother was born, he was christened as Orval Reese Osmon. A second son came along three years later. He was named Carl Duayne Jr. We in the Osmon family never understood how you can be a junior unless your name is exactly the same as your father, but I guess in those days you could do anything you wanted.

When the depression hit, home building stopped and for a number of years my father fed his family by hunting birds and deer. He also trapped possum in the marshy area between the Lake Michigan lake front and the bluffs of Zion, the same area Loren worked his mink traps 20 years later.

When President Roosevelt started his New Deal program and the Civil Conservation Corps was formed, Dad was hired as a foreman by the U.S. Government to head up a crew in the Northern Illinois area. Under his guidance, Camp Logan, an Army base located between Zion and Winthrop Harbor was built on the lake front as a firing range. Subsequently, it became an important training area as our troops prepared for WWII. He also built a huge cement parking lot on the lake front at 21$^{st}$ Street. Because of the rising lake level in recent years, this parking lot is gone now. But for many years it provided a wonderful parking area for hundreds of Illinois folk to safely leave their car before the long walk down to the water's edge. It also became the turn around point to which I jogged when I started my rehabilitation after surviving rheumatic fever.

In the early 30s, my Father's wife, Libby, contracted cancer. Dad took her to California in hopes that she could be saved, but to no avail. He grieved for many years over her loss. He proceeded to raise two teenage boys by himself until he met my Mother. They married in 1935. My Mom always said it was the dark eyes, the wavy dark

119

hair, and the handsome, rugged look that attracted her to my Dad. (My son Ted has a lot of the same physical features as my Dad. I believe my son Chris picked up his entrepreneurial and building skills.) I was born in 1937. Unfortunately, my Mother and Father divorced in 1939. I don't know what happened for sure to their relationship because neither of them ever talked about it.

Carl Van Osmon, Sr., 1950

My Mother was awarded custody, but throughout my life my Dad lived in Zion and played a very active role in my care. Dad married again, this time to a lady who became his business partner as well. During World War II, they owned and operated "The Victory Inn", a tavern north of Wadsworth Road on Sheridan Road. Their tavern was outside of the city limits so alcohol could be served.

On Saturday mornings when no customers were there, Dad picked me up at my home on Enoch Avenue and took me back to the tavern where he would cook breakfast. He taught me how to hold a cue stick, pick out the best shot, and showed me how to line up the balls for a clean stroke. I would be allowed to practice on his beautiful pool table. I loved doing that and would play for hours.

Sometimes Dad would give me a roll of nickels to play the slot machines. By the end of fifteen minutes, all the nickels would be gone. I clearly recall my Father sternly lecturing me.

"Son, these aren't called one armed bandits for nothing. The reason I have them is that they make money for me, not for the people who play them. The longer you play the more money you will lose."

This was another lesson I learned from this worldly wise man. I still avoid slot machines to this day even though I have visited Las Vegas numerous times. I can always picture my Dad shaking his head "no" as I reached up to put a coin in the slot.

About 1951 the State of Illinois declared slot machines illegal so a major source of his profit was gone from the tavern business. Dad was tired of the long hours from early morning until late into the night, so he decided to sell the tavern and build a motel. In the summer of 1952, I proudly helped him build that motel.

That summer I became closer to my Dad than I had ever been before. Working together, hand in hand, to create a beautiful building that still stands and operates today was an accomplishment I still cherish. More so I cherish the time I had with my Dad. How wonderful it would be if all young boys could spend a summer working hand in hand with their fathers. It would create a tight bond between them which is too often lacking in today's world.

## Mortar and Muscles

The body is an amazing organism of bones, muscle, and tendons. It is so adaptable that men and women have learned to live in extreme heat or extreme cold and survive well. They can also go for long periods surviving food deprivation and torture and still bounce back. Wounds and punctures of the skin can heal without a doctor's medication. So it was with the screaming muscles that resulted from working with my father.

At the end of the first day, I was absolutely exhausted. My Dad drove me home that night. I left my bike at the work site. The next morning I could barely move. Dad was there early to pick me up and we went through the same routine again. By the end of the day I was once more exhausted. Again Dad drove me home. This continued all week. By Friday evening I felt I could get home on my bike, so I pedaled home.

After a weekend spent mostly in bed to recuperate, I felt much better. During the second week I was actually starting to catch on to my Dad's routine. While he was getting ready to work and laying out his plumb lines, I hauled his blocks to the proper spot and spaced them as he liked. Then I mixed up a batch of mortar and had it at the ready the minute he was ready to start. During the day I anticipated whether or not he would want blocks or mortar next. As a result I stopped wasting precious minutes doing tasks out of sequence. Slowly my muscles began to adjust to the new work loads and I felt myself becoming stronger. By the third week I had improved so much I could keep up with him.

One day he totally caught me by surprise.

"Sonny boy, you're doing fine now keeping up with me with the mortar and blocks. How would you like to try laying some block?" he asked warmly. "You may have to do this someday to make a living."

"Dad, thanks. I'd like to give it a try," I replied in a manner not nearly as cocky as the first day of work.

Under his guidance and patience, I actually became a decent block layer. Of course, my work was on the back side of that motel, but as I drive by it when I am home for a reunion I know that my own personal handiwork is part of that building.

My Dad did one thing which really won my respect and admiration. While I was laying block, he mixed the mortar and hauled blocks to me. That gesture endeared my Dad to me in a way I can never put down in words. He showed me some respect and treated me as an equal by allowing me to do the skilled work while he did the manual labor. I'll always love him for that.

## Basketball in the Park

It was now early July and my body finally adjusted to hard manual labor. Loren and I talked on the phone several nights a week as I related to him the agonizing routine I went through each day.

He in turn told me how he ran his trap lines and hunted for crows and pheasants. Also he played basketball at Shiloh Park several evenings a week in pick up games.

"C'mon, Moose. Arvid, Paul, and I are there almost every night. Remember our pledge to stay in shape!" he reminded me.

As if I need reminding. "I'll start next week. Hopefully I haven't lost my shot," I laughed.

The following Monday as soon as my Dad and I were through with work, I hopped on my bike and headed to the Shiloh Park. I ate a sandwich and an apple on the way. Loren and Paul were waiting for me.

"It's about time, Moose," needled Paul. "We thought you were going to wimp out on us." The memory of Paul's being voted off the freshmen basketball team had long been forgotten and we were close friends again.

"Hey, some of us have to work for a living," I shot back in jest. I knew Paul had worked hard since he was a young boy.

We banged and knocked into each other for a good two hours. Finally, with all of us covered in sweat, we hopped on our bicycles and headed down to the lake front. Lake

Michigan was never warm. But it did have varying degrees of cold. The cold water actually felt good on my aching muscles as we plunged in for brief dip. Later we laid on the warm sand and talked baseball, football, and girls... the favorite topics of most teenage boys.

We met at the park three or four times a week for the rest of the summer and cycled down to the lake afterwards. Not only did we get in better shape from this effort, but we further forged a bond between us that carried us through some tough times in the future.

## Check Up

Before my sophomore football season could begin, I had to clear another hurdle: the annual test for my heart and legs.

"Robert, it's about time we go to see Dr. Kalem again. I'll make an appointment for next week," my Mom said firmly.

The thought of being checked again for my fitness to play sent chills up my spine. I couldn't give up football at this point.

"Oh, Mom. I don't have to go," I pleaded. "I worked with Dad all summer hauling bricks and mixing mortar and I never had any problems. Why don't we skip it?"

My Mother was like a bulldog. She didn't give an inch. She reacted sternly.

"If you want me to sign off on your authorization to play, you are going to get that exam. We'll discuss it no more."

Reluctantly I nodded in agreement. Early next week I found myself once again in front of Dr. Kalem going through tests. I felt my heart beating stronger than usual and tried to calm down my sense of unease. Finally the tests were over.

"Robert," Dr. Kalem pronounced, "you are fine. Your heart continues to be strong. The nerves in your legs still don't respond like they should, but it is not so bad to stop you from playing football."

I leaped off the table with a yelp of joy. I'm still on the team! Bring on the sophomore season.

## Bad News Travels Quickly

The tryouts for the Junior Varsity team started in the middle of August on the Zion practice field. The very first thing we heard when we reported for the two a day drills in the fall was that Evan Ellis had been promoted to Assistant Varsity Coach.

"Oh, great," I told Loren. "I thought we were done with him after freshman year."

"For gosh sakes! Don't worry about it!"

"When we move up to the Varsity next year, he'll be on our butt again. What a rotten deal."

"Anything could happen by next year," Loren countered irritably.

"I guess you're right." I wasn't consoled easily.

"Let's make the best out of this season."

Loren was right, of course. No use spending time worrying over some perceived problem in the future. Besides Coach Ellis was only the assistant. I had a good rapport with Coach Rushforth and he was still the Varsity head coach.

Dick McGrew was the JV coach. He was a quiet, insightful man. He was very handsome... always well dressed and dapper. I knew Coach McGrew couldn't be as tough or sarcastic as Coach Ellis, so I looked forward to playing the new season with enthusiasm.

## The First Crack in the Pledge

The team faced a real disappointment on the very first day. Arvid Detienne announced to us all that he was not going to play football anymore.

"My Mother feels that football is too dangerous. She doesn't want me to get badly hurt, so she won't give me permission to play."

"But Arvid," I implored with urgency. "We really need you out here."

"I'm sorry," he told me with obvious disappointment in his voice, "but I won't be out there this season."

"What about the pledge you took with us last fall?"

"There's nothing I can do about it, Moose."

Other members of the team talked to him at great length as well. Several of us went so far as to agree to come to Arvid's home and talk to his Mom directly on how much it meant to us to have him on the team.

But it was to no avail. His Mom stood adamant against football, and that was the end of Arvid's athletic career at Zion Benton High School.

Arvid and I continued our friendship, but I was disappointed not to have him on the team. I always felt he could have been an outstanding player and would have helped us immensely.

But one of the amazing things about this team was the fact that every time we lost somebody for one reason or another, someone else came along and filled in very nicely. In this case, Bill Hosken was moved from the guard spot into the wingback position and filled that slot in an excellent fashion. He was the fastest man on the team, and as a result our reverses often made big yardage. Also his experience as a lineman suited him well at the wingback position since he was used heavily as a key blocker in the Single Wing formation.

## Dick McGrew

Dick McGrew, our new JV Coach was liked by all the girls at the school. He spent too much time talking to them for my liking. I would have preferred the same interest in football. Coach McGrew eventually became a Hall of Famer in the State of Illinois because of his coaching successes in basketball, but frankly he didn't know much about football. Too often he found reasons to miss one or two practices every week. His heart was just not in football.

We also learned that Coach McGrew was miffed that Evan Ellis was promoted over him to the assistant Varsity coach position, especially since he coached at Zion several years longer. How that decision was made, I do not know. But I suspect the selection was made on ability and not on longevity. No matter what the reasoning for this promotion of Evan Ellis, it was to have a dramatic effect on the team while we were sophomores and on the team again when we were seniors.

On the afternoons that Coach McGrew didn't show up, Loren and I took over the backfield and ran plays for an hour or so. Paul drilled the line in blocking and tackling. Then together as a team we ran plays the best we knew how. Even when Coach McGrew was there, there was very little guidance. On the one hand, I liked not being yelled at all the time, but on the other I was distressed that the team was not showing progress.

We had a good cadre of returning players, although once again we had only a total of 15 players turn out for the team. The Harbor Boys had a disproportionately large number of players once again. In fact, they made up the entire left side of the line. Phil returned at the left end position. He was ready again with his now to be expected tirades against the refs.

"I hope there are better refs this year. The fifteen yard penalties are killing me," he chortled. To this day, when he walks into a room, I start to smile. I always thought he could have been a stand up comic like Jerry Seinfeld.

Leon started at left guard and Bogie was our center. Bob started at the right guard position and again was our best all around lineman. He was off the ball so fast after the snap that the referees often flagged him for being offside. In the prior year Ellis several times ran on the field and had to explain to the refs he wasn't offside, he was just quick off the ball.

Paul anchored the right side of the line at tackle. True to his word, he kept himself in great shape all summer working on cars. He was big, strong, and an able leader on the field. We all looked to him with respect. I wished we had about four more like him.

Bobby was back at tailback, Loren at quarterback. Bill took over at wingback, and I filled the fullback spot.

Much to our surprise Middy came out again and showed signs of becoming an excellent running back. Without Ellis as our coach, he may stick around for the whole season this year I thought to myself. He sure could be an asset to this team if he really tried.

So hope sprang anew in my heart. I sincerely felt we had the makings of an excellent team. Once again, alas, reality caused my expectation to fall flat on its face.

## The Lost Season

We opened the season with an away game against Highland Park, one of the schools in the Suburban Conference made up of schools with a 2000 student enrollment in the suburbs of Chicago. Whoever scheduled them for the opening game must have been a little crazy. But considering all that, our defense played very well and held the Little Giants to two TDs. Unfortunately our offense didn't function well at all. Coach McGrew was of no help during the game, at halftime, or afterwards. We lost 12-0. It was another moral victory for holding a much bigger school to a low score.

Next were the Libertyville Wildcats. We did not play them the year before even though they were in our conference. The story was about the same. We really played tough on defense, but the offense showed no consistency. We lost 14-0. Coach McGrew's lack of knowledge concerning the Single Wing really began to create a sense of disgruntlement among the team. No one liked to get yelled at by Coach Ellis when we were freshmen, but none of us liked losing either. We quickly realized that we were going nowhere with Coach McGrew.

The third opponent was Horlick of Racine at home, the same school the Varsity crushed the previous year. We were so inept it almost made me cry. It's one thing to play well and lose. It's another to play pathetically the whole game. We needed coaching leadership. We lost to Horlick 22-0. Three straight shutouts. This was not a good sign.

Dan Loblaw's article in the Waukegan News Sun summed up what many people were thinking.

*"After a promising end of the freshmen season, the JV Zee Bees have floundered through their first three games. In fact, they are yet to score a touchdown being shut out by all three opponents. How disappointing after what appeared to be great potential after their late season success last year."*

## Loss of a Staunch Supporter

One event happened at the Horlick game over which I still feel badly. Since we all performed so poorly, Coach McGrew took some of the starters out of the game to let some of the substitutes play. As I walked to the bench I took off my helmet and slammed it to the ground in disgust. My Mother was sitting in the stands and it was the first time she ever saw me taken out of a game. So she immediately came down out of the stands to find out why.

"Robert, are you all right?" she asked.

"Yes, Mom. I'm fine," I answered shortly.

"Are you hurt?" she asked concernedly.

"No, Mom. I'm not hurt," I replied curtly.

"Then why did the coach take you out of the game, son?" she went on innocently.

My patience wore thin at that point. I was a little embarrassed having my Mom asking me these questions during a game in front of our bench. So I decided to end it quickly.

"Because I stink. I'm playing lousy. That's why the coach took me out. Now go home and leave me alone."

I saw the hurt in my Mother's eyes as her shoulders slumped and she slowly turned around to go back into the stands. Immediately I regretted what I had said. She was a loyal supporter and simply wanted to know why her baby boy was taken out of the game. It was the motherly thing to do. I knew I had crossed the line.

When I got home for dinner, I immediately apologized, but the damage was done. She never came to another game. She always asked me how each game came out, wanted to know how well I played, and told me how proud she was of me, but she would not come near that football field again. After 50 years, I still regret that outburst of impatience on my part.

## The Wheel of Fortune

It was a balmy fall weekend, one that signaled that the end of the swimming season was near. I was lying along the side of the pool at Lynn's when I heard Kay Starr's words coming from the phonograph set up near me.

> *"The Wheel of Fortune,*
> *Goes spinning around,*
> *Will the arrow point my way?*
> *Will this be the day?"*

The irony of her words caused me to snap in frustration.

"Yeah, right, Kay. That damn arrow seems to be pointing every where except at this team. What did we do to deserve this situation?"

Yes, I was feeling sorry for myself and my team. Nobody wanted to suffer through three more games like the last three.

Fortunately a lovely smile from a beautiful young girl can quickly improve any young man's disposition.

"Would you like anything from the kitchen?" Lynn asked sweetly. "I can bring you a sandwich if you like. You don't look very happy."

Betty Rae and Joyce chimed in with the same thoughts. "This is supposed to be a party and all of you act like it is the end of the world. Come on and dance. That should help."

Bogie, Paul, and Leon were up immediately and started swaying to the beat of the song with the girls in arm. I still couldn't muster enough positive thought to get into the festivities. I still had a big crush on Joyce, but I was in no mood to pursue her today.

"Sorry I'm such a grouch. I can't seem to get over how badly we are playing this year. I thought we'd be much better," I explained solemnly.

"It's that damn coach of ours," Phil groused. "He doesn't know beans about football and doesn't show up to practice half the time. Last week I was hurt so bad I asked him for a ride home and he told me to find someone else. That wasn't his job."

Leon chimed in. "I hope something changes soon... or this season is going to be a total loss."

"I know you'll do much better in the next game," Lynn offered. "We'll all be there to cheer you on." She softly put her hand on my shoulder and gave it a pat. "But for now, why don't you relax and let's enjoy the evening."

"Thank you, Lynn. You're great!" I answered appreciatively. "Now where is that sandwich?"

## The Coach Puts Me on the Spot

The following Monday night the Bears highlights TV show became a forum for Loren and me to bitch, loud and long.

"This is really getting to be a bad situation," I said forlornly. "Some guys are talking about quitting because the coaching is so bad."

"I know."

"We've got to keep the good players we have together or as seniors we won't stand a chance. What are we going to do?" I asked worriedly.

Loren replied with concern in his voice. "I don't know. Maybe having Ellis as our coach wasn't so bad after all. At least we were learning something under him."

Loren's Dad suggested we both go talk to Coach Ellis and tell him our concerns. I thought about it, but somehow going to Coach and squealing on another coach didn't seem the right thing to do.

"I'm sorry, Mr. Stried," I said. "Ellis would have my head if I tried to tell him that we didn't like McGrew as our coach. He'll tell me to quit whining and start playing football instead."

And then, when the sky often seems the darkest, something happens to bring on the dawn. God steps in through divine intervention to make everything right again. Thank God for divine intervention and his concern over Zee Bee football.

The next day at school, I was walking down the hall on my way to my next class. A too familiar voice behind me stopped me in my tracks. I had no doubt who it was without even looking.

"Moose. Come in this room for a minute. I need to talk to you," Coach said sternly.

Oh oh, I thought. Now what did I do? While I often saw Coach Ellis in the halls at school, I seldom talked to him or him to me. A nod was about the extent of our communication. When possible, I avoided him completely.

He guided me into his room and shut the door. I began to sweat.

"Tell me what is going on out there with the JV football team," he said as he scowled at me. He slammed his books on the desk. "I expected much better things out of all of you this year. Not only have you not won a game yet, you haven't even scored a touchdown in three games."

"How do I get into these things anyway?" I asked myself. On the one hand I don't want to be a tattle tale, especially not to give an opinion about a man who is a respected teacher and my coach. On the other hand, I am not happy with the way the team is coached. I could see us disintegrating out there. Coach McGrew simply was not doing his part and someone ought to be told.

"Give me the straight story," growled Coach Ellis. "I want to hear it… now!"

I took a deep breath, praying I wasn't going to pay dearly for this. "Coach, Coach McGrew really doesn't know beans about football. He has zero enthusiasm for what he is doing," I complained openly.

Coach Ellis nodded his head in concern.

"He misses practice once or twice a week. Paul, Loren and I take over to run the drills and plays. And during the games he never gives us any guidance."

My emotions began taking over. I was on a roll and I wasn't about to stop.

"Frankly, I think we are going backwards. We're definitely not getting better. Some of the players are talking about walking off the team if things don't improve."

The Coach looked surprised that I was willing to be so frank with him. "Go on," he said.

"The guys want to play football," I said with a little more confidence, "but what we're doing now is a bunch of baloney. If something doesn't change soon, this season will be a total waste."

I wanted to get it all out if I was going to tell him anything at all. The Coach stood up.

"Thank you, Moose. That's all I wanted to hear," Ellis stated without expression. With that he strode out of the room leaving me standing there alone somewhat befuddled.

I told Loren about this conversation on the way out to practice. "Did I do the right thing?" I asked him.

"If Coach asked you directly what was going on, and you told him the facts, then you did the right thing," Loren answered. "As long as you told him the truth, this will come out okay."

"I pray you are right, my friend," I said hopefully. "I pray you are right."

## Playing Against the Big Boys

That same afternoon, as soon as were finished with our calisthenics, Coach Ellis called the entire JV squad over to the Varsity practice area. "Boys, I need to work the Varsity on both offense and defense, so you're going to be their opponents," he explained.

What? I thought. We're going to get killed! The Varsity has players like Co-captains Don Bogue and JT Birmingham. Tom Douglas is a terror at tackle. They are going to wipe the field with us. Is this what our talk was about this afternoon? I wanted a change, but this is not what I had in mind. What have I done?

Coach Ellis took over the JV while Coach McGrew stood around watching. Coach lined us up first on defense. He told the Varsity to start running their complete set of plays, but he stayed with us on defense. "I know you must feel intimidated by these seniors. But remember these guys put on their pants one leg at a time like you do. I'm going to show you how you can compete against them."

Well, that's a new approach for him, I thought. He actually seemed concerned about us. But the harangue didn't change while we were on the field. "Are you gonna let that guy beat you down? What the heck kinda tackle was that... looked like a ball bouncing off a cow! Are you ever gonna do what I showed you... or do you not understand? Awww... my goodness... what a poor effort that was!"

But, we learned and learned quickly. Coach showed us how to best defend against blockers and how to set up for a tackle. He told us how to look for clues where the play was going and how to anticipate them. He knew we were in awe of these older seniors, but encouraged us to do our best. This was a new role for our former freshmen coach.

The first plays the Varsity team ran, we were overwhelmed. The difference between seniors and sophomores in high school is dramatic. Tom Douglas blocked me on one particular play and I thought I was hit by a Mack truck. "You gonna let him plaster you like that, Moose? Get up and get your stuff together!"

JT was a high stepping, fleet tailback who was tough to bring down. He scored the first three times he carried the ball against us. The last TD, he ran right at Middy and then jinked left, leaving Middy grasping at air.

"You left your jock on the field that time, Middy!" needled Ellis. "Ho Ho Ho!"

We put up token resistance while they ran at will right over the top of us. It was definitely discouraging.

After about an hour of defense, Coach switched us to offense. Running against these guys wasn't much fun either. The linemen overwhelmed our line and Bobby and I were often tackled in our own backfield. But Ellis stayed with us, patiently coaching us and showing us the correct way to run the plays. When he finally let us go after about another hour, we were a bedraggled and worn out bunch. Coach McGrew dismissed us all and we were glad to head to the showers.

When we came out for practice the next night, Coach Ellis again quickly brought us over to the Varsity area and we went at it one more time. I cringed at times when he got on Middy.

"Oh my God! That tackle will go on the books as the worst ever. I thought you wanted to play football, Middy! This isn't roundball, you know!"

I thought to myself, you keep that up, Coach, and Middy won't be around very long.

Tom blocked me hard again and sent me careening backward.

"Hey Moose... am I gonna have to rename you Mouse? What the heck kind of defense was that?" The needle never stopped.

It rankled me at first... but then, strangely... I smiled and got up more determined than before. Coach Ellis showed me how I could keep Tom Douglas away from my body using my forearm and get in position for the tackle... at least some of the time.

Coach made us scrimmage against the Varsity virtually every single night for the rest of the season. As we continued to face these bruisers every evening, something began to slowly change. We got tired of the seniors pushing us around and began to fight back.

We started to gain confidence, particularly on defense. Slowly at first, but more and more as one by one some of us made good tackles on JT. Even our offensive plays began to gain yardage. I found if I kept my head down and plowed forward as hard as I could, I made consistent gains. The linemen were beginning to make better blocks as well.

By the end of the week, we were starting to shout encouragement to each other.

"Philibuck, nice tackle."

"Good block, Paul."

"Moose, good run."

"Good pass defense, Loren."

"Nice fake, Middy."

Bogie had the opportunity to play defense against his older brother at center. By the end of the second week, he was playing him tough also. That must have made for some interesting conversation at the dinner table at night.

Unfortunately Middy didn't see things the same way. He came up to me one day in gym class and announced he was leaving the team…again.

"Moose, I told you I didn't like playing for Ellis. He's on my butt constantly."

"Hey… he's on everybody's butt," I said concealing my frustration.

"Yeah, but he's always ragging on me about quitting last year… so I say the hell with football. I don't need his needling every night."

"Okay, Middy, if that's the way you feel about it," I said sadly.

While I was in sympathy with him about Ellis' constant harangues on us, I began to realize that I would rather have a demanding, dedicated coach than an uninterested, lackadaisical one. I was slowly beginning to appreciate what Coach Ellis had to offer us.

"We'd all like you stick it out with us," I said. "You're a darn good player… and we need you."

"It's not worth it," said Middy. He turned around and left me there in the gym.

When Coach found out that Middy dropped off the team again, he scoffed, "If he can't take it out here like the rest of you do, then he shouldn't be here anyhow." And that was the end of it.

By the end of the third week, we all were actually looking forward to scrimmage against the older players. We were beginning to realize that we could hold our own against them. The Varsity was showing signs of respect as well.

After one particular play where I fended off Tom Douglas and dropped JT for no gain, Tom looked at me with a big smile and said, "Moose, you are starting to play like you really mean it out here. Good job!"

That small comment meant the world to me.

As we improved against the Varsity, we also improved in our own games. Even though we still weren't getting much coaching or guidance from Coach McGrew, we carried with us into the game the things Coach Ellis taught us. Our games started to be fun again.

About this time Dru Ellis gave birth to her second baby girl. Mary Beth was born on October 2, 1952. Coach Rushforth made the announcement in practice one night.

"Coach Ellis won't be with us for several days. His wife gave birth to their second little girl last night."

"Wow! How about that Loren?" I said as we were stretching out. "Another girl! How many do you think he'll have?"

"I dunno. There are three boys in my family."

"And there are three in mine. I guess from now on the odds are in his favor to have boys," I prophesized. How wrong I was!

Lake Forest made the mistake of sending their B team to play us since we lost so badly to their starters in the two games we played against them as freshmen. While the B team was not a bad group of players, after playing against our Varsity, playing these guys was a relief. We beat them 9-0 controlling most of the game with a steady offense. Our defense showed signs of becoming a force. They came close to our goal line only once. Everyone on the team was making solid tackles and showing the benefits of playing against the Varsity on a daily basis.

Then Warren came to town and we tied them 7 – 7. It was a good battle that could have been won with a few breaks. But we weren't getting killed anymore. We were playing like a team and getting better every game. Everyone was enjoying being a real team once again.

The last game of the season was again against Lake Forest. This time they played their first team. We fell 19-6, but two touchdowns didn't come against us until the last quarter. We were in the game until the final whistle. Our defense was really tough for three quarters. A penalty and a fumble did us in. Only a 13 point difference! We were getting closer!

Paul was such an aggressive player and improved so much during these scrimmages that he was elevated to the Varsity team. We were all proud that one of us had received that honor. Fortunately Coach Ellis allowed him to play in our JV games when it didn't interfere with his Varsity practice. Paul played with the first team quite a bit in the second half of the season and was the only sophomore to be awarded a letter in football.

The Varsity still had a couple of games to go when our season ended, so we continued to scrimmage against them. Coach Ellis took us over completely. McGrew never even showed up the last two weeks of the season. Obviously there were some hard feelings between these two coaches.

While I did not see it personally, some of our teammates told me that one day Coach McGrew and Coach Ellis got into a shouting match in the boy's gym. Ellis had his coat off and was ready to start swinging away at Coach McGrew when the janitors broke it up. Undoubtedly it was about the JV football team and the way we were handled.

This bad blood lasted for the next two years. There were several more verbal shouting matches that made everyone cringe. The animosity between the two coaches was evident to anyone who cared to notice. I was concerned that the bad blood between them during our sophomore year might affect our football team during our senior year. Only time would tell.

### JV Basketball

Coach McGrew was also the JV basketball coach. Paul, Loren, and I all wanted to play basketball again as sophomores. But I had some concerns. I prayed that Coach McGrew didn't put two and two together and figure out it was I who had told Coach Ellis what was happening with the JV football team. Secondly, since I had missed most of my freshman basketball season, I knew my skills weren't up to what they should be. Thirdly, unlike the JV football team which was all sophomores, the JV basketball team included juniors.

It would be no easy task to make the team under any circumstances. I didn't want my disclosure to Coach Ellis to complicate my goal. Fortunately, Coach McGrew hadn't learned of my session with Ellis and he needed extra players so the team would have enough players to scrimmage.

I was picked for the team. So were Paul and Loren. Middy came out and immediately reestablished himself as one of the stars. It was good to have us all together again.

Coach McGrew knew his basketball very well. Led by our juniors the team won the North Suburban JV League. I played enough to keep me happy, mostly in mop up roles. Occasionally in a tight game I played when one of our better players fouled out. I knew all along this wasn't my sport. It was a fun game, but I realized I better plan on sticking with football if I planned to make any mark at Zion. Paul and Loren played much more than I and made a major contribution to the success of the team. Frankly, I was happy to sit the bench and be content as a sub.

At the end of the first semester I again got Loren pumped up for his finals and once again he came through with flying colors. I received an A minus in Latin so my Mom was happy. Thus we both would be eligible for the next football season. After the strong showing we made in the last three games, we were all fired up and ready to be on the Varsity the following fall season.

## End of Semester Celebration

We were once again in Betty Rae's barn for our end of first semester celebration. How lucky we are, I thought as Loren, Paul, and I walked in, to have such a fun place to have our parties and how nice that Betty Rae's Mom was willing to do all this work. The music had already started.

*"How much is that doggie in the window? (Arf! Arf!)*
*The one with the wagglely tail.*

*How much is that doggie in the window? (Arf! Arf!)*
*I do hope that doggie's for sale."*

Each time the song came to the Arf! Arf! part, Leon,
Phil, Loren, Paul, Bill, Bogie and I would let out the most
God awful yowls and yelps ever heard in the world of
dogs.

"I can see why Patti Page never hired you guys to be
her backups for that song," Betty Rae laughed. "That was
terrible!"

"Hey, don't give us that static or I'll turn out the lights
again," said Leon jokingly. "What would your Mom say
this time?"

"No, please don't," Betty Rae squealed. "She may not
let us have any more parties if you do."

Leon laughed and walked toward the light switch.

"You little devil," scolded Betty Rae. "You're going to
get us all in trouble one day."

Leon faked turning out the lights and laughed. Joyce
walked in with a tray of cookies and Cokes for everyone,
and set them on the big picnic table in the corner. We
immediately forgot about the lights and went for the
cookies. I offered one to Joyce.

"Say, Joyce…I heard that selections for cheerleader
will be coming up soon."

"Yes," said Joyce demurely.

"I know you've been working hard with the
cheerleaders club over these past two years," I said as I
started munching a big chocolate chip.

"It's been a lot of fun."

"Do you think you'll be selected as a junior?"

"I really don't know," said Joyce. "I hope so."

Modesty was always one of Joyce's endearing traits. I
was glad I found something Joyce would talk to me about.

"I'll be pulling for you," I said trying to put on a
winning smile. I still had the crush and tried to please her
whenever I could.

"If you're pulling for me… maybe I'll make it," she
replied with a smile that thrilled me.

I wasn't done yet. "Hey, guys, who here wants to see Joyce be one of our cheerleaders next year?"

The big cheer that went up told me the response was unanimous. "I guess you've got it made," I offered in support.

"I wish you guys were on the selection panel," said Joyce with a smile.

Phil had an idea he threw out. "You want me to intimidate any of the teachers on the panel? I could threaten to trash their car if they don't vote for you."

"Yeah," said Leon. "Maybe I could hustle one of the junior cheerleaders. I'd promise to give them a ride in my chick car if they vote for you."

Joyce laughingly replied, "Thanks, but no thanks. I think I'd better earn this on my own."

I saw Arvid standing alone at the side of the room. Since he left the team, he seemed to hold back and wasn't as much "one of the gang" as before. I walked over to him.

"What're you doing these days," I asked.

Arvid looked at me, his loneliness penetrating his gaze.

"I've been working," he said, "... trying to save up enough money for a motorcycle."

"Hey," I exclaimed, "a Harley?"

"Whatever I can afford," said Arvid. "I want to try racing 'em."

"Sounds like fun," I said.

Paul walked up and slapped Arvid on the back. "You know... we'd still like to see you around... even if your Ma won't let you play football."

"Darn right," I said.

"That's good," said Arvid, "but it's not the same."

"Well, make it the same," said Paul.

Arvid smiled. "I'll try."

The rest of the evening was spent dancing, singing, eating, and enjoying each other's company. Arvid seemed to take part more than before. I was glad Paul and I talked to him. I didn't want to lose a good friend, even if he didn't play football anymore.

## The End of Sophomore Year

Loren chose to play baseball again in the spring. Our sophomore squad had a very good season and Loren was one of the better hitters. Middy was the star pitcher and the best hitter on the team.

I continued to participate with the track team. I improved in both the shot and discus and began scoring points for our team in our track meets. It was an honor to represent ZBTHS in each of these events. I never scored enough points to earn a Varsity letter, but it was a thrill to know I was contributing. I was happy to add my JV track letter to my collection of growing awards.

But my heart was still set on a much higher athletic achievement. My goal was always the North Suburban Championship in football. I began to run as much as possible as part of my conditioning program, even though I did not compete in any running events. I knew the coming fall would be a challenge.

Phil made his mark running the low hurdles. After finishing first, second, or third in several meets, Phil earned enough points to be the only sophomore to earn a letter in track. I was very pleased for him and proud of his accomplishments.

Bill was very competitive in the sprints and Dick ran the relays. It was great having football teammates and good friends on the track team with me.

About that time Bogie began dating a soft spoken and lovely girl...Kay Kern. Kay was a deeply religious young lady and well liked by all of us on the football team. She attended all of our home football games and was an avid supporter. So it pleased all of us when they started going together.

"Hey, Bogie, did you know Kay and I went all the way through Lakeview together?" I asked him one day in the hall. "In fact, she used to come to my birthday parties when we were little kids as well."

"Yeah?"

"I've always liked her."

"Well... don't like her too much," smiled Bogie.

"She's all yours, Bogie," I laughed punching him in the ribs.

"Well, thanks. We always have fun together," Bogie responded in a happy voice.

Class officer elections took place and one of my long time friends from Lakeview was elected our new president. I really enjoyed my role as president for two years, but it was now time to turn over the reins to a new leader. None of the original four officers ran for reelection.

I had one more duty to perform as president before stepping down and that turned out to be surprisingly pleasant event. The incoming class of freshmen was brought to the high school from the various grade schools for a day of orientation. Each class president got up and said a few words regarding what the new class might expect. I was asked by the faculty to talk about the various athletic teams which would be available to each of them. I said I would gladly do so.

Bogie came up to me a few days before the assembly was to take place. "My sister, Barbara, is going to be a freshman next year. She'll be at the assembly, so if you get a chance, please say hello and make her feel welcome," he asked me as a friend.

"Sure, Bogie, I'll be glad to," I answered. "Anything for a teammate."

After we made our speeches and the teachers finished their briefings, it was time to seek out Barbara Bogue. After looking at numerous name tags as I wandered through the crowd, I finally found her talking with some of her friends. I was thunderstruck! Bogie's sister Barbara was a doll to put it mildly. She had a sweet, angelic face, a voluptuous figure, and a beautiful smile. I knew from the moment I met her that this was someone I wanted to date and get to know better....a lot better!

"Uhm, hi, Barbara, my name is Bob Osmon," I stammered. "Bogie asked me to find you and answer any questions you might have for next year."

When she smiled at me, my heart absolutely went into a flutter. "Dick told me a lot about you, Bob... I'm glad to meet you," she replied sweetly. I had almost forgotten Bogie's given name... Dick.

I spent as much time with Barbara as I could answering questions and offering advice on what to study in her freshman year. Finally the orientation period was coming to an end and I knew I had to break it off. But I didn't want to.

"May I see you sometime this summer?" I asked hoping beyond hope for the right answer. "My Mom bought a car this spring, so I can drive down the Harbor to pick you up."

She looked at me shyly. "Sure," she said.

"Maybe we could go to the beach or a movie sometime."

"I'd love to do that. I'll need to ask my parents, but since Dick knows you, I don't think they'll object."

"Great!"

"Besides my Dad knows your Dad very well. He's done some plumbing for him in the past."

Under my breath, I said, "Thank you, Dad."

In a demure, yet forthright manner, she said she would look forward to seeing me this summer. I knew I was hooked. She probably knew it too.

As I walked away, suddenly I got a guilt pang right in the solar plexus. What about Joyce? Was I cheating on her, I wondered. How could I be cheating on her when we only dated once? Any overt attention in this relationship had only been one way. Besides, she was now dating an upper classman, so I reasoned that I was in the clear. It would be nice to have a girl friend for a change... one who returned my affection. I wondered if Barbara was the one.

**********

# Chapter 6
# Junior Year – 1953

As I entered the Highland Park Hospital again early the next morning, I couldn't help but wonder what the Coach's situation might be today.

"Would he be worse..... maybe confined to bed?" I asked myself. My heart was full of so many emotions that I could barely think. I don't think I can stand to see him die in front of me. That would be too much to bear.

But, my job was to cheer him up, not come in with a dour look. So I formed a quick prayer in my mind and said in a low voice, "Dear Lord, help me to be your candle today in Coach Ellis's life. Help me to make his day brighter. For all he has done for me, let this day be a small thing I can do for him." A feeling of calmness came over me. With a deep breath, I walked up the steps and through the automatic doors.

"Moose. I'm over here," came the familiar voice. There he was again, wearing the white hospital gown with the ankle weights at his side. He also had on the old baseball cap he wore every day for four years while he was coaching us. It actually was a little comical. "Dru found my old CSU Bears cap, so I thought I would wear it today. Pretty cool, huh?" he said with great relish and a goofy look on his face.

And I had been worried about cheering him up. "Hey, Coach, you look like you're set to take the field," I hailed him cheerily. "You ready for your hikes up and down the hallways?"

"As soon as you get these things on me. I've been waiting for you for over an hour. I ought to make you run laps for being late for practice," he said with a big grin. With that, he let out one of his big guffaws. "Ho! Ho! Ho!" he roared, his top teeth jutting out over his lower ones.

I couldn't help but chuckle. This man is really amazing, I said to myself. No self pity here whatsoever. Should I ever be in a situation like this, I need to remember the way he is handling himself. I should do so well.

Off we went again, up and down the halls, about six times. It was a slow shuffle, but nonetheless, it was a steady shuffle. As he gripped my arm, I thought to myself what a role reversal this was. As a teenager I never imagined that I would be helping this man in any form or fashion. He was such a strong personality that I believed he would never need help from anyone. Now I was in the prime of my life with no doubts about my capabilities or health. I realized that if Coach was in this condition at so young an age, someday it could happen to me. So I told myself to pay attention to how he was acting so I would remember his role model if a similar situation affects my life.

Near the end of his sixth trip up and down the hall, he told me he was tired and needed rest. I helped him back to his bed and watched as the nurses gave him his medicine and tucked him in, like a mother would do her little son. As he started to drop off to sleep, once again he uttered his favorite play call, "Moose up the Gut". With a silly grin on his face, he slipped into deep breathing.

"Moose up the Gut," I repeated wistfully. It was both a blessing and a curse. This particular play resulted in both my highest and lowest points while playing Zee Bee football. I wondered if he realized that. I needed to talk to him about a few things when he awakened. With that, I slipped back into my own reverie.

## Summer Employment

I was in a dilemma what to do during the summer of 1953. The motel that my Dad and I worked on the previous summer was long completed. Dad now devoted full time to making this venture a success. No more building anything with him. I asked him to inquire with some of his friends and find out if any of them needed a good laborer. It seemed construction was down that year, so no one needed any additional help. I tried the Park District to see if any jobs were available, but no luck there

146

either. Then through the grapevine I heard that a Dairy Queen which recently opened was looking for help.

I immediately hopped on my bike and rushed down to the store. It was located on Sheridan Road and 23$^{rd}$ Street, so it was only a few blocks from my house. Doc Studebaker, the owner, interviewed me and asked if I could work six days a week, Monday through Saturday, from 10 AM to 6 PM. I told him I would, so I got the job. It was modest pay, but it brought in money for clothes and helped my Mom at home with groceries. So I was elated to get the work.

It also worked perfectly for the workout schedule I planned for myself to prepare myself for next year's football. I got up about 7 AM, grabbed a quick bowl of cereal and ate some toast, and then headed out to the backyard. I did about 30 minutes of calisthenics and lifted weights.

My weight was a single bar with two #10 cans filled with cement on each end. I made them during gym class in seventh grade and now they were really of use. After about a dozen exercises, I took off running around the temple site, the place where my Mom took me as a baby to see the fire. From my house, around the temple site and back was about 2 ½ miles. I didn't push myself too hard because I knew I had a full days work ahead, but still got a good workout.

After I returned home, I showered, rested a bit, and headed down to the Dairy Queen. It was a fun job. We were always busy. Soft serve ice cream was a novelty in those days and the smooth texture of the Dairy Queen blend was very popular. I learned to put the curl on top of the cone as well as anyone in the DQ organization.

Many friends came by each day so I saw everyone in town all summer long. It was a super place to work. At the end of the day, if there was any mix left in the machines, I was allowed to pull it out and take it home as it couldn't be reused. So my Mom and I always had a freezer full of the best ice cream in the world.

We also had car hops in those days. The customers didn't even have to get out of their car if they didn't want to do so. The girls who worked as car hops took the cones or shakes from me on a tray and attached the tray to the car hooking two claws over the open window. Roller skate service hadn't started yet in Zion, but car hopping was considered very cool among teenagers.

After work, as in the previous summer, I headed down to the park and played basketball until dark with Loren, Paul, and any other teammates who could make it that night. After our customary dip in Lake Michigan to cool off, Loren and I headed home. I bolted down a late dinner and hit the sack, looking forward to doing it all again the next day.

Life was good in Zion during those days. Of course, Sunday was reserved for church. Great schedule! Great routine! Great life! I was happy. I was making money and getting physically stronger each day. There had to be a dark cloud on this horizon somewhere. And there was!

## Hammered Again

Loren, Paul, and I were playing basketball in the evening at the park one warm summer night in July. Coach Ellis showed up unexpectedly and made his way to our court.

"Moose," he bellowed loud enough for everyone to hear. "Where're you working this summer? Are you working for your Dad again?"

"No, Coach. My Dad retired from construction work."

"So what're you doing?"

"I took a job with the new Dairy Queen on Sheridan Road," I answered proudly. "It's a great place to work."

He came down on me like a ton of bricks. "What?" he yelled in a nasty voice. "You're working in a damn ice cream store! You should be working in hard labor somewhere, doing work that will get you in shape for football." He shook his head vigorously in disgust.

The three of us looked at him in amazement. I had no idea what to say.

"Hell, when you report for practice this fall, you'll be a piece of flab and not worth the effort to suit you up." With that he turned and walked away, leaving me standing speechless, as he did at the Kenosha game when we were freshmen.

I raged at Loren for 20 minutes. "What in hell does this guy want from me? I'm working to bring in money to help my Mom, I'm working out with weights and running every morning before I go to work, and I'm playing basketball every night. No matter what I do, I will never please this guy," I said in disbelief.

Paul advised calmness. "Take it easy, Moose. He must have a good reason for being so concerned. Remember everything is football with him."

"Who in hell does he think he is? He doesn't run my life. I'll do damn well as I please."

"He didn't even give you a chance to explain your workout routine. Sometimes he's really unfair," Loren responded sympathetically. "The heck with him! Give it your best effort this summer and be ready for him in the fall."

"I'm already doing that," I countered irritably. "I damn well don't like his talking to me that way. Someday he and I are going to have it out."

"Don't do anything rash. Remember our pledge," Loren cautioned.

"Yeah! Yeah! I understand," I replied impatiently. Slowly I calmed down.

Even though I said he wouldn't get to me, I worked even harder for the rest of the summer, mumbling to myself the whole time about this damn critical coach I was destined to play for. When the middle of August rolled around, I was ready. As in the prior years, another surprise waited for us as the season started.

But first I once again knew I had to take the dreaded heart and legs check up. Again I protested to my Mother that I didn't need it, but I knew from the start my pleas would fall on deaf ears. While my heart was in a nervous state of affairs, I passed again with flying colors. Somehow God gave me a strong constitution and a determined will. Together these traits kept me on the path to recovery.

## New Head Coach

Evan Ellis was promoted to head coach during the course of the summer. Joe Rushforth, the former head coach, decided he did not want the responsibility of the head position anymore. So in an agreement made at the end of the school year, Coach Ellis and he swapped jobs. Coach Rushforth was now the assistant and line coach. Coach Ellis was now head coach and handled the backs.

Great, I said to myself. Isn't this going to be fun? At least now I know why he was so uptight this summer. He knew he was going to be the head coach and he wanted the team to be as good as possible. Looks like two more years of harangue and harassment. I guess I'd better grit my teeth and get used to it. He's not going away. Maybe as head coach he will yell at someone else for a while.

I knew from the moment that Coach Ellis was announced as the new head coach that Middy wouldn't come out. And I was right. He wouldn't even consider it. We all knew how strong minded Middy was, so none of us even tried to talk him into playing this year. Besides we had two good tailbacks.

But then we suffered an even bigger blow to our team. Bob Lee announced he would not play football this year. I went to talk to him immediately.

"Moose, my church doesn't believe in violence," he explained to me quietly. "They feel it is against the good book."

"It's a game, Bob," I said.

"I love being on the team with you guys, but I can't go against my religious beliefs. Please don't be mad at me for it."

"Well, damn, Bob," I said irritably. "What about the pledge we made two years ago. You were one of the biggest supporters for it."

"I know. I know."

"Now you're backing out as just as we finally are going to be on the Varsity. Please reconsider," I begged with utmost sincerity. "Hell, next to Paul, you're our best player."

Bob's shoulders slumped as he put out his hand to grasp mine. "I'm sorry. I sincerely am sorry." He turned and walked away.

I immediately went to the Harbor Boys fully intending to enlist their help.

"Leon… Bogie… Phil. You guys grew up with Bob. Don't you have any influence on him? What's going on?" I yelled as I threw up my hands in disgust.

Bogie was a very devout Christian himself and stepped up to offer an explanation.

"Bob belongs to a very conservative, fundamental church in the Harbor and this is part of their belief. Frankly, I'd be very reluctant to pressure him to go against his religious beliefs. He must feel terrible about leaving us as it is. But I'll explain how much we all want him to be on the team."

All three of them talked to Bob at various times, but when religion played that strong a role in a person's life, we had to respect his feelings, no matter how adverse the consequences to us. None of them were able to change his mind.

During the very first day of practice Coach Ellis called Loren, Bill, and me over for a meeting. "Boys, I need your help. I have a very good senior backfield set for this year, but I'm hurting for linemen… especially since Bob Lee has decided not to return to the team. I would like each of you to learn to play some line positions as well as your backfield spots. I want Loren and Bill to work at the guard spots and Moose at tackle. It could really help us out."

Frankly, I was not elated about playing in the line, but I did agree he had the backfield well set. LeRoy Cliff, Larry Peterson, George Doty, and Karl Holzman, all seniors, played together since they were freshmen, and were a smoothly functioning unit. They were Coach Ellis' first team at Zion, so he knew their abilities well.

George was the best athlete of the four and played fullback. He had great speed and agility. But he was prone to injury.

Larry was the brains of the team and had an excellent knowledge of play calling. Tall and slender, he was the quarterback.

LeRoy was the sparkplug of the team. He always had a smile on his face and loved competition. When the team was in difficult straits, it was always LeRoy who pulled everyone up.

But Karl was the man who made the team go. He was solidly built, a steady, consistent runner, and a good passer at the tailback position.

All four of them acted as mentors to the juniors. They willingly took time to show us how to block, handle the ball, tackle, and do all the little things that we had not learned the previous year. Karl in particular was a wonderful teammate. He always encouraged us to keep up the good work and offered guidance at every chance. This special attention to us was both valuable and appreciated. All four of them earned the respect of every junior on the team.

The starting lineup began to take form.

From the juniors Paul filled the right tackle spot. Bogie became the center. Phil backed up both ends. Bobby Young backed up the tailback. Leon filled the left guard spot. Bill, Loren, and I worked out each day splitting time between running backfield plays and learning the linemen responsibilities. I became the backup for fullback and both tackle positions.

There was one new player who reported for practice who made a huge impact on our team. He turned out to be exactly the replacement for Bob Lee we needed. The previous spring Evan Ellis spotted John Jecevicus in the hallway one day and asked him if he had ever played football. John said he hadn't but might be interested. He was a big, strapping, Lithuanian farm boy, used to hard work and strong as an ox. He was about 6'1" tall and weighed in at 190 pounds of solid muscle. Coach got him to agree to come out for football with the caveat that when the crops were ready to be harvested, he would be allowed to take off to help his Dad.

This arrangement turned out to be an excellent compromise. I always thought of John as a man mountain and he filled the end position on both offense and defense in an outstanding manner. Coach immediately nicknamed him "Lugan". I surmised that was slang for Lithuanians. Didn't matter. That was his new name.

The two a day practices started. Bill and Loren learned to be guards, and I learned to play tackle. Then from time to time we also practiced at the backfield positions. Kind of a jack of all trades, but master of none situation. Although I was skeptical at the time, it turned out we all started in the line at different times during the year due to injuries to the first stringers. After a season of playing in the line as juniors, I believe it made all three of us a lot tougher as backs when we were seniors. Coach made a good decision.

## Joe Rushforth

If Evan Ellis was the brains of the coaching staff, then Joe Rushforth was the heart and spirit. He exuded enthusiasm with everything he did and everything he said. He loved his players and treated us all with great respect. Since Joe was the line coach, it didn't take long for me to realize that being out of the spotlight from Coach Ellis for a while might not be such a bad thing. I'd still be playing football, but without all the harassment.

Joe was the Captain of Zion's first team in 1940. He played two years at Waukegan High School and was a star there as an underclassman. Handsome and well built, with Nordic God type of looks, Joe was a terror on the football field.

When Zion first opened in 1939, he was required to attend the new school, but there was no football team in that first year. In the second year, a team was formed and coached by T. Ray Miller as Head Coach and Hubert Pearce as Assistant Coach. The team was made up of a bunch of young players, many of whom never wore a

Joe Rushforth, High School Years 1939-41
Captain of Zion Benton's first football team
Later head Football Coach 1950-52
Inducted into Zion Athletic Hall of Fame

football uniform before. Zion's first football team set an excellent standard for all the future teams to follow. Joe played fullback on offense and tackle on defense. My brother Carl played both offensive and defensive end. Phil Anen's cousin, Ken Johnson, played center on that first ZB team. The team ended their first season with a 5-2 record and lost to Lake Forest, the Lake County Champion, by a score of only 14-7.

Joe went on to Northern Illinois State Teacher's College (Now Northern Illinois University) in DeKalb, Illinois. He became the first string fullback in his freshman year and went on to earn three letters, earning All American honors in his junior year. He enlisted in the Marines in 1944. His knees were injured during training, so he never saw combat, but served until the end of the war. He returned to get his teaching degree at DeKalb, but his football playing days were over. He met his lovely wife Nancy there and married soon after graduation. He took his first teaching position in Galena, Illinois coaching all sports. Joe came to Zion as the head football coach in the fall of 1950.

His very first team was on the way to the North Suburban Championship when a serious injury occurred to L.T. Bonner, a terrific running back who later went to the University of Illinois. (L.T.'s claim to fame was scoring three touchdowns against Michigan one year. He also is in the Illinois Referee's Hall of Fame.) The offense was built around L. T. and in his absence, the team couldn't move the ball. They ended up losing only to Lake Forest and Crystal Lake, the Zee Bees perennial nemeses. The conference championship trophy was not yet in the Zion showcase.

There was one incident that happened involving Joe, Phil and me that Phil and I still chuckle about years later whenever we are together. In those days the helmets were heavy, hot, and bulky so we took them off whenever we could. One day Joe explained to the defensive linemen how to break a double team block, i.e. when two offensive linemen are both blocking on one defensive lineman.

"Moose and Phil," said Joe. "Get over here and let me demonstrate the moves to make when someone tries to double team you."

"Sure, Coach," we answered obediently. "Should we put on our helmets for this drill?"

"No," he answered impatiently. "I'm going to slowly walk through this move."

Naively, Phil and I both got down in a four point stance like sheep being led to the slaughter. When the ball was hiked, Joe first came at me and gave me a forearm shiver that bowled me over. He turned to Phil and with both his hands came up under his shoulder pads, lifted him off the ground, and dumped him on his back.

"Now that's the way to break a double team," he shouted with fire in his eyes. "Do you want me to show you again?"

After a few moments when the stars finally cleared from Phil's and my head, we got up with a dazed look and said, "No, that's okay. Coach. We've got it!"

Fifty years later Joe still looks like he could do the same move to us again. At least now we would be wise enough to put on our helmets. I hope!

## Barbara Bogue

During the summer I managed to meet up with Barbara several times. Once we went to the beach for an afternoon at Illinois State Beach Park and once we attended a church picnic. She was such a sweet, soft spoken young girl that I knew I wanted to spend more time with her. Barbara became, in reality, the first girl I could truly call a girlfriend.

I still carried a torch for Joyce and became tongue tied most the of the time I was around her, but as I spent more time with Barbara, my focus began to change.

Earlier that year when I turned 16, my Mother bought a used 1947 Chevrolet. It was hardly a beauty to look at, but to us it was wonderful. It meant no more hauling groceries home from Kroger's on Friday evenings, and no more walking to church on brutal cold Sunday mornings. The car gave us the freedom to do things which was otherwise unavailable.

In the first weekend that we owned the car, my Mother asked me to drive from Zion to the South Side of Chicago to visit one of my cousins who was an airline pilot with TWA. Although I was a nervous wreck driving down Chicago's Cicero Avenue, I made it there and back without a scratch. Sort of like baptism under fire.

I also discovered how nice it was to have a car when you are starting to enter the dating scene. The United States, particularly the Western states, was developed based on use of the automobile. While I know this country needs to take a good look at rapid transit in the metro areas for the future, for the sake of young men and women everywhere in the country, I pray automobiles never disappear.

In Zion we had a little inside joke among teenagers that went like this. When a young man wanted to spend some private time with his girlfriend in a romantic setting, he would ask, "Would you like to go see the submarine races?" The girl usually played along with the game.

"Where are the submarine races held?" she would ask innocently.

"Why along the shore of Lake Michigan. Haven't you ever seen them? This is an event you wouldn't want to miss."

The girl then agreed to go see the submarine races. There were many good, isolated parking spots along the lakefront of Lake Michigan, so it was no problem to pick out a secluded area. Alcohol was a total no no in Zion and none of us even knew what drugs meant in those days. Since there was never any vandalism and anything inappropriate going on, the police never bothered anyone. It was ideal for young boys and girls to get to know each other.....much better.

After finding a secluded spot, the boy would put his arm around his date's shoulder and pull her close.

Eventually the girl would ask, "So where are the submarines?"

The answer was, "Oh, they are out there. You just can't see them because they're underwater." Then nature took its course.

I clearly remembered what I learned from my previous debacle with Joyce and my Mother's stern lecture. I did not try to kiss Barbara on the first, second, or even third date. But finally one evening when I took her home, it just kind of happened. Like it was supposed to do.

"Bob, I have had a wonderful time with you this summer. Thank you so much for all the fun things we have done," Barb said sweetly as she gave me a soft, tender look.

"Barb, I, uh, er, uhm," I stuttered like an idiot. Finally I got it out. "May I kiss you goodnight?"

Without giving me an answer, she reached up, put her arms around my neck, and gave me a soft, lingering kiss. I felt like I had been shot to the moon. As the Jimmy Dean song goes, "She had kisses sweeter than wine." I drove home that night in euphoria.

Loren, Betty Rae, Barbara, and I double dated numerous times. Now that I had a girlfriend and a car, double dating was a fun thing for the four of us to do. One evening during the summer we went into Riverview Park in Chicago and had one of the best times I can ever remember. We rode the Parachute Drop, the Bobs, the Shoot the Chute, and the Whirl, a device that would spin around quickly and the floor would drop out from under you. The riders were flattened against the wall by centrifugal force. Loren and I particularly liked this ride because the girls' clothes would be tightly molded against their bodies... which made the ride particularly appealing. I suggested another spin, but both of the girls were wise to me after the first ride.

One of my favorite photographs from my high school years was taken at Riverview that summer. The setting was a mock up of a Western saloon. The girls hopped up on the bar while Loren and I stood behind them. Because of our religious backgrounds and being from Zion where bars were forbidden, this was very risqué for Loren and me. I still have that photograph in my possession, and every time I see it I can't help but think of good times we so thoroughly enjoyed during that period of our lives. It was a period of innocence and good clean fun.

Doubledate at the Saloon: Left to right: Betty Rae Birky, Loren Stried, Bob Osmon, Barbara Bogue

Dates during the football season were great times as well. The girls went to the games with their other girlfriends. Then Barb and Betty Rae met Loren and me in the parking lot behind the boy's gym after the game. We drove to Rooks' Restaurant which was located on the far side of town at 30th and Sheridan Road. This was definitely the teen hangout after football games. We would all jam together at tables and booths and relive the game for hours. The fare for the evening was always a huge burger, large order of fries, and a chocolate malted. We sang the school song several times, yelled impromptu cheers, and enjoyed being teenagers.

Since the Rooks had a daughter, Rosie, who was a year ahead of us, they understood teens and never were upset at our antics. The worst damage we ever did was to loosen the caps of the salt and pepper shakers so the next user might get a plateful when he used it. But, in retrospect, I suspect the Rooks family was wise enough to retighten all shakers after a Friday night game. The restaurant stayed in business for many years until they sold it to a Chicago group several years ago. When I drive by it now on my trips back home, the building brings back many great memories of our times there.

When we finally left Rooks, I first drove Barbara back to Windy Harbor, and then Betty Rae out to Russell. On the drive back to Zion Loren and I dissected the evening's game from beginning to end until we knew precisely everything that had gone well and everything that had not gone well. It was good preparation for what was to come in the following year.

**The Season Begins**

The headlines of the Waukegan News Sun's sports page didn't paint a very rosy picture of Zion's football fortunes for the '53 season.

*"Zee Bees picked for last place in the North Suburban Conference. In Ellis' first year as head mentor of the Zion football team, he faces a dire situation. Lacking in depth in the backfield and only two returning veterans in the line makes his start appear to be a dim one."*

Dan Loblaw's newspaper column was considered gospel in our parts of Illinois, but no one liked his analysis one bit. It went on.

*"But there are a number of juniors from last years JV squad, led primarily by big and burly Paul Jackola, who could make a difference. Loren Stried, Bill Hosken, and Bob Osmon, all backfield men last year, are learning to play linemen positions and could fill in well as the season goes on. Time will tell. But Ellis has his work cut out for him."*

The first opponent for the '53 season was Grant High School. I sat the bench most of the game, but did get in on a few plays at tackle. Loren played some at guard and was used as the middle linebacker several times. Our backfield performed well and we came away with a 13-6 victory. Not overwhelming, but any victory is a good one.

The next week we played Barrington at home. Barrington entered our conference one year before and was a powerhouse. They had a running back who was fast and very shifty. Their fullback was a big bruiser who also had speed. Add to that a good line and we were no match. They beat us 26-0. I played some at tackle and Loren played quite a bit at center linebacker.

Loren told me afterwards, "Moose, their fullback came through the line and I had a clear shot at him. I hit him as hard as I could and he bounced me straight backwards. I hardly slowed him down."

Their fullback was about 220 pounds while Loren weighed in about 145 soaking wet. But Loren was not about to accept that disadvantage as an excuse.

"I'll get him good next year," he promised.

"I know you will, pal," I nodded confidently.

After the game, the Barrington coach came to our dressing room and told Coach Ellis and the team how impressed he was that we kept fighting to the end with great spirit and determination. That became a trait of all of Coach Ellis' teams.

## Concern About Lynn

Loren, Phil, and I were standing at our lockers during the lunch hour replacing our books from morning classes with the books for the afternoon classes.

"Has anyone besides me noticed that Lynn doesn't seem to be her old self recently?" I asked my friends. "She normally is so upbeat and smiley, but since we started school she seems a little down."

Phil immediately agreed. "Yeh, I noticed that too. I cracked a joke in History class this morning and she didn't even laugh."

"And yesterday in homeroom she wasn't saying hello to everyone like she normally does either," Loren added. "What do you suppose is bothering her?"

"Well, frankly, I don't like it when one of the girls in our group is feeling down. I think we should ask her and maybe we could help," I offered.

Both Loren and Phil agreed. Phil thought for a moment.

"Hey, we're all in Social Studies together last class. Let's talk to her afterwards."

As we entered the classroom for our last class, I observed Lynn more closely than normal. Yes, I said to myself, something is bothering her. She is definitely not the Lynn I know.

After the class was over, the three of us encircled her outside in the hall.

"We have noticed that you have been down since school started," I began slowly. "We're all concerned and would like to know if there is anything we can do to help."

We could see tears come to Lynn's eyes. Mine misted over a little also. I wasn't used to seeing her like this. She hesitated to say anything at first, but then realized she was among friends, so she slowly started to tell us what was causing this change from her normal self.

"Ever since Tom Douglas left for college out in Colorado, I have really missed him. I have an empty feeling without him. Being guys you may not understand."

To tell the truth, I didn't really understand, but that wasn't the point. Lynn was hurting and being there for her was what was important.

"Tom is a terrific guy," I volunteered.

"We'll make sure you're part of any activity we're involved in," Loren added quickly, seeing her sadness.

"I'll drive out to Colorado and drag him back home for you if you want," Phil promised trying to get a small smile from her.

It worked. I saw a little smile start to creep in at the edges of her mouth.

"Seriously, Lynn," I said with as much sincerity as I could muster. "We all think the world of you. If you're unhappy, then we're unhappy. You're one of us and don't ever forget it."

"You guys are great," Lynn said with deep feeling and emotion. "I'm blessed to have friends like you. I'll eventually get over it."

"You'd better," retorted Phil. "It's a long drive to Colorado and I'm running out of gas money."

With that comment he coaxed a full smile out of her. We each gave her a small hug and headed out for practice. Breakups due to graduation when upper classmen went off to college were tough...more so than I realized at the time.

We made sure the other guys on our team understood her feelings and over the next few weeks we all went out of our way to talk to her a few minutes each day. We wanted her to understand that friendship was important in good times and bad times, like on our football team.

## Failure at Fullback

The next week the game was against Crystal Lake on their home field. Early in the game, our senior left tackle was hurt and I was inserted in that position. Actually I felt I played rather well. I made several good blocks on offense and twice on defense I broke into their backfield to make a tackle behind the line of scrimmage. Coach actually stopped to tell me I had made some good plays as we were walking into the locker room at halftime. Hmm, I thought. Maybe this is where I should have been playing all along.

I started to really gain confidence in my play at tackle when early in the fourth quarter George Doty was hurt.

"Moose, get in there at fullback for George," Coach yelled to me on the field.

"Yes, sir," I yelled back with a feeling of trepidation. I thought...Oh, oh! Am I ready for this?

I lined up in the backfield in the fullback position. Since I had not practiced there very much, I was a little nervous. My first Varsity game as a fullback. I prayed I would do well. Crystal Lake was leading 6-0 in the middle of the fourth quarter when we finally put a good drive together.

First Karl ran several times gaining seven or eight yards. Then I plunged for the first down. We repeated this sequence of plays several more times. I became more comfortable after making several first downs with "Moose up the Gut". I thought, "Hey, this is kind of fun."

But as we got closer to the end zone, the yards became tougher. We finally worked it down to the two yard line with fourth down coming up. Larry called my play and I knew I had a chance to be a hero. As we broke the huddle, I quickly glanced at the hole into which I was supposed to run. There I saw four of their biggest linemen bunched right at the intended hole and the two line backers stacked right behind them.

My God, I fretted to myself. They know exactly where I am going to run. Should I call time out and ask Larry to call another play? I was just a junior and didn't want create any confusion. I also knew better than to deviate from the drawn play because if I did and it didn't work, Coach would be on my butt something fierce. So I said nothing. I gritted my teeth, received the ball from Bogie, and drove as hard as I could toward the line.

I felt a surge as I hit the line and initially thought I was going to make it. But the surge stopped and an overwhelming force picked me up and shoved me back. I was short of the goal line by inches. We lost the game 6-0. I felt terrible. I knew I let down the entire team.

In the locker room, Ellis unloaded on me. "Moose, what the hell is wrong with you? You had the chance to tie the game and you hardly made an effort. My grandmother could have hit the line harder than you did! You've got to plow into the line like you mean it. I get so disgusted with you," he snarled and stomped away. He sulked on the bus all the way home.

"Loren, I did my best," I said sincerely as I felt tears coming to my eyes. "I just couldn't make it."

"You hit that line as hard as you could. You don't have anything to be ashamed of," Loren offered sympathetically.

Paul extended his understanding as well. "Moose, they had too many linemen all in one place. John and I moved two of them out, but we couldn't get them all. You made a good effort."

The hell with being a fullback, I told myself. I want to go back to tackle. Nobody sees what they do.

I did go back to tackle. George recovered and took his spot at fullback once again. In the next game against Warren, we tied 6-6. I played tackle the entire game and knew I played well. I was really enjoying playing the tackle position and began to think that maybe this is where I belonged. Coach Rushforth's daily instruction and inspiration by treating me with respect was paying off.

The next game was against the Scouts at Lake Forest. I played the entire game at both offensive and defensive tackle. We played them tough for three quarters. We were tied going into the fourth quarter, but some offside penalties prevented us from moving down the field. It was a 14-14 score with a few minutes to go. Coach called for a screen pass. While the timing for the play in the game was probably a good one, it was unfortunate that one Lake Forest player was not fooled. The pass sailed right into his arms and he took off for a 60 yard TD. Another tough loss, 21-14. Lake Forest beat us again. But we were getting closer. Only a seven point loss this time. To Loren and me, that was encouraging.

## The Snakemobile

I was humming Perry Como's latest hit as Loren and I parked my Mom's Chevy in front of Lynn's home. Our season was a lot more enjoyable as juniors than it was the year before.

*"Don't let the stars get in your eyes,*
*Don't let the moon break your heart.*
*Love blooms at night, in daylight it dies,*

*Don't let the stars get in your eyes."*

Lynn was having a middle of the season party just as the leaves were turning those magnificent reds and yellows. Many of us were invited to share the wonderful ambience of her parent's home and enjoy Lynn's sincere hospitality once again.

"I've noticed that every time Barbara Bogue's name is mentioned, you let the stars get in your eyes. What gives?" Loren laughed at me.

"I think I'm in love. I think about her all the time," I readily admitted.

"Oh ho!" needled Loren. "I thought you were the guy who would never fall in love. What does Bogie think of you dating his sister?"

Before I could answer, we heard the screeching of tires and the whine of a hot engine as Leon charged into the parking area just off the driveway. Arvid was in the passenger seat with him.

"Hey, it's the Snakemobile and the biggest snake of them all," laughed Loren as Leon hopped out of the car.

For his 16th birthday in the spring Leon's Dad gave him a 48 Hudson Commodore 8 Cylinder, fender skirts, dark blue, four doors, with seats that had cushions you simply sank into. To complete the image of decadence, Leon had the entire car upholstered in leopard skin. The word got around quickly among the gals of ZB High.

"Be careful if you get into Leon's Snakemobile. Once you're in there, it's really hard to get out and that could be a problem when Leon starts to get amorous," one of his previous girlfriends told everyone. "And especially don't get into the back seat unless you intend to stay for a while."

Of course, Leon knew this was the gossip being spread around about him, but it didn't deter him one iota. In fact, he considered it rather prestigious to have such a notorious reputation. All of the boys envied him... particularly Arvid who loved cars and motorcycles.

## The Snakemobile

"So what were you guys talking about when I drove up?" he asked as we started up the driveway.

"I asked Moose what Bogie thought about his dating Barbara," Loren explained with a little needle in his voice for me.

"Actually I have no idea. Tell you what. At the party today, why don't one of you subtly ask him how he feels? Then afterwards let me know," I suggested willing to let someone else do the work to find out how Bogie might feel.

"Sure, Moose. Glad to help you out. Anytime," Leon chuckled.

Lynn met us at the door and welcomed us like royalty. It appeared she realized Tom was gone for good and made up her mind to move on in her life. It was great to see her in high spirits once again. She had definitely regained her enthusiasm for life.

"So glad you all could come today. The weather is perfect for one last dip in the pool. Help your self to some Cokes and chips. The sandwiches will be out soon."

Leon immediately spotted Bogie and Kay standing together across the room and in a loud voice bellowed, "Hey, Bogie! Moose wants to know how you feel about his dating your sister."

"Leon," I exclaimed in exasperation. "You've got the subtlety of a sledgehammer."

Bogie chuckled softly. "Well, she seems very happy...and my parents seem pleased about it."

"I can't see why!" laughed Leon.

"Frankly, I'm proud to have her dating Moose."

"So what if I ask her out sometime?" Leon asked jokingly, knowing he'd get a rise out of Bogie.

"First of all I'd weld all the doors to the Snakemobile shut and then throw your keys away. Does that give you an idea how I feel?" Bogie immediately replied in mock anger.

Everyone in the room had to laugh out loud including Leon. In Zion and Windy Harbor, brothers protected their sisters in every way. But I got the answer I was looking for. Bogie approved!

## The Cutest Cheerleader in the North Suburban Conference

We found out during the summer that Joyce was selected as a Varsity cheerleader. I looked around for her. Normally she was always present by the time the rest of us arrived.

"Where's Joyce?" I asked.

Lynn replied, "She had to do some things with her parents this afternoon, so she'll be a little late."

"It's great she was selected to be a ZB Cheerleader!"

"It's terrific!" exclaimed Lynn. "She's so enthusiastic in front of the crowd. I really enjoy watching her."

"So do I," I quickly replied. "For that and other reasons."

"Hey," Phil said "Let's surprise Joyce when she comes in. Let's give her a cheer for a change."

"Great idea, Philibuck. Let's hide in the back room when she arrives," I said supporting his idea.

A few minutes later we heard her car pull into the driveway. We all scurried into the back room and tried to be silent, which wasn't easy with our crowd.

Joyce walked in and with her always bright, bubbly personality asked, "Lynn, where is everybody? I thought I was going to be the last one."

Cheerleader: Joyce McEwen

With that we all burst from our hiding place and started to chant, "Zee Bees! Zee Bees! Sting'em! Sting'em!"

That cracked her up and she about fell over laughing. "Yikes, you guys are good," she chortled. "Glad I didn't have to compete against you."

"We're real proud of you, Joyce," I said sincerely knowing I had the agreement of all the guys present.

"Thanks guys. I'll do my best to make everyone cheer real loud," she promised blushing a little from all the attention.

I still had more to say. "Furthermore, Leon, Phil, and I have decided that you are without question the cutest cheerleader in the North Suburban Conference!"

With that Joyce blushed heavily and stammered a bit. "Uhm, thanks... but aren't you stretching it a bit?"

Phil stepped forward and in an exaggerated indignant manner asked, "Are you doubting our abilities to discern who the good looking cheerleaders are in this conference? I'm crushed by your assertion."

"I'm sorry," laughed Joyce. "You're right. If there are any three guys who know how to make a girl feel special, it is you three. So I will just say thank you."

With the three of us mollified, the party got back in full swing. Another great evening at the Reinier's.

## The Coach Makes Some Changes

Much to my surprise, Coach Ellis started making changes as we approached the last three games of the season. After stretching and calisthenics, we gathered around Coach to hear what he had to say about the next game.

"In an effort to give George a little rest and reduce his chances of injury, I'm going to start Moose as the left defensive linebacker. I'm also going to have him start calling defensive plays," he said in an authoritative voice.

Then he turned to me with a snide expression on his face. "You think you can handle it?" he asked with a challenge in his voice.

"Yeah, Coach. I can handle it," I answered quickly. I was caught off guard, but I was determined not to show it.

Moving me back to linebacker made good sense and I was glad to be able to play in my old position. But the fact that he also gave me defensive play calling duties really surprised me. I wondered why he made that decision. In the past he tightly controlled every defensive formation we used.

Loren by now was well established as the center linebacker. He always came in on defense for Larry while Larry talked over offensive strategy with Coach Ellis.

"Okay, pal. It's you and me again on defense together. Let's kick some butt," I yelled at Loren. It was fun to have my old buddy playing right next to me again.

"It's great to have you back, Moose. Let's do it!" he yelled back.

Unfortunately yet another negative event put a big damper on the team's goals for our senior year. Bobby apparently came to practice several times with alcohol on his breath. He was warned by the coaches not to do it again. But one evening during practice, Coach Ellis called the team together.

"Boys, I am sorry to have to tell you this, but Bobby Young has been dropped from the team."

We all knew why.

What a blow! "Darn it, Loren," I complained later that evening as we were watching the Bears highlights. "For three years we planned our team for our senior year and now our best back has been kicked off the team."

"Well, when we lost Arvid, Coach moved Bill back to wingback and he's done great at that position," said Loren hopefully.

"Yeah... and when we lost Bob Lee, Lugan came out and filled in perfectly. But who in the world do you see can play tailback for us now?"

Loren said calmly "Guess we'll have to wait until next year to find out. Coach always seems to come up with someone to fill these empty spots."

We had a home game against Woodstock and everything clicked. Our backfield was really smooth. Karl had a great game running up big yardage. The defense played very well, and we beat the Blue Streaks 20-6. I felt very comfortable at linebacker and made several good tackles. My defensive calls consistently were the right calls at the right time. Ellis was in a great mood. There were pats on the back all around including even a few for me for my defensive work. I was very pleased, but I knew any rapport I had with him because of one game wouldn't last.

## Homecoming

Barb, Betty Rae, Loren and I double dated for the homecoming dance after the Woodstock game. The boy's gym was decorated in a festive way. With the big win now on our record, it was a happy crowd of teenagers that evening. My Mom bought me a new suit just for this event as the only other I ever owned was the one I used for my eighth grade graduation. Both Barbara and Betty Rae looked beautiful. We danced to the "Bunny Hop", the "Stroll" and the "Conga", forming a line that stretched around the gym several times. Life was good and getting better. I wished the football season lasted all year long.

## Onward and Upward

We next played McHenry at the Warriors home field. In the first half I made several good tackles and intercepted a pass. I felt quite good about my defensive performance. True, I missed one major tackle which would have nailed them deep in their own territory, but it was really my only mistake. It must have been the one Coach saw. We went into the locker room at halftime leading 7-0.

I had my head down as Coach ranted and raved about how terribly we all were performing. "You all are playing like you never saw a football before. We should be beating these guys by three touchdowns. Our blocking and tackling are terrible. Moose, you could have pinned them down deep in their own territory which would have given us a chance to score. But, no, you tried to arm tackle the runner and he made a first down," he yelled loudly.

With that he picked up a huge chunk of chalk from the blackboard tray and screamed, "Moose, I get so damn mad. You tackle like an old lady."

With that he cocked that catcher trained, rifle arm of his and fired the chunk of chalk in his hand right at my head. I looked up just as he threw it and all I saw was a big, yellow missile rocketing right at my head. I jerked to the right and the chalk exploded against the locker next to me. The players near me jumped back in astonishment.

If that thing had hit me, I would have been out cold for the rest of the game. My first thought was to say, "Gosh, Coach, I don't know if you noticed or not, but we are winning. What are you so mad about?" Fortunately, I stifled my mouth or I may not have lived to see another game.

In the second half, Larry broke his collarbone on a hard block to the defensive end. But when he came to the sidelines to tell Coach he was hurt, Coach thought he was just faking.

"Get away from me. I don't want a penalty at this point. Get back in the game," Coach yelled at him.

Larry reluctantly went back into the game. When we finally had to punt, he came back to the sideline. "Coach," he said firmly, "I think my collar bone is broken and it hurts like heck. What does a guy have to do to get out of a game?"

Unmoved Coach turned to Loren and said sarcastically, "Stried, get in there for Peterson. Seems he doesn't want to play anymore." Coach was tough on everybody.

Loren became the first string quarterback in addition to his line backing duties. While I was sorry for Larry that his season had to end this way, I could see that giving Loren a full game of experience as the Varsity quarterback might pay big dividends for us next year.

We eventually won the game 13-7 and we were a happy group headed home that night. But memories of that chunk of chalk plagued me all the way home. When was I ever going to please this guy? How can I be so elated to play for him in some games and virtually hate his guts in another? Was there a pattern here that I wanted or didn't want? I didn't have the answers.

Our last game during our junior year was an away match at Libertyville. This one we won rather handily with a 20-7 victory. My defensive play calling and tackling were definitely getting better. After the game, the Coach did a strange thing... he complimented me.

"Moose, you're improving with each game," said the Coach. "Try to remember what you did this year so you can start at a higher level next year."

I decided that a back handed compliment was better than none at all. Especially realizing the source.

With our class teaming up with the seniors, the team ended up with a record of four wins, three losses, and one tie. At last a winning season. Certainly a lot better than anything we put together by ourselves. We beat the pre season picks by a wide margin.

The seniors provided excellent guidance and leadership all season long. Everyone appreciated their positive attitude.

Karl was as fine a teammate as you could ever want to know. At the end of the season he was selected as an All Conference tailback and it was well deserved. Years later we were all saddened when Karl passed away at an early age.

Larry was another super guy and later became a dentist in town. George often took time to show me how to handle the ball and get off the mark quickly. LeRoy kept everything loose for the entire team. He became the head football coach at Zion a number of years later and brought a championship to the school in 1969. He won many titles after that and ended up in the Zion Sports Hall of Fame. Their friendship and encouragement were a blessing to us all. It also paid big dividends for the Zee Bees the following fall.

Our third year of playing football was now over and there was only one year left. Based on our record to date and the loss of some of our best players from that original freshman team, there was not a lot of optimism in the school regarding great success for the following year.

But Loren, Paul, the other members of the team, and I pledged to each other three years before that we would do everything in our power to become conference champions. We were not about to give in to negative thinking. If all the games were preordained as to the winner, there would be no need to play the game at all. By all accounts we were consistent losers and no one would pick us as winners next year. In particular, no one would ever pick us as champions. But in our hearts Loren, Paul, and I knew that we had one more chance to prove ourselves.

The three of us called a meeting of all the junior lettermen and talked over how we could best prepare for the fourth and final season of our football careers at Zion. Bogie, Leon, Phil, Bill, and John all wanted a great senior season as much as Loren and I did, so all were present.

"Guys, you all remember how bad we were as freshmen and sophomores. This year we got a taste of what it was like to win and I know you all loved it as much as I," I enthused. "So let's reinforce our goal to go all out for the championship next year. I'm sure no one else would give us much hope for doing this, but we've been getting better every year and next year just might be our time. Waddya say?"

Everyone nodded their heads in agreement.

"We should meet down at the lake front and run plays and do wind sprints," Phil recommended. "Running in the sand really builds up the calf and leg muscles."

"Yeah," Paul agreed. "And remember we all are going to have to be iron men next year. There aren't many players on the JV squad, so we'll probably not have two full teams again next season."

"Paul's right," I echoed. "It'll be the eight of us and maybe four or five juniors. That's it."

"Do you think there's any chance we can get Middleton out next year? Since we lost Bobby Young, we need a good tailback," said Loren.

"You know how Middy feels about Ellis," I replied quickly. "I doubt if he'll even consider it."

Loren was quiet for a moment. I knew he must have something up his sleeve. With a thoughtful expression he related his plan to us.

"We all know Middy has a big ego," Loren stated. "So first of all several of us should needle him about not really being a great athlete unless he plays football."

"That ought to raise his hackles," I said.

"Then we'll have some of the girls tell him what a great baseball and basketball player he is," Loren continued, "and how wonderful it would be if he played football too."

"Think that'll work?" I asked.

"It's sure worth a try," said Bogie.

"But let's make sure he knows it's because we need him out here. Before the end of the school year, each of us should talk to him at least once about coming out next fall," I stressed.

"Good idea," said Paul. "I'll try to talk to him as soon as I can."

"And, Leon, try to be at least a little bit diplomatic," I said.

"Waddya mean, Moose? You know me!"

"You're right. I do know you, and that's why I mentioned it."

Everyone had a good laugh. A few of the guys punched Leon playfully.

We all agreed to make an all out effort to get ourselves in the best shape possible. Once again we formed our circle and placed our hands on top of each other. "Go Zee Bees! Sting 'em! Sting'em!" With handshakes and back slaps, we broke as a team with a determined mind set. Nothing less than a winning season would be acceptable. And we had to beat Lake Forest! But the North Suburban Championship was the ultimate goal.

## Second Semester – Junior Year

The balance of our junior year brought some disturbing events and changes. First of all, Fred Stanton, the beloved Athletic Director, Head Basketball Coach, and Head Baseball Coach of many years retired. There was much speculation who would get what assignment and we all lined up supporting different men for the different positions. But the powers that be made the decision without help from us.

Coach McGrew was promoted to Athletic Director and both head coach positions for basketball and baseball. Because of the animosity between Coach Ellis and Coach McGrew, I didn't think this arrangement would bode well for the football team. But then, I also believed these were mature men and neither would allow personalities to interfere with their professional performance. How wrong I was.

Paul, Loren, and I decided not to play JV basketball that year. To put it bluntly, none of us wanted to play for Coach McGrew. We organized our own intramural team and called ourselves the Red Raiders. My Mom bought some Tee shirts, dyed them bright red and put taped numerals on them, the same as our football numbers. We also picked up John Jecevicus, and Bill Perry, my cousin who was a sophomore tackle on our football team, so we had plenty of size.

Ron Peterson was a good friend of us all, so we invited him to join the team to play guard. Although he was slight of build, he was a very good shot from outside the free throw line. He became our playmaker.

It was so much more fun to play intramurals. I was the self appointed Captain and held practices when we could get a court in the girls' gym. Everyone played in every game and the scoring was about equal except for Ron. He led the intramural league in scoring. The Red Raiders went undefeated for two years.

**Our First Attempt**

Loren and I sat together with Phil, Paul, Loren, and Leon at the game in the boy's gym. Zion won another close game and Middy scored 26 points. Middy was clearly the star of the basketball team. He was very quick, a great dribbler, and could shoot from all over the court.

"Man, he's good. I wish I could move like that," I said to my friends with a little envy in my voice. "We need to get him out next fall. He could really help us."

"Let's catch him at Rooks tonight. He normally goes there after the game," Loren offered. "We're going anyhow, right?"

We all shook our heads in agreement.

Later at Rooks' Restaurant we just finished our shakes and burgers when Middy walked in with some of the other basketball players. They took a table near us. Normally he had one of the better looking girls in the school on his arm, but this particular night he was without a date.

Leon wasted no time. He sauntered over to Middy's table in his usual cocky manner with the three of us close behind.

"Hey, Middy," said Leon. "Good game tonight!"

"Thanks," said Middy with a little smile. "26 points tonight. Looking to score more next game."

"So, since you're so good, where's your date tonight?" Leon asked, firing the first shot.

"I didn't feel like having a date tonight. What's it to you?" he snapped back.

I said to myself, Uh Oh! So much for diplomacy. I wonder where this is going? I could hear Paul and Loren suck in their breaths.

"You know why you don't have a date tonight?" Leon continued in an openly antagonistic tone. "Because you are not a football player. That's why!"

I could see the blood rising in Middy's face.

"Yeah, you're good in basketball and baseball, but chicks really dig football players." Leon didn't pull any punches. "And since you've quit on us twice, all the women know that."

Middy didn't expect a personal attack on his manhood like this. I wondered how he would respond in front of everyone.

"You're lucky anyone goes out with you!" smirked Leon.

With that Middy jumped to his feet with his fists clenched.

"Take it easy, Leon," said Paul. "We're all friends you know."

"Okay... okay."

"You know Middy," said Phil. "You have to be tough to take the shots we take out there. You might be a great athlete... but come out next fall and prove to us you are."

"You all know the reason I quit," Middy spat back at us.

"Yeah, but it's not a very good reason," I said. "You oughta be out there for the team... whoever the coach is."

"I'm as good as any of you," Middy retorted angrily. He faced off with Leon.

"Yeah? Then come out and prove it!" said Leon, sticking his face into Middy's.

Paul quickly stepped between the two of them. Leon and Phil spun around and walked away before Middy could respond again. Middy stood there, staring after Leon and Phil, an expression of rage on his face. Loren and I took the good cop approach.

"Middy, don't worry about what those guys said," Loren counseled him.

"But we really could use you out there next fall," I added. "You'd make a great tailback for us."

"Give it some thought," Paul advised and slapped him on the shoulder.

It was very obvious Middy was steaming. We left him there in the restaurant and went out to our car. Leon and Phil were waiting for us.

"Good job, you guys," I said sarcastically. "You sure handled that diplomatically."

"Hey, Moose," Leon laughed. "You wanted to get his attention? We got his attention."

"I'll bet he's thinking about coming out right now," grinned Phil.

"That or he's thinking of a way to catch you in a dark alley somewhere and pound the stuffing out of you," I replied half laughing at the whole scene.

"No way!" said Leon cockily. "Let him try. I'd kick his butt and he knows it."

"But if he got mad enough to show up on the football field, then it worked," said Phil. "Right?"

"You're right," Loren agreed quickly. "Let's hope it did the job."

Silently I hoped it would also. But I knew we had to keep trying. It would take more than one effort to get Middy out in the fall.

# The Great Zion Fire

In January Loren and I drove out to the ZB/Barrington basketball game at Barrington. He and I tried to attend every game we could. It was fun sitting in the stands screaming for the Zee Bees. Besides, I could observe Joyce far more clearly than I could during football games. I still had a crush on her, I guess...even though Barb was my girlfriend.

The Zee Bees lost a close game that night, but it was exciting. When the game was over Loren and I were milling around on the floor talking to some friends from Barrington when an announcement came over the loud speaker.

"Attention Zion students. It has been reported that a major fire is burning in downtown Zion. The Zion Department Store is in flames. All of you have been requested by your principal Mr. Pearce to return home immediately so your parents will know you are safe."

Loren and I looked at each other in shock. Then we sprinted to my car. We drove home that night in record time.

"My gosh. Our home is only a block from the Zion Department Store," Loren expressed with concern. "Do you think it could spread that far?"

"I don't think so, but if it's as windy in Zion as it is out here, who knows how far it can spread?"

"I'm sure my Dad is spraying down our home with water right now. Could you speed up a little, Moose?"

I pressed down on the accelerator a little harder. "You know, Joyce's Dad's business is right across the street, isn't it?"

"It is. I think I saw the cheerleaders leave right after the game. Hopefully she got the word somehow."

"Well, let's pray that the damage isn't too bad," I said anxiously. "And that everyone gets home safely."

The Zion Department Store was a huge wooden structure located on Sheridan Road, Zion's main thoroughfare. It stretched from 27th Street on one end to 26th Street on the other. It was laid out so that as you passed from one end to the other you actually walked from one different department to another. It was very old and had a wonderful wooden smell to it as you entered. My first meeting with Santa Claus was in this building. My Dad bought my first bicycle for me in this store: a Schwinn complete with fenders, brakes and handle bar tassels. My Mom bought my 8th grade graduation suit here. There always seemed to be something magic to me every time I walked through it. It was sad to think it was burning.

Little did we realize how bad it was. From the time we hit Lewis Avenue about two miles from downtown Zion we could see the red glow in the sky.

"Whoa, Loren. That doesn't look good. That fire must be eating up the entire store."

"Gosh, I hope Joyce's family store isn't ruined. Maybe we can find her and help out."

By the time we hit Shiloh Park, a few blocks away, we were stopped by the Zion Police Department and told we could drive no further. So we parked the car and hightailed it the rest of the way. As we turned the corner of Sheridan and 25th Street, we stopped dead in our tracks. Before us was the biggest conflagration I had ever seen in my life. It was surreal.

"The whole store is going up," Loren shouted over the roar of the fire and the noise of the fire engines.

"It looks like the road is burning it's so hot," I yelled back. "Can you see McEwen's Store from here?"

"Not yet. We need to get closer."

The streets were covered with hoses, water, firemen, police cars and spectators, but the two of us wound our way through all of this to get near to McEwen's. Finally we saw it was not afire. We spotted Joyce nearby. We sprinted over to her.

"Joyce! You all right?" I yelled at the top of my voice.

She nodded yes vigorously. What a relief! But as we moved even closer we could tell she was in distress.

"I haven't been able to find my Dad yet... and I'm afraid the flames are going to leap the road and burn our store," she yelled fighting back the tears.

181

"Can we help?" screamed Loren.

"Find my Dad so he knows I'm okay. The firemen have hosed down the store, so I think it's safe for now."

So off we went again through the tangle of hoses and equipment. Anything for one of our friends that meant so much to us. After failing to spot Mr. McEwen on our initial run through the maze, we finally spotted him on the other side of 27th Street helping the Zion firemen trying to save Bickett's. We ran up to him breathing heavily and coughing from all the smoke.

"Mr. McEwen, Joyce is on the other side of the street near your store. She's safe, but I think she's scared. She wanted us to find you."

"Thanks, boys. Can you guide me back to her?"

"Sure. Follow us."

I could see the relief in Joyce's eyes as her Dad came into view. They hugged tightly for a few minutes. How wonderful to see such a good daughter/father relationship. Loren and I were pleased that we could help...even in a small way.

We stayed with Joyce well unto the wee hours of the morning. Loren left for a few minutes to check his own home, but returned quickly when he found it safe and sound. His parents were out somewhere watching the fire he presumed.

Before we parted, Joyce gave us both big hugs. "You two were great to stay with me tonight. I am blessed to have friends like you," she said in total sincerity.

"And we're blessed to have a friend like you," I said. "God bless...good night... and be careful."

Loren and I shook hands, gave each other a pat on the back which meant more than any words could have said, and headed to our own homes.

The aftermath was devastating. Fire trucks came from every town in Lake County and from several in the Chicago area. But they couldn't pull off a miracle. The Zion Department Store burned to the ground and engulfed the basement as well. For years there was a huge gaping hole and a huge eyesore in downtown Zion. Eventually it was replaced a by a number of smaller stores, but none of them ever had the same charm or ambiance.

The fire burned so hot that the pavement on Sheridan Road caught fire. All the store fronts on the other side of the street were charred, but fortunately did not burn down. McEwen's received similar damage, but was open for business the following Monday. The stench of fire permeated downtown Zion for months afterwards. It was a devastating setback for Zion and its residents.

Fortunately, Zion, like many other Midwestern towns of the time, had an indomitable spirit and soon bounced back to thrive again.

## The Junior Talent Show

The entire gang was up in Betty Rae's barn on the second floor singing along with great gusto with the Chordettes.

*"Mr. Sandman, bring me a dream (bung, bung, bung, bung)*
*Make him the cutest that I've ever seen (bung, bung, bung, bung)*
*Give him two lips like roses and clover (bung, bung, bung, bung)*
*And tell him that his lonesome nights are over!"*

"Hey," Phil said with great enthusiasm. "We should enter ourselves in the Junior Talent Show. Who could possibly sound better than we just did?"
This elicited groans from all corners of the room.

"You've got to be kidding," Leon observed sarcastically. "We sound like the Hounds of the Baskervilles on a full moon night."

"But, Leon," said Loren with a little needle in his voice. "Chicks love singers."

"Hey," said Leon with a big laugh. "You're absolutely right! That's a good point!"

Lynn stepped up and offered, "Seriously, Betty Rae and Bob, why don't the two of you try out for the Emcee positions for the Talent Show. You're both good speakers on your feet in front of people. I think you two would do a terrific job."

Kay, Joyce, and the rest of the guys all chimed in. "Great idea. You two would work well together. Do it!"

I looked at Betty Rae and she looked at me, neither of us speaking. Finally she said, "Well, I'm willing to try if you are."

I thought about it for a few moments and said, "What the heck. Why not? Nothing ventured, nothing gained. Besides it might be fun to get up in front of everyone and try to be funny." So we shook hands and the deal was made.

During the second semester, the Junior Class traditionally organized and ran the Junior Talent Show. The primary reason for Talent Show was to give the Junior Class a chance to raise money for the Junior-Senior Prom, to be held late in the spring. It also created a showcase for the more artistically talented students in the school to demonstrate their skills.

Betty Rae and I tried out to be the Co-emcees for the show and much to my surprise, we both were chosen. I had no doubt she would be selected as she was an outgoing, vivacious and confident young lady who spoke very well. I was still pretty rough around the edges so I had my doubts about my being accepted. But once we were selected, we both took our assignments very seriously and worked hard at the job. Betty Rae took care of the professional responsibility introducing each act as it came up in the program.

I tried to be the comic relief. I came up with some of the corniest jokes you can imagine.

"My Mother came home from work the other day," I said in a deadpan manner, "and when she opened the oven, there was a mouse in it."

Betty Rae acted very concerned and asked, "Oh, dear, Bob. Did she shoot the mouse?"

"No, by the time she got her gun, it was out of her range."

The groans were louder than the laughter. With one exception. I could hear Coach Ellis out in the audience loud and clear over anyone else. "Ho! Ho! Ho!"

I thought, well, at least Coach has my sense of humor.

Later he asked me with a big grin on his face, "Moose, where in the world did you get those terrible jokes? Out of Captain Willie's Whiz Bang? (This was a joke book popular in the 20s.) My grandmother could tell better jokes than that!"

My obsession with doing this show exactly right led to the one and only major disagreement that Loren and I ever had in our four years together. Betty Rae, Loren, and I were at practice for the show several hours after school and decided to go for burgers at Rooks. It was still rather early in the evening as we got up to leave. I got the idea that this would be a perfect time for Betty Rae and me to go over our lines and cues so we would have it down pat on stage. I made the mistake of assuming that Loren would be bored to death hearing us go over the same line several times, so I took him home first and then drove out to Betty Rae's home where we practiced for several hours. Bad move! While it wasn't intentional, I really hurt Loren's feelings.

Early the next morning at school Loren confronted me.

"Moose, I really didn't appreciate your dropping me off last night and then taking Betty Rae home. How do you think that looks when my best friend and steady girlfriend are alone for two hours?" he asked.

"Gosh, I had no idea you'd take it like that. I was trying to save you from having to listen to us practice for two hours," I explained earnestly.

"I could've stood it... I guess."

"Nothing happened I assure you!"

"Well, I hope not! If I couldn't trust you, what would be the point of our friendship?" he shot back.

"I agree. I'm sorry! For gosh sakes. Don't overreact!"

"I'll tell you something. I didn't like it one bit," he countered and stomped away.

"Gee whiz, sometimes the most innocent things I do get me in trouble," I remorsed.

So we both stewed about it for several days. Since we never had a disagreement of any kind before, I really didn't know how to handle it. But I knew we couldn't go on like this. Our friendship was far too important. I caught Loren at his locker one day after school.

"Look, pal. I'm sorry. I wasn't thinking. I won't ever do that again. Let's shake and have this over with."

Loren broke out in a warm smile.

"Maybe I did overreact. But since you promise never to do to it again, let's get back to being friends."

With a sigh of relief I strongly shook his hand and suddenly we were back to normal. Moose and Loren. Loren and Moose. Best buds again.

The show turned out to be a big success. We made lots of money for our prom. Betty Rae and I received many accolades from teachers, parents, and classmates for our performance. Betty Rae was particularly smooth and calm on stage. It was obvious she was headed for some type of public relations job in her life.

I learned first hand what it was like to stand in front of a crowd of people and try to be entertaining. It was a small step at that time, but it paid large dividends later in my life. My military duty assignments often required me to give presentations to numerous Navy seminars, large and small, with Admirals and Congressmen often in attendance. I seemed to handle these briefings with ease. One never knows where seeds sown in our young lives will eventually bloom in our adult lives.

## Lynn Gives It a Try

After the Junior Talent Show a group of us were sitting around a large table at Rooks talking over the performance. Lynn, Betty Rae, Barb, Joyce, Loren, Phil, Bogie, Kay, Leon, and I were just finishing up our fries and burgers when I thought it might be a good time to bring up our idea for the gals to participate in getting Middy out for football.

"Girls, we all have a favor to ask of you," I said matter of factly.

"Uh oh... what can this be?" asked Betty Rae cautiously.

"You all know Bobby Young was kicked off the team for drinking," I said. "He was a terrific tailback. We really don't have anyone who can fill that spot."

"But we all think Middy could do it if he really wanted to," said Phil.

Loren immediately jumped in. "And we want one of you to volunteer to talk to Middy to try to find a way to get him to come out."

"Who wants to volunteer?" asked Leon.

"What do you want us to do?" Joyce asked with one eyebrow going up suspiciously.

"What influence could we have on Middy?" asked Betty Rae.

"Listen," I said emphatically trying to contain myself. "You know how Middy has great pride in his athletic skills..."

"If one of you could come up with a way to stroke that ego," said Loren, "maybe you could convince him to come out next fall."

Lynn was sitting at the table quietly taking this all in. I could see she was considering it.

"I could try," she voiced sweetly. "I've always had a good relationship with Middy... he might listen to me."

Later that week I was walking with Lynn along the hallway in the high school when we spotted Middy at his locker.

"Waddya think, Lynn?" I asked. "Are you ready?"

"Now is as good a time as any," she smiled confidently.

We walked up to Middy together. Lynn was in perfect form.

"Oh, Middy. You played so well last Friday night," intoned Lynn with her sultry, honey laden voice. "You're the star of the team... and I'll bet you make All Conference."

Middy looked at me suspiciously.

"Thanks, Lynn. I'd like that," Middy replied somewhat modestly for him.

"Oh, I know you'll make it, Middy," said Lynn. "Nobody can block your shot. You're so quick."

"No one has blocked it yet."

"And you're such a good baseball player too! It must be great to be so good in two sports," she cooed softly.

"I'll be the starting pitcher for the Varsity this spring," Middy stated candidly. "We should win a lot of games."

"You might be selected to All Conference in both sports. Wouldn't that be something?" offered Lynn enthusiastically.

"Yeah, that would be great!" Middy replied with a big toothy grin.

"It's too bad you don't play football too," Lynn said in a disappointed tone.

I immediately saw Middy's eyes lock onto mine. He knew I was behind this talk. I tried to keep my face as impassive as possible. After what seemed like a long time, he looked back at Lynn.

"If you played football, you could be the first athlete from Zion Benton High School to ever be selected All Conference in three sports," explained Lynn in a completely innocent voice. "Wouldn't that be wonderful?"

Lynn, you're beautiful, I said to myself. I couldn't have scripted it better.

"Yeh, that'd be terrific. But I don't know that I want to play football next year."

"Oh come on, Middy," cooed Lynn. "I think you'd look super in a football uniform."

Middy puffed up a bit and shuffled his feet nervously.

"You'd be famous at ZBTHS."

"I'll think about it," he said in a dismissive manner as he walked away.

As Lynn and I walked down the hall toward our next class, I couldn't contain my enthusiasm any longer.

"Lynn, you were great! Man, that was perfect. After that, he'll definitely think about it. You said exactly the right thing."

Lynn smiled sweetly. "Anything I can do to help the football team."

"You were a big help."

"Now he'll think I was flirting with him," said Lynn with mock concern.

"Well... you were... weren't you?"

She slapped me playfully on the arm. We both laughed as we entered the class room.

## Double Dating

Later that spring, Betty Rae, Barb, Loren, and I went to Lake Geneva, Wisconsin to hear Louis Armstrong. I never saw a professional performer before in my life. Louis was such a big star at that time, I couldn't believe we had the opportunity to see him up close.

The concert was held at the Riviera, a luxurious, beautifully decorated circular structure built on the waterfront in downtown Lake Geneva. For years it hosted big bands from Miller to Dorsey. Folks from Milwaukee and Chicago drove several hours just to see these stars perform.

Louis Armstrong didn't disappoint any of us. He put on a two hour show that was terrific. We were all so excited about seeing him that none of us stopped raving about his performance all the way home. It was a memorable evening.

In the spring Loren played baseball and I stuck with my shot and discus on the track team. He became a starter and I earned points for the track team in every meet. We both were awarded our second Varsity letter.

At prom time the four of us double dated again... Loren and Betty Rae... Moose and Barb. Loren and I rented tuxes for the first time in our lives. Our Mothers said we both looked handsome. The girls were absolutely beautiful and wore lovely off the shoulder dresses.

Loren and I couldn't have been any more pleased with ourselves. We had the best looking dates at the entire prom. We had several professional photographs taken during the course of the prom and received copies a few weeks later. I still have these photos in my possession and still get goose bumps when I look at them. Life was good for teenagers in 1954.

Prom May 1954
Left to right; Loren Stried, Betty Rae Birky,
Barbara Bogue, Bob Osmon

Afterwards we went to Lynn's home for a very late dinner and early breakfast. We all dragged home at five in the morning. A good time was had by all. Our junior year ended in great fashion.

**********

# Chapter 7
## Senior Year – 1954

I was sitting in Coach's room in the hospital all morning thinking about Zion and our unaffected way of life in the 1950's. How special that time was in our lives.

Coach slept for about six hours. I had some lunch and dozed myself for a bit. Suddenly he awoke with a jerk and gruffly told me he was hungry.

"Get the nurses in here, Moose. I want to eat," he ordered.

So off I went again to get his food. The nurses rushed in with a tray of chicken and corn. I watched him hungrily wolf down his plate and settle back.

"Coach, I was reminiscing a bit about our junior year. Do you remember much about it? That was your first year as head coach," I reminded him.

"Of course, I do," he chuckled and was off and running. "Do you remember the time when Larry Peterson tried to come out of the game holding his arm? I thought he was trying to talk to me about what play to call."

"I remember that well, Coach."

"Back then he would have drawn a penalty for talking to the coach. So I told him to get back in the game and walked away from him. Later after we finally punted the ball, Larry came out and told me he thought he had a broken collar bone. He said 'Gosh, Coach, what does a person have to do to get out of a game?'"

This was followed with howls of laughter with those buck teeth in full view. Coach obviously relished in telling these stories.

"And how about the game at McHenry?" Coach continued. "Their field was high in the middle and slanted down toward both sidelines. So after the first half, we lined up left or right so we could be running our plays down hill all the time. I don't think they ever figured out what we were doing." Another guffaw!

"Do you remember throwing that big chunk of chalk at me in the locker room at halftime?" I asked cautiously. "If you had hit me, I would have been out for the rest of the game."

"Moose, I was trying to get your attention. You looked like you were asleep back there instead of listening to me," he explained.

"It got my attention, Coach!"

"Then there was the time at home when we were playing Barrington. I wanted to get some of my starters out so they could rest a bit. After several plays, I noticed they were all still standing around instead of sitting. I walked over to them to find out why. There were all the cheerleaders sitting on the end of the bench. Ho! Ho! Ho!"

"I must've been in the game for that one."

"Well, I laid into 'em and told 'em never to sit on my football benches again. Can you imagine that? Cheerleaders sitting on the football team's benches," he snorted. "Ho! Ho! Ho!"

"They were a nice distraction."

"You bet...but I didn't want you guys thinking about girlies in tight sweaters...I wanted you thinking about crushing the other team!"

I smiled. "I know, Coach."

"And for the homecoming parade, LeRoy Cliff wanted to build a float for the Lettermen's Club. All it would be was an outhouse with a sign saying 'We'll Drop'em.' Ho! Ho! Ho! I should have allowed LeRoy to do that. It would have been a big hit," he laughed as if it happened yesterday.

This went on for about thirty minutes which ended up with my laughing so hard there were tears coming to my eyes. He had a way of embellishing each story that made it hilarious. Finally the extended effort caught up to him and he quickly slipped into another deep sleep.

The quietness of the room enveloped me. The contrast from the recent hilarity was very profound and slowly sedated my mind from the reality of the situation. Gradually I too slipped into another deep set of memories. These were more vivid than any I had since I had arrived. I was saving the best for the last.

# Captain Paul

The summer of 1954 passed rather much like the previous summer. I worked at the Dairy Queen six days a week, lifted weights, ran around the temple site every morning, and played basketball at the park almost every evening. About once a week our group of guys and gals met at the beach or had a party at Betty Rae's or Lynn's home.

My Dad took me to several Cubs game in Chicago and we enjoyed Osmon family picnics at Shiloh Park once a month. My Mom and I attended the Memorial Methodist Church every Sunday (at one time I had thirteen years of perfect attendance). I continued to be active in the MYF which met every Sunday evening at the church. Loren, Betty Rae, Barbara and I continued to double date, enjoying picnics, the beach, and horse back riding. Life was good and it was an idyllic summer, one that young men and women from a small town in Illinois can remember with great appreciation.

But always in the forefront of both Loren's and my mind was how our football team would perform in the fall. We waited three years for this very special moment, our senior year and our final season of football at Zion Benton Township High School.

The previous spring Coach Ellis called in all the lettermen and told us it was time to vote for the Captain of next year's team. "Boys, the Captain position is a very important one. The person selected to this role will act as your team representative for the entire season. He needs to be someone who can be a leader both on and off the field. So select well."

Paul played a lot as a reserve tackle on the Varsity when he was a sophomore and was the only one of us to earn a letter that year. He played virtually every down both on offense and defense as a junior. He was also a steady leader on the field and very well respected by everyone on the team. In my mind there was absolutely no doubt he should be our Captain. I knew he would represent us well.

When the votes were counted, Paul received all the votes but for one. That one was for me. Since I had not voted for myself, I knew exactly where that vote came from: my loyal and true friend Loren. It was meant as no disrespect to Paul, but was simply Loren's way of expressing his friendship to me.

It is not often one has a friend like Loren in one's life. When someone like him does come along, they are few and far between and should be cherished. I continue to appreciate my present relationship with him as we always spend time together whenever I come back to Zion for a visit. But the biggest display of friendship and loyalty he was to make on my behalf was yet to come.

## Arvid Detienne

About a month before we went back to school for our senior year, a terrible tragedy occurred which affected us all deeply. Arvid was riding his motorcycle on Highway 41, a major thoroughfare between Chicago and Milwaukee, when he apparently lost control. His bike skidded under the wheels of a big semi truck and he was crushed to death. Everyone on the team felt terribly about this accident and we all attended his funeral.

It was hot day in the cemetery, the smell of fresh cut grass permeating the air. I stared at the coffin with the flowers on it… trying to realize that our good friend was in it. It seemed unreal. After the brief ceremony, my teammates and I gathered under a tall oak tree near the burial site. We all showed the grief and emotion stirred by the loss of our close classmate.

"Arvid was a good friend," I said.

"And an excellent teammate," said Loren

"I can't imagine that we've lost him," mourned Paul.

"Who could think his life would end like this," said Phil stifling a tear.

To the man, everyone nodded in silent affirmation.

"What's so darn maddening about all this," Paul said in an agitated state, "is that his Mother bought him a motorcycle to keep him away from football."

"She was afraid he'd get hurt," said Leon voicing the irony we all felt.

"I've owned scooters and cycles all my life," said Paul. "You never think much about getting hurt on 'em."

"Arvid and I were good buddies... even when he wasn't on the team," said Leon. "Cars and women...that was what we liked! It really hurts to lose a friend like that."

"I talked to him a lot about coming out again for football after freshman year," Paul said sadly, "but he never seemed interested any more. What a waste of life."

"And we sure could have used him on our team," Loren said.

"We can't bring him back," Bogie said softly, "but let's all say a prayer for his family and be glad we had the chance to know him."

Bogie led us all in prayer. The silence continued long after we all murmured "Amen!" No one really wanted to leave with such sad memories. Finally I broke the silence with a few last words.

"We have another reason now... to do the best we can this fall," I said emotionally. "For Arvid."

"For Arvid," everyone muttered.

## Bonding at the Beach

Around the middle of July Loren, Paul, and I telephoned all our players and asked them to come to the lakefront several times a week for some preseason training. No one needed to be reminded of our pact from the year before. Everyone was enthusiastic about participating. Phil, Leon and Bogie drove up from the Harbor. Bill and John drove in from their farm jobs. No one saw Middy all summer long, so we had no idea what he was going to do. We could only hope for the best.

Several of the juniors joined us as well. There in the deep sand on the shores of Lake Michigan, we jogged, sprinted, ran plays, and threw the football to each other, trying to build up stamina and endurance for the upcoming season. We all knew that we would have to play both offense and defense during the season. We did everything we could to avoid injury by toughening our bodies as much as possible.

The team met two or three times a week over the course of the summer, especially late July and early August when it was really hot and muggy. We all wanted to be ready. As a side benefit to becoming more physically fit, a renewed sense of camaraderie developed between us all. We had been friends and teammates for three years. We were headed into our fourth and final season... the last one in which we would all be together. Looking back, I believe these workouts on the beach of Lake Michigan further brought us together as a tight knit unit and cemented the close friendship we would need to get us through the season...a closeness that carried us through some extremely discouraging setbacks.

## One More Exam

The way my Mother walked in our front door from work told me I had no chance of getting out of this annual exam of my heart. When she had her mind set on something, no one or no thing was going to change it, come hell or high water.

I knew I was in good shape, but I also knew my Mother would insist that I take the heart exam like the doctor had ordered years before. As the day approached to go to his office, I began to dread it more and more. What if, this year, of all years, he finds something? I couldn't take it. Now that I've come so far and worked so hard. God just couldn't do this to me.

"Robert, it's time to go. Quit dilly dallying around and get moving. This is very important." My Mother left work early just to go with me to this exam. She was in no mood to hear me procrastinate.

I knew better than to argue with her at this point. "Okay. Mom. Let's see what happens this time," I responded reluctantly.

As I once again climbed the stairs to Dr. Kalem's office, disturbing memories of four years prior flooded into my thoughts. I grew even more apprehensive. I felt something foreboding about the whole place.

"Robert, good to see you again," Dr. Kalem started in a cheerful voice. "We have some new, modern equipment this year, far more sophisticated than in the past, so if anything is wrong we should be able to detect it fairly easily."

"Oh, that's just great," I mumbled to myself. "Just what I wanted to hear."

He hooked me up to all kinds of cords and devices and turned on his machine. I could feel my body tense up and I began to sweat a little. The test took about five minutes, but seemed like five hours.

"Let me check out these printouts and I will let you know how you are in a few minutes."

It seemed like another five hours passed. Finally he walked back in the exam room with a grave expression on his face.

"Robert, something is wrong. The printout doesn't read the way it is supposed to. I'm not saying anything is wrong with you, but I'm going to have to send these into Chicago to get an expert's reading. I should have it back by the end of the week," he said matter of factly.

"What!" I yelled as I jumped up off the examining table. This was just too much to take. "Practice starts next week. You're going to keep me hanging until then?"

"Now look, young man. This is your life I'm dealing with. I'm not going to okay you for football until I know absolutely your heart is fit and ready to go. So go home and I'll call as soon as I know the results."

Despondently I dragged down the stairs even slower than I came up.

"What a bunch of garbage, Mom!" I said with tears in my eyes. "You know I'm fit. I couldn't do all the running in the sand this summer that I did if I weren't. This can't be happening."

"The Lord works in strange ways," said my Mom. "If he wants you to play, you will be fine. If not, he has a reason why not. So put your trust in the Lord and we'll pray for the best."

For the next few days I was beside myself with anxiety. I shared my anguish with Loren.

"While I feel terrible for you, I'm pretty much in agreement with your Mom," said Loren. "You can't do anything about it now anyhow, so keep working out, praying, and leave it in God's hands."

I did keep working out and I did keep praying. Finally the Friday afternoon before Monday practice was to begin, my Mom got the call from Dr. Kalem. I watched her face intently to see any signs of sadness or glee. Dr. Kalem must have explained the entire procedure to her it took so long. Finally I saw her break into a smile and my heart leapt with joy.

"Thank you, Dr. Kalem," she said into the phone. "I know he'll be happy to hear that."

"What? What?" I yelled as she hung up the phone.

"Dr. Kalem says there was a small error in the printout, but it had nothing to do with your heart. He has cleared you to play football this fall," she exclaimed.

"Yahoo!" I danced around the room for five minutes. This time it was a short five minutes. I immediately called Loren.

"Hey, my friend. Guess what," I yelled into the phone. "I'm clear to play football. It was the stupid machine that made the error, not my heart."

"I never had a doubt. But it is good to hear it officially. We start on Monday."

"I'll be there. With bells on! Go Zee Bees! Sting'em!"

**Our Final Season Starts**

The first two weeks of practice in the fall of 1954 brought the worst weather we experienced in four years. It was very hot, muggy, and our old practice field was as dry as a bone. The dust got in our mouths and eyes, and made everyone miserable. And as if that weren't enough, Evan Ellis made us even more miserable.

"Moose, move your butt. Anen, keep your hands up. Hallgren, can't you pull any faster than that? We look like a bunch of old ladies out here. Do you all realize we have a season starting in three weeks?" Coach ranted and threw the usual snide and acerbic taunts at us.

Coach Ellis started off as intense as I ever saw him. He seemed to rage at us from the moment he walked on the field until the moment he walked off. Our two a day practices were brutal and everyone's butt was dragging at the end of the day. Tackling, blocking, running; nobody was exempt. It was as if something was eating at him and none of us knew what it was. Maybe it was the promotion of Coach McGrew to Athletic Director. Maybe it was just his desire for us not to embarrass ourselves on the field. A few of us even considered the remote possibility that he believed we might have a shot at the championship. But no one knew for sure. Whatever it was, he was driven. And we paid for it in sweaty, dirty, and bruised bodies.

## Single Wing 1954

X
**Fullback**
**"Moose" Osmon**

X
**Halfback**
**"Middy"**
**Middleton**

X
**Wingback**
**Bill Hosken**

X
**Quarterback**
**Loren Stried**

X
**End**
**"Lugan"**
**Jecevicus**

X
**Tackle**
**Paul**
**Jackola**

X
**Tackle**
**Bill**
**Perry**

X
**Strong**
**Side**
**Guard**
**Larry**
**Laird**

X (boxed)
**Center**
**"Bogie"**
**Bogue**

X
**Weak Side**
**Guard**
**Leon**
**Hallgren**

X
**End**
**Herman**
**Swanson /**
**"Philibuck"**
**Anen**

In my opinion, the team shaped up very well. The seven of us who were together since freshmen year all landed starting positions. Phil was our starting defensive right end. Leon was our pulling left guard. Bogie was at center. Paul was starting at right tackle on offense and left tackle on defense. Lugan was starting at right end on offense and left defensive end. In the backfield, Bill nailed down the wingback slot and played defense at the left halfback position. Loren had the quarterback job on offense and played both as defensive center linebacker and defensive guard. I was set at fullback on offense and as the left linebacker on defense. But there was still great consternation over who would be our tailback. We had no idea who would fill that critical spot when we first reported for practice.

## The New Tailback

On the day equipment was being issued in the boy's gym to the candidates for the 1954 team, in walked Middy and went straight to the coaches' locker room. We all stopped what we were doing and watched him.

"Coach Ellis, Coach Rushforth, I'd like to play on your team," said Middy straightforwardly. "I know I quit the team in previous years, but I want another chance to prove myself."

Neither Coach Ellis nor Coach Rushforth was very positive about it when he first approached them

"I don't know, Middy," said Coach Ellis gruffly. "These boys have stuck it out through all the ups and downs of this team... they may not want you coming out now."

"What makes you want another chance?" asked Coach Rushforth with a skeptical tone in his voice.

"I know you need a tailback. I can play that position if you give me a chance."

"So, now that you're a senior, you want to be a big hero out here," Coach Ellis sneered at him. "There's a lot more involved in playing football than being a big hero. You have pay your dues... you have to block and tackle."

"I know that, Coach."

"We'll think about it," Ellis replied in a curt manner. "Come back in two days."

Two days later Middy came back to the coaches' room. He had no idea what their decision would be.

"If you miss any practices without our authority, you will be dismissed from the team," stated Coach Ellis. "If you start to clown around at practice or display any poor sportsmanship on the field, you will be dismissed."

"I understand, Coach," said Middy looking a bit miffed.

"If you think I'm just talking, may I remind you what happened when you didn't show up for a basketball game as a freshman?"

"I remember that, Coach," replied Middy with a determined look on his face.

"You'll be expected to hustle, block, and tackle just like everyone else out here on the team. You'll get no special treatment," Coach Rushforth added with gruffness in his voice. "We don't need any prima donnas on this team."

"If you're willing to accept those conditions, then go suit up," Coach Ellis growled with no nonsense in his eyes.

Middy wasn't used to being talked to in that manner. It grated under his skin. But his desire to be part of the team overcame his irritation. He agreed to accept the conditions laid out by Coach Ellis. Although he didn't know it at the time, it was probably one of the best decisions he ever made in his life. Both for himself and our football team. He left the coaches' office with a grim smile on his face.

"Okay, you guys," grumbled Middy, "are you happy now? I'm here."

"Welcome back, Middy," said Leon in his caustic way. "I'm gonna give you a big hit during tackling practice as a welcome back present!"

Middy glared at Leon.

"Come on, guys," I said. "Remember... we asked him to come back..."

Paul walked up to Middy and stuck out his big hand. "Welcome back, Middy," he said. "Good to have you with us. Now let's go out and see you play some ball!"

"Thanks, Paul," said Middy, still glaring at Leon. "This time, I'm staying... no matter what."

But Coach wasn't about to make it easy on him. One day there were about ten new shoulder pads laid out in the locker room. Coach Ellis told the seniors that if they fit, pick up the new pads and use them. Middy picked up one pair and put them on. When Ellis saw this, he ran over to Middy and yanked them off over his head stinging his ears.

"You don't deserve these pads," snorted Ellis. "These go to someone who has been on the team for the past three years busting his butt out at practice every night and taking his lumps in the games."

Middy knew without a doubt at that point that Ellis meant everything he said. He absorbed the insult without a word.

There were mixed emotions among some of the players about having Middy out there with us. On the one hand, no one denied that he was a terrific athlete, and we needed a good tailback. On the other hand we knew he was cocky and had a big ego. We were concerned about his gelling with the team. We were such a close knit group that some of the team wasn't sure he would fit in with us. Middy would have to earn the respect of the team. But we all were willing to give him that chance...even Leon.

## The All Slow Team

Coach Ellis immediately started teaching Middy how to play the tailback spot. Middy was so quick and so shifty in his moves he really didn't have much trouble picking up the system. My job on many plays was to get out in front of him as the lead blocker when he swept around the end. Because of his speed, he would often overrun me. On the one hand Coach Ellis told him he needed to better judge his speed and follow his blockers, but on the other hand was constantly on my butt to run faster.

"Moose, get your fanny out there quickly, pick out a man to block, and be aggressive," hollered the Coach.

I ran as fast as I could.

"We've got a tailback with a little speed now, so you've got to pick it up."

The Coach's frustration with my lack of speed came to a head one day in a manner funny to my teammates, but not to me.

I tried to get downfield to throw a block into the defensive halfback to spring Middy free. I heard Middy behind me.

"Come on Moose...move it!"

I pushed my legs as fast as I could go and sought out a halfback to block. Middy became impatient and passed me. The halfback made the tackle.

Again the clipboard! Ellis threw it at me and snorted, "Moose, if the North Suburban Conference picked an All Slow Team, you would be the unanimous choice for All Conference."

Well, of course, my teammates thought this was funny as could be and I heard about that for weeks. "Moose, All Conference All Slow." It made me that much more determined to hustle my tail out in front of Middy and show Coach I could make my blocks.

Had I been more knowledgeable about aerobic training, I would have realized that the long slow running I did all summer long prepared me for only one thing: long, slow running. What I should have been doing is running short wind sprints to improve the bursts of speed I needed to get through the line or lead an end sweep. So I continued to be the slowest back in the conference as the season approached and suffered every afternoon from the barbs of the coach's needling.

Actually there was a great benefit in my life due to long slow running. At age 70 when I take the endurance test on a treadmill trying to reach capacity of my peak oxygen consumption, I always max out the test without ever reaching the highest heart rate for my age. In short, this means I have a very strong heart. I attribute it to all to that long distance running I did as a teenager to strengthen my legs and heart trying to recover from the rheumatic fever. What doesn't kill you makes you stronger.

**The Team Fleshes Out**

Another unexpected source of talent came from Herman Swanson. During the summer his Dad moved to

Zion to accept a new job. Herm played basketball and ran track at Kenosha High School for three years. He was tall and lanky, about 6' 2" and ran like the wind. His pass catching ability became a great asset to us. He was also an excellent punter, a skill we lacked on our team. So Herm was installed as the starting offensive left end and became our kicking specialist.

Herm also was our starting safety. His speed and height made it virtually impossible for opposing teams to try to throw deep against us. Herm was always on them like flies on flypaper. His addition to our team was a blessing. He filled a significant hole in our defense.

Herm was very personable and had an easy laugh. "Guys," he said to all of us in the locker room one day, "I know most of you have played together for three years, but I think I can help you if you'll give me the chance."

That immediately won over many of us. We knew we could always use more talent on the team.

"I didn't play football at Kenosha because the basketball coach wouldn't let me," Herm relayed to us. "But I've always wanted to play football."

But, of course, before he was given that chance, he too had to suffer the slings and arrows of Evan Ellis' tart tongue. "You look pretty damn skinny to me, Swanson! You don't look like a football player. Can you even catch a pass?"

"Yeah, Coach. I can catch a pass," Herm answered defiantly. "But all we ever do is run, so what difference does it make?"

We all snickered at this response. We could all see he was definitely a Kenosha bred boy.

"Run out there, Swanson," yelled the Coach.

Herm took off like a gazelle. Ellis delivered a bullet pass that would have ripped my head off. Herm caught it and trotted back with a smile. He tossed the ball back to Ellis.

"Good catch," mumbled Coach begrudgingly. "Now let's see you do it in a game."

The juniors brought a number of very good players into the mix and filled our team weaknesses perfectly. Bill

Perry, at 200 pounds, played quite a bit with the Varsity the previous year. He was installed at left tackle on offense and right tackle on defense. Larry Laird, about 140 pounds but tough like Leon, started at right guard on offense and was our defensive nose guard on the 5-3 defense. He moved over to left guard on defense when we moved into 6 man line and Loren moved in at right defensive guard.

Julian Emanuelson, about 180 pounds, was a strong, aggressive player who could play both tailback and fullback, so Ellis slated him as the number one sub for both positions. He also was the starting defensive right linebacker. Bill Rymer, a transfer from Chicago's Lane Tech, about 165 pounds, was the backup wingback and filled in as a defensive back in any position. Jerry Koskinen, a 180 pound tackle, performed well at either tackle position both on offense and defense when he was called on to do so. Bob Schmidt backed up Bogie at the center spot.

We started the season with a lineup that had eight senior veterans, two inexperienced senior players, three starting juniors, and a bench of three junior substitutes. There were no second or third teams. The prediction that Coach Ellis made while we were freshmen came true. The 13 starters had to be iron men. And iron men we were. We all played virtually every down and yet suffered only one season ending injury the entire fall.

The team was formed. The offense was set. The defense looked intimidating! Our Coaches were prepared. The die was cast. There was nothing to do now but go out and play the games. Let the season begin!

**Preseason Predictions**

I picked up the Saturday Waukegan News Sun from the front steps and immediately opened it to the sports page. There in headlines was the estimate of the Zee Bees fortunes for the 1954 season.

*Zion Football Picture Looks Trifle Better*
*By Dan Loblaw*
*"Football has been a sport badly neglected in recent
years at ZBTHS. A comparably small group of courageous
youngsters have kept the school from fading out of the
conference gridiron title over the past five campaigns. With
them as Seniors, ZBTHS appears to be making a
comeback.*

*Coach Ellis says "If we are able to develop a smooth
operating offense with this group of backs, the Zee Bees
might well blossom into a full-fledged contender. We
possibly have sufficient material available to provide one
of the most formidable forward walls in the school's
history."*

Wow, I thought. I never heard him sound so positive.
You would never guess these were his feelings by the way
he has been haranguing so far in practice. I read further.

*"But, if our offense sputters the club could end up at the
bottom of the heap. We won't know how good we are until
we hit the field."*

"Now that's more like our coach," I scoffed loudly.
"The bottom of the heap! That's probably what he really
thinks of us. What a tragedy it would be if that happened
to us. All this effort and work down the tubes. All we can
do is our best."
There was more.

*"Lake Forest is the team to beat. This Zion club hasn't
beaten them since I have been at the school. I believe
Libertyville and Crystal Lake also will be strong
contenders. It could be a surprising season."*

So our task was laid out for us. Were we up to the
task? That was the unanswered question.

# Grant Bulldogs – Off and Running

The season opened at home under the lights on a Friday evening. The Grant Bulldogs were our opponents. We beat them the year before at their field, but each new season was different. Their quarterback was Bobby Klaus, who later went on to the Cincinnati Reds as a shortstop. He was virtually a one man show. Stop him and we win the game. (I got to know Bobby fairly well in later years. He played shortstop for the San Diego Padres before they became a Major League team while I was stationed in San Diego for several years. He provided me with free tickets to his games and I cheered him on to bigger and better things. Bobby eventually became the starting shortstop for the Cincinnati Reds until a player named Tommy Helms came along and took over his position).

We took the field in our new deep maroon and white uniforms. I loved the white stripes on the arms of our maroon jerseys and the way the white pants set off the dark color. Ellis particularly liked the way our uniforms looked under the lights. He said it made us look like the Chicago Bears. That was very intimidating to the other team.

I was extremely proud to wear my uniform and reveled in having a big number 44 on the front and back of my individual jersey. I was now following in my Brothers' footsteps. I was thrilled to be representing ZBTHS on the field of combat as a football player. I finally reached the level of competition I yearned for all my life. Now I had to live up to my own expectations.

"Okay, Loren. Here we go!" I breathed excitedly as we formed up for the announcement of the starting lineup. "This year it's on our shoulders."

Loren was as pumped as I. "Let's hit it, Moose. All the way this year!"

When the announcer was calling out the names of the starting lineup, he came to Loren's name and instead of pronouncing it as "Streed", with a long E as is correct, he said "Stride" with a long I. You could hear Coach Ellis' laugh all over the field. "Ho! Ho! Ho! Loren Stride. We must have a new quarterback on the team." At that point, Loren got his new nickname. "Stride" it was for the rest of the season.

Before the game started, I heard from the stands a cheer that cracked me up. I had a number of close friends who came to every single game, home or away. They made up a cheer that went like this. "Rock'em. Sock'em! Set him loose. Give the ball to good old Moose." Their voices rang loud and clear down on the field and I couldn't help but laugh. It became a favorite with the crowd. I heard this cheer during many of our games during our senior year. It was great knowing I had friends like that in the stands rooting the team on to victory.

The referee blew his whistle and Herm boomed the kickoff deep into Grant's territory. We stopped them cold. We got the ball back quickly on the punt. On the first play I led Middy around right end and got a good block on the defensive halfback. Middy took off in a sprint and scored a 67 yard TD. Unfortunately it was called back due to a penalty. But we served notice.

"Nice block, anyway. Moose," said Middy as we ran back to the huddle.

Maybe Middy was loosening up some. I didn't expect his comment... but it was welcome.

Wow! I said to myself. If Middy can score like that, we can beat anyone this year. We then went on a 67 yard drive which ended when Middy threw a 24 yard TD pass to Bill Hosken. He can pass too, I thought! This is great!

Late in the first quarter, Middy threw a perfect pass to Herm which should have been a touchdown. Unfortunately it was just off his finger tips and Herm couldn't pull it in. Oh, oh! I thought to myself. He's going to hear about that one.

In the second quarter Bill took a reverse 27 yards to the eight yard line. On the next play I took it in with "Moose up the Gut". My first Varsity touchdown! What a thrill that was! I was filled with elation.

Later in the quarter Bill scored his second TD running another reverse. We went into the locker room with a 20-0 lead. You wouldn't know it by Coach's tirade. He started on Herm.

"I thought you told me you could catch a pass! What the hell was that feeble effort I just saw out there? Do that again and I'll send you back to Kenosha."

I saw the redness creep into Herm's face and knew he was both embarrassed and ticked off at being singled out like that by Coach Ellis. I could only chuckle and say to myself, "So Herm, welcome to the team. You're now officially one of us."

As we filed out of the locker at the end of the halftime intermission, I went over to Herm and patted him on the back.

"Herm," I said. "He treats us all that way."

"Don't let him get to you," encouraged Paul. "That's just the way Coach shows he likes you."

"Funny way of doing it," muttered Herm.

"Don't let it get you down," said Loren. "We need you."

Herm smiled grimly.

"Guess I'd better get used to it. All of you have had three years of this crap...I'll do better for you."

The final score came on a safety in the second half. We beat Grant 22-0. We dominated them both offensively and defensively.

Our defense consisted basically of two formations: a six man line with two linebackers or a five man line with three linebackers. I was allowed to change the defense based on the down and yards to go. But Coach didn't allow me to crash linebackers. He told me only he would call for crashes when he felt it necessary. But our defense was so dominating he saw no need to do so throughout the game.

The one other defense we sometimes used was an eight man line at the goal line. But it wasn't necessary in this game. The shutout was really satisfying for the defense. Philibuck and Lugan were rock solid as defensive ends, our defensive line was almost impenetrable giving up a total of only 67 yards, and our defensive backs shut down their passing attack totally.

In the locker room, Coach Ellis expressed his pleasure.

"Boys, we played well out there tonight. I particularly was pleased with the defense. But we've got a long way to go. Crystal Lake comes here next Friday and you know they're one of the preseason favorites."

Just hearing the name of Crystal Lake put a chill down my back. I never played well against the Tigers and I clearly remembered what happened last year. Maybe this year it would be different.

The atmosphere at Rooks was festive. Lots of loud laughter and good natured jibes thrown back and forth to each other.

The burgers and fries tasted great!! There is absolutely no feeling like the feeling of winning when you know you have worked hard to deserve it.

Barb and Betty Rae were excited for us.

"Bob, it must have been a thrill to score that first touchdown tonight," Barb said with a beautiful smile. "I was so happy for you."

"And you made some wonderful tackles out there tonight, Loren," Betty Rae yelled over all the noise. "You guys looked great."

"Hope we'll be enjoying these celebrations many, many more times this year," I told them between big bites of a burger and slurping down a big chocolate malt. "I love winning."

Ahh, but if I could have foreseen the clouds of darkness at that time, my mood would have been far more subdued.

## Crystal Lake Tigers – The Dream Dims

Zion never beat Crystal Lake in seven previous encounters in North Suburban Conference play. If there was ever a time to do it, there was no time like the present. It was a home game and all our friends were there to cheer us on.

Early in the first quarter, we fumbled the ball deep in our territory and the Tigers recovered on our 12 yard line. Four times they were repulsed with no gain. Unfortunately, on their fourth down, we were hit with an offside penalty which moved the ball down to the goal line. The Tigers scored on the next play. The extra point was no good. Not a great start at all.

We received the kickoff and started working our way downfield. Several plays later, Loren fooled their defense by calling a pass on first down.

"Running Pass Right! Running Pass Right! On Two! Let's get back into this game," he encouraged.

Middy received the ball from Bogie and took off to the right as if it were to be a running play. At the last minute, he pulled up and fired a pass back to Herm Swanson who was standing in the left flat all alone. Herm cradled the pass in his arms and raced 70 yards for a score leaving everyone in his dust. He made good his promise to do better.

Not bad, I thought. Our new players are making an impact tonight. We lined up for the extra point.

The call was "Moose up the Gut." As my eyes quickly flicked over the defensive line, I could clearly see I was in trouble. Crystal Lake stacked three of their linemen right in the hole to which I was headed. In addition two linebackers were up snug right behind them.

This is the same situation as last year, I quickly analyzed. They know exactly where this play is going and are ready to stop it.

My intuition told me to call time out and recommend we try to run Middy around the end. But I knew Ellis would have a fit if I called time out unnecessarily on the field. He reserved that privilege for himself, Loren or our Captain. I doubted that Paul could see the big picture from his tackle position and Loren had to concentrate on calling cadence. So I sucked it up and hit the hole just as hard as I could. Just as in the game the previous year, I felt a surge as our blockers made their initial thrust, but I was pushed back. I twisted and turned trying desperately to find the slightest hole to get through, but it was to no avail. Again I was stopped inches short of the goal line. I was sick to my stomach about it. I let my team down again.

I could hear the groan of the crowd as I lay there on the ground in frustration and mental agony. I wanted to burrow down deeper so no one would ever see me. It was one of my darkest moments ever playing for Zion.

Suddenly I felt someone grab my shoulder pads and yank me upright. It was Paul. He knew what I was feeling at that time.

"C'mon, Moose. They had that hole plugged from the start," he encouraged sympathetically. "We'll score a lot more TDs before this night is over." With that he punched me in the chest and I couldn't help but smile a bit.

We do have another half to go, I reasoned to myself. Maybe he's right. Hopefully we can pull this one out. In the huddle, I let Loren know the situation.

"They're stacking the line on me. Until they spread out a little, I'm not going to gain many yards up the middle," I said mournfully. "I'm not sure what we should do."

Loren nodded in understanding. "Let's see what Coach comes up with at halftime."

Coach opened up on us all at halftime. "None of you are blocking, none of you are hitting, and you look like little old ladies out there. Moose, we badly needed that extra point and you went down like a sack of potatoes. I thought you were a fullback?" he ranted and raved. "My Grandmother could hit that line harder than you do."

In the second half we opened up a little with more sweeps and reverses, but they seemed to know our every play. They stuffed us every down. Four times in the second half we were inside their 30 yard line and couldn't score. Once Middy scored on a 12 yard scamper, but it was called back for a penalty. One of our passes was intercepted. Fortunately our defense was rock solid in the second half and they gained virtually nothing. But our offense couldn't punch it in. Bill and I together gained only 10 yards the entire game. Middy gained 124 yards which was quite an accomplishment, but scored no touchdowns that counted. The game ended 6-6 and I was sick to my stomach. Our first conference game against one of the two favored teams and we ended up with a tie. More importantly from a personal point of view, I failed to score the extra point which would have been a victory for Zion.

I wanted Middy to know how much I appreciated his effort, so I walked up to him in the locker room after I showered. "You did great tonight, Middy...it was my fault. We shouldn't have run up the gut...I should have called time out and changed it to an end sweep with you carrying."

Middy nodded. "If it weren't for the penalties, we wudda won by two TDs."

The team went to Rooks that night with our dates, but it was not a happy place that evening. No laughing, no cheers, no songs. Just an agonizing and subdued atmosphere. This was not an auspicious beginning to our big dream.

## "Moose up the Gut"!!

As soon as we finished our calisthenics on Monday afternoon, Coach called us over to him. "Moose, you should have made that extra point Friday night. Two years in a row you haven't gained the two yards we needed for the score."

"I know, Coach."

"A performance like that is not acceptable. So tonight we're going to have a little personal training for you."

Coach turned to the team.

"I want all the first team except Moose to line up on defense. The JV team will be on offense...with Moose."

Everyone looked at me with apprehension as they lined up in a defensive formation. I fought back the tears that crowded to my eyes.

"I want 'Moose up the Gut' called until I say stop."

He stared at us all with a ferocious look.

"If the defense gives Moose more than three total yards on any of his carries, you'll be running laps the rest of the evening. So make this for real."

I knew I wanted to win the Crystal Lake game as much as anyone and was steamed that I was being designated the goat. For the first time ever in my relationship with Coach Ellis, I knew I had to stand up for myself. If I didn't, I would be his doormat for the rest of the season and more so, for the rest of my life. I overcame all the frustrations and bitterness stored up for the last three years and let it rip.

"So why in hell am I the only person who's getting this crap? The line didn't open a hole for me! This is really unfair! Isn't this supposed to be a team effort?" I shouted at Ellis as loudly as I could.

Coach first looked at me in surprise, and then his expression turned to controlled anger.

"You're doing this because you are the one responsible to make the play work. And you haven't done it two years in a row."

My voice increased a level of pitch. "Let me tell you something, Coach. Not only did everyone on our team know where the play was going, but so did everyone on their team."

"Maybe running against our line will teach you how to hit a line when we badly need a score!" he shouted back at me spitting out his words.

"They were stacked in the hole with three linemen and had two linebackers snubbed up right behind them. Hell, everyone in the stands knew where the play was going. How would you expect me to gain anything?" I spat back at him sarcastically.

Coach was getting really angry now. He stalked over to me and poked his finger against my chest.

"Because this is our bread and butter play and if this one doesn't work, we may as well not even walk on the field. If they load the hole you are headed for, then you just have to find another one!"

"Yeah,right, Coach! Any time I hit a different hole, you chew my butt for not knowing the play. You want it both ways."

Now I knew I was on a roll. Coach stood staring at me, his hands on his hips. I decided to keep going since I was letting it all hang out.

"Why in hell don't you design a play that looks like I am going up the gut, but in fact I hit the line somewhere else?" I yelled. "Wouldn't it make sense to try to fool the defense once in a while instead of always using brute force?"

With that he really exploded. "Don't you tell me how to do my job! I'll tell you what to do and you do it."

"They're dug in two deep just waiting for me," I continued without fear. "Waddya expect?"

"If you can't do it, I'll find somebody else who will," he reacted vociferously.

I knew at that point I had better back off. I saw the cold anger in his eyes and decided to shut up. I never would win an argument with Coach. But I was furious! How unfair to be singled out!

In the huddle the JV quarterback called "Moose up the Gut" as ordered. I took the ball and slammed into our line as hard as I could, but against Paul, Bill, and Lugan, backed up by Julian, I went nowhere. Again I slammed into them. Nothing. Again I slammed into them. Nothing. Each time I hit the line I was getting madder and madder. Again. Nothing. Again. Nothing.

Finally after the sixth futile effort to try to gain the needed two yards, I was absolutely livid. My stomach was in knots and my mind was a boiling pot of emotion and resentment. I'd had it with Ellis and his bullying techniques. Totally disgusted and furious with the humiliation I was experiencing, I was on the verge of telling Coach Ellis to take his damn football and shove it where the sun doesn't shine. Just before I opened my mouth with the words that could have sealed my fate for the remainder of the football season, my old buddy came through for me once again.

"Hey, Coach," piped up Loren. "How about letting me go over and block for Moose? I'll bet he and I together can gain some yards against the first team."

Immediately everyone on the field became deathly quiet. No one had ever challenged Ellis' authority before. All eyes, including mine, turned to Coach. I saw nothing but fire and brimstone in those eyes. He looked as if he was ready to rip Loren apart from the top of his helmet to the bottom of his cleats.

I said to myself, "Oh, Loren, you just walked into the lion's den. You are going to get chewed to pieces by him. I appreciate your loyalty, but this battle is between him and me." I knew that Ellis knew that Loren and I were best friends. But to go against Coach in the middle of this tense encounter was going to set him off like no one had ever seen, I reasoned to myself. This is not going to be pretty.

But an amazing thing happened. As we all stood there frozen waiting for his emotional outburst to start, I saw a change come to Coach's demeanor. I think I actually saw a twinkle come into his eyes.

Considering the highly emotional atmosphere at the time, he said in a fairly calm voice, "Okay, Stride. If you want to block for Moose, you go right ahead and do it."

We all stood agape! Did we hear right from the coach we thought we knew?

Then he turned to the defense and snapped with a snarl, "If you allow Moose one yard, one yard, you got me? You all will be running laps." He hadn't relented one iota.

Loren came into the huddle and put his arm on my shoulder. Our eyes met. Mine were filled with appreciation and admiration for this noble gesture on his part. He nodded knowingly.

Then he got into the middle of the huddle and yelled at all of the JV players, "Come on everybody. Let's block for Moose. Let's show the first team what we can do together."

He turned to me with a smile, friend to friend, with his hand on my shoulder pads and said, "Moose, we can do this."

At that point I couldn't help but laugh out loud. If my old buddy Loren was willing to face the wrath of Coach Ellis and put his body on the line for me against the first string defense, then the least I could do was to give it my best shot.

"You're damn right, pal," I chortled with renewed enthusiasm. "Let's show those guys what we can do!"

Suddenly football was fun again. It was as if we were freshmen once more and just learning to play football. I knew darn well we would never gain a yard against the first string line, but frankly I didn't really care that much anymore. My buddy was with me and the two of us were giving it our best. That was what mattered. So I took the ball and followed Loren into the line as he ordered. Of course, we were stopped cold, but it didn't mean a thing anymore.

I jumped up and yelled at my friends across the line, "Yeah, you got us that time, but we're coming at you again. We're gonna kick your wimpy butts."

Again and again and again Loren and I hit the line together, harder and harder each time, but to no avail. Paul, Lugan, Bill, Julian, and Leon were as impenetrable as a rock. The JV line on my side was more in my way than a help. But Loren and I were now laughing and totally enjoying what we were doing.

Finally Ellis called out, "Okay, Moose, if you hit that line like that on every play, we'll never have a problem scoring from two yards out."

To which I replied under my breath, "Yeah, if they don't stick their linemen and linebackers right in the hole... like Crystal Lake did."

As I walked off the practice field with Loren, most of the team came up and told me that was a lousy thing for Ellis to do. None of them blamed me for not making the extra point. The linemen knew that Crystal Lake had plugged the hole before we ever ran the play. I was greatly mollified to know my teammates stood with me.

Middy trotted up and walked with us.

"Coach is still the same guy I can't stand," he snorted shaking his head. "He shouldn't have singled you out that way."

"It made me madder than hell, Middy," I snapped with anger still in my voice. "But I'll get over it."

"And we'll win more games when Moose is mad," observed Loren.

All three of us laughed.

**********

# Chapter 8
# Warren Blue Devils

It was about noon on a Friday. Loren, Paul, and I were eating our lunch together in the school cafeteria watching the howling wind and rain outside with a sinking feeling.

"This is the most miserable weather I've ever seen," Loren lamented as we watched the skies open up with an almost monsoon downpour. "I hope we're not going to play a game in this slop. Warren's field is nothing but a cow pasture anyhow, and this rain will make it one giant mud hole."

Warren was the only school we played on a school day afternoon. They had no lights, so night games were out. The school football field resembled more of an open piece of grazing land than it did a football field. It was lumpy and uneven. Not a fun place to play under the best of conditions. Our practice field was better than their playing field and that was not saying much.

"Who makes the decision whether the game should be rescheduled or not," Loren asked me in an agitated manner. "This kind of weather could really screw up our ball handling."

"McGrew... and he won't give us a break," I replied sarcastically.

Paul snorted, "Well, for once I'd like to see him do the right thing."

"Don't count on it."

Sure enough, at two o'clock came the announcement that the game would go on as scheduled. We were dismissed from class and begrudgingly trooped to the locker room to pick up our gear and board the bus. It was not a happy group of Zee Bees that afternoon.

Phil commented sarcastically, "Today we not only have to fight Warren's lousy field and their biased refs, but now we have the miserable weather to deal with also. This should be a fun game."

Leon added, "Besides none of the good looking honeys will come out to watch a game in weather like this. I wonder if McGrew thought about that."

"Get your mind on the game, will you?" said Loren irritably.

The hour's ride to Gurnee was quiet and subdued. The normal banter we shared was missing. It was as though each of us somehow knew we were being forced to play a game that would have a calamitous result on us all.

Further we could tell by the furious look on Coach Ellis' face and his seething manner that he too was not happy with this decision. I was sure that McGrew and he had a few harsh words for each other before we left the school.

The mood on the bus matched the dreariness of the weather. The rain continued to come down in sheets and the wind howled. Throughout the bus could be heard the mutterings and concerns of my teammates.

"Who would be stupid enough to have us play a game in this weather?" groused Philibuck.

Even Lugan who rarely talked expressed his thoughts. "They'll probably plow Warren's field after this game and get it ready for the fall planting."

"Maybe we should have brought our bathing suits instead!" Herm growled.

"You guys… get ready," said Paul with authority. "We might not like it, but we're gonna play this game!"

The Warren Blue Devils were considered to be the doormat of the league. Warren was the smallest school in the league with the worst facilities. But they did have one very special player. His name was Tucker Howard. He was Warren's quarterback and was capable of breaking a game open by himself.

I knew Tucker personally because of the time we spent in the same patrol in Boy Scout camp at Camp Indian Mound in Oconomowoc, Wisconsin. We bunked in the same tent for two years in a row. The second year our softball team was undefeated as I pitched and he played shortstop. Also the two of us entered in ten events at the end of the two week period to test the skills we learned the prior two weeks. Between the two of us, we won every single event, from canoe racing to life ring throwing.

After Boy Scout camp, I stayed in touch with him and would often go to Gurnee to visit and enjoy his Mom's home cooking. Furthermore, he was the steady date of Ann Loblaw, who was Dan Loblaw's niece and grew up in Zion. She moved to Gurnee with her family after eighth grade. I knew her from my days at Central Junior High. So I often saw her as well and maintained an easy going friendship. But because of this experience and our ongoing friendship, I knew how good Tucker really was.

"As long as we can keep Tucker in check, we can win this game in spite of the rain," I said.

"I know," agreed Loren. "He's their only threat."

"The rain'll mess up their passing game more than it will our running game," I said more with hope than conviction.

"You're right. We'll just have to play our game no matter what."

Finally we arrived at the visitor's locker room. Coach Ellis kept us inside until the very last minute. "Boys, we've played in the rain before. Let's not let this storm stop us. Backs, you need to be very careful handling the ball. It will be very slippery. Bogie, do your best to keep the ball dry and ask the refs to wipe it off for you before every play. This is an extremely important game for us. Let's give it our best and go home with a victory," he encouraged.

It almost sounded like he was pleading.

As we walked outside, the wind and rain hit us in the face like an evil force. By the time we got to the field, we were soaked to the skin.

The field was even worse than we had anticipated. There were pools of water standing in many parts of the playing surface, a number of them several inches deep. Trying to run warm up wind sprints was absolutely ridiculous. We slipped and slid so much it looked like a Keystone Kops movie. Even worse, the chalk markings designating the yard markers and goal lines were virtually obliterated.

Paul came over to Coach and lamented, "Coach, we can hardly get any traction when we try to block each other. Executing our plays is going to be impossible."

Coach replied with gritted teeth, "Well, they have the same conditions we have. Do your best."

## The Game Begins

I could tell by the sound of the "Pumpf" on the ball that Herman nailed the kick off. However, as it reached the peak of its flight, a sudden gust of wind stopped it dead in the air. It came down back toward us. Warren had a first and ten on our 45 yard line, a mere five yards away from where Herm kicked off.

Oh, great, I thought. This is going to be some kind of game.

Neither team went anywhere. It was three plays, punt. Three plays, punt. Three plays, punt. Miraculously Bogie did a terrific job of centering and the backs never fumbled the ball. But neither did Warren, so it was a complete stalemate until late in the second quarter.

We were on our twenty yard line when disaster struck. The down was third and three and we desperately needed a first down to get out of our own territory.

"Moose up the Gut," Loren barked loudly. "On one."

As we came up to the line, Loren saw the Warren players stacked right in the hole where I was to run. I saw them too. We had a check off play which called for Middy to receive the ball instead and appear to run into the line. He was supposed to stop short and loft the ball to Herm coming across the middle.

"Check red!! Check red!!" Loren called into the howling rain.

Not a bad call, I thought. This might catch them unaware. But I was concerned whether or not Middy caught the check off. He still hadn't learned all the nuances of our offense. Additionally the wind and rain were wildly distracting. I was tempted to call timeout to clear up the situation. But Ellis harped at us that only our Captain and the quarterback could call time out. I knew it needed to be done, but I was reluctant to be singled out again by Coach Ellis. So for the second time in our brief season, I chickened out and remained silent. I regret that indecision to this day.

Bogie did the right thing by centering the ball to Middy instead of me. As I feared, Middy did not pick up on the check off call and was caught by surprise as the ball sailed by him toward the end zone. Pushed by a big gust of wind, the ball rolled furiously down the field with Middy chasing after it, a number of Blue Devils not far behind. As the ball rolled into the end zone, he finally fell on it. It saved the touchdown, but was ruled a safety against us. We went into the halftime locker room down 2-0.

I never saw Coach so agitated. He paced the floor like a wild man, but really didn't say much to any of us. I surmised that he was still angry about the decision to even play the game and worse, he wasn't sure what to tell us to do in the second half. Nothing made sense. We couldn't pass with the wind whipping around like a gale. We couldn't run because it was impossible to get our footing. He was completely frustrated.

Finally as the time neared for us to return to the field, he called us together. "Boys, I know it's difficult out there. But we have got to move the ball. Stride, don't do anything fancy. Just keep running Moose and Middy, and hopefully something will break."

**From Disaster to Anguish**

The cold, miserable, soaking and dreary day we once again faced on the field contrasted greatly with the warmth of the locker room. The rains eased slightly, but the playing surface was a total quagmire. We didn't even try to clean our cleats before taking the field.

This time we received the kickoff and slowly our size and determination began to show. We actually picked up a few first downs before being forced to punt. The conditions weren't any better, but the heart and soul of this team was beginning to materialize.

Warren turned to Tucker to try to bring them out of their morass and he ran the ball three out of every four plays. But our defense was stifling and they never made a single first down. After each exchange of the ball, we moved closer and closer to the Blue Devil's goal line. Only some questionable penalties and deep muck kept us from scoring. Finally in the fourth quarter the most bizarre event that I have ever seen in high school football happened before my very eyes.

We had a first down on the 50 yard line when Loren called, "409 Sweep. 409 Sweep. Moose, I can take the defensive end by myself. You lead Middy up field. Tucker is the defensive back on that side. Take him out for us."

I nodded my head in agreement. Good play, I thought. Tucker, here I come.

Middy received the ball and the two of us headed to our right. Loren easily cleared out the defensive left end and I turned up field looking for my old tent mate and present enemy. I saw his eyes watching Middy a few steps behind me. I took one extra step to be sure I was in range of him and threw one of the best body blocks I ever made right into his midsection.

"Oof," he grunted as he went down and watched Middy slog on by. "Nice block, Moose."

The two of us watched from the muck and slop as Middy had nothing but clear field before him.

"Well, Tucker, old pal, I guess this means the game. You'll never score on us after this TD," I needled.

As I got up on all fours, I saw the referee on the far side of the field raise his arms signaling that Middy scored a touchdown. I saw Middy throw the ball down and start back up field for a celebration. But quickly I realized that something was amiss. The referee who was only about halfway down the field was yelling something we couldn't hear. I saw some of the Warren players race down the field and fall on the ball. Finally it dawned on me. The referee furthest from the play ruled that Middy had not crossed the goal line before he threw down the ball. Thus it was not a touchdown. It was ruled a fumble. Warren recovered and it was now their ball.

Phil was the first one down the field to confront the referees. "Are you crazy? You can't even see the goal line standing on top of it let alone calling it from way back there. He was across the goal line. Are you blind?"

Ellis was close behind racing onto the field. "You've been screwing us this entire game with your one sided penalties. The other ref clearly signaled a touchdown. You can't take it away from us. This is rotten. This whole thing stinks."

The argument continued unabated for at least 20 minutes. Both coaches, both referees and both Athletic Directors got involved. Ellis and Rushforth were so livid that their faces were red with anger. I think if Ellis had a gun, there would have been a dead referee on the field.

In the meantime we huddled up trying to stay warm and discussed it among ourselves.

"I know I was over the goal line," Middy lamented.

"I saw the ref on the far side signal a TD for us and he was down on the goal line," I offered in support.

"I know that damn second ref was too far away to see anything," Phil added vehemently. "I'm going to nail that SOB before the game is over."

"Gang, be calm. We still have to finish this game," Loren advised wisely.

The decision went against us. The head referee was adamant that Middy did not cross the goal and awarded the ball to Warren. Somehow we had to pull it together and win this game.

We stopped Warren cold on three plays and once again they had to punt. We got the ball back on about the 40. Steadily we moved downfield. I could feel the momentum building. The spirit and character of this team was clearly evident.

It was third and one on the ten yard line when Loren called "Moose up the Gut". The hole opened beautifully. I plowed ahead for nine yards giving us a first down on the one yard line. Victory once again was in our grasp.

Then the feeling of helplessness engulfed us one more time. The same head referee who didn't give us the touchdown called a 15 yard penalty on one of us but wasn't clear as to who it was against or why.

Out on the field again came Ellis. "What in hell are you doing to us?" he screamed. "You're the most chicken shit ref I've ever seen in my life. I'll write the conference and have you blackballed for the rest of your career."

Joe Rushforth finally dragged him off the field, but not until Coach vented his spleen. It was a miracle we didn't get another 15 yard penalty.

Loren huddled us up. "Guys, we are still in it. 409 Sweep. 409 sweep. Moose, take Tucker again like before."

Again Middy followed me to our right and I cut up field. Again I smashed head on into Tucker enough to get him out of the way for Middy to sprint on by. But this time their secondary was ready and brought him down with only a 14 yard gain. Two yards short of a first down. Fourth down on the 11.

In the huddle Loren called for the Buck Lateral. Not a good call, I thought. Takes me away from the blocking position and relies on handling the ball twice. Again I thought seriously about calling a time out. But once more I didn't want to violate the rules of the coach and get my butt chewed for causing a delay at such a critical moment. I remained silent. Again I regretted my decision.

I plunged straight ahead into the line handing the ball to Loren as I went by. He pitched the ball to Middy going wide. But Warren wasn't fooled. Without Loren and me leading the way for him, he was nailed at the line of scrimmage. Warren's ball.

There was less than a minute to play and I was virtually in tears. The up and down emotions we experienced were overwhelming. We were desperate. I tried to needle Tucker into making a mistake.

"Hey, Tucker, I hear Annie is hot for some other guy now. Too bad you're such a loser," I threw at him hoping to break his concentration.

Tucker, in the totally confident manner typical of an excellent athlete, looked at me and smiled. "Moose, who's winning this game?"

The comment struck a deep wound into my heart. The game ended. Warren – 2. Zion -Benton - 0

## The Coach Shocks Us All

As we all slogged back to the locker room with heads hung low and nothing to say to each other, I dreaded the coming onslaught of vituperative comments about our play. I had been here before. We played our hearts out and had only a losing score to show for it. But to everyone's amazement, a major change was evident in Coach's attitude from the moment we all filed in and plopped down on the bare benches.

"Boys, I want you all to know how proud I am of all of you. You played like champions out there today. Under the most adverse conditions I have ever seen, you never gave up and kept coming back time after time."

We stared at Coach in disbelief.

"Even though two lousy referee calls went against us, you kept your spirit up and gave it your best," he said in a softened and subdued voice. "We were knocking at their door the entire second half."

His words were surprising but did little to cheer us up.

"There's one more thing I want you to know." Coach took a deep breath and let out a sigh. "Today we became a team. Today we played like every coach wants to see his team play. Today you all stuck together and no matter how the rest of the season turns out, you will always remember this game and how you became a team. Thanks for giving me the honor of being your coach." With that he turned and walked away.

Total silence encompassed the room. What? Did I hear him right? It was an honor for him to be the coach of the team that just lost to the worst team in the league? The emotion of the game and the sense of depression that was prevalent made his comments incomprehensible to me at that time. Frankly, it wasn't until years later that I truly understood the real import of his words.

Then another shock hit us. Loren stood up with a dejected expression and looked at all of us still drooped over where we plopped down in misery. "I lost the game for us today. I shouldn't have called the check off play ...I shouldn't have called the buck lateral when we only needed two yards. I'm sorry! If anyone else wants to take the quarterback position I'm willing to step down."

I was off the bench in a flash. "Hold it! You didn't lose the game for us today. The stupid decision by our Athletic Director to even play this game and the stinking calls by that damn referee is what did us in. You've been our quarterback for three years and I'll be dammed if we're going to change now."

In unison everyone clearly responded in the affirmative. I walked to Loren and put my arm around him. "Hey, my friend. You called them the way you thought best. Those plays worked before in games and they could've worked today. You're not at fault for anything."

I paused to make sure my message sunk in. "Think how Middy feels!" I said trying to divert his attention.

I glanced over in Middy's direction. I saw Paul, Phil, Bogie and Leon all around him giving him what comfort they could. Loren and I joined them.

"Hey, Middy, it was a lousy call. We know you scored," I offered sympathetically.

"You're damn right I scored," stated Middy with obvious frustration.

The ride home was the most miserable experience I had in four years of playing football for ZBTHS. I was sick to my stomach for Coach Ellis, the team, Middy, Loren, and myself. What a lousy turn of events.

The rain stopped just as we were pulling into the parking lot back in Zion. That just added to our pitiful state of mind.

We lost to the worst team in our league. How could we ever overcome the sense of shame? There was no celebration at Rooks that night.

**********

# Chapter 9
# Redemption

Saturday broke as a beautiful and clear day. Loren and I were in my Mom's old Chevy headed down Sheridan Road toward Lake Forest. We were lamenting the game from the day before.

"Why in hell didn't McGrew postpone yesterday's game until today?" I groused to Loren. "We would have beaten Warren by three touchdowns."

Lake Forest was scheduled to play Woodstock on that Saturday afternoon, and since we were playing the Scouts next, it seemed like a good idea to me to check them out. Maybe I could pick up a tip from their style of play which could help us beat them. It would be wonderful to beat them at least once in our four year career.

"We've allowed only 8 points so far, and yet we have a 1-1-1 record. 0-1-1 in the conference. How could that be? Is our offense really that bad?" I asked emotionally clearly showing my frustration.

"The tie to Crystal Lake didn't hurt us as much as the loss to Warren," Loren analyzed. "If we just had the tie, we'd be tied with Crystal Lake in second place right now."

"It seems ludicrous to think about winning a championship let alone becoming All Conference selectees," I complained loudly. I wasn't about to be mollified.

"At this point there are only two undefeated teams and we have yet to play them," said Loren, not about to think negatively. "So we're a still big factor in this conference race."

"If we keep playing the way we have, no one will even know who we are by the end of the season. Osmon and Stried? Who the hell are they?" I said mockingly.

"Sometimes you really tick me off," said Loren irritably. "You're crying as if our season is over...and we still have five games to go. I'd really like to beat Lake Forest. How sweet it would be for us blue collar guys to knock off the rich kids just once."

"Yeah... that would be great."

"They're a darn good team, but not unbeatable. We almost got'em last year. A win against them would make our season... whether we win the championship or not."

"I know. I know." I reflected on that a bit as we sat at a stoplight waiting for the light to turn green. "Loren, I'm sorry I'm bitching so much. I'm down on myself because I feel I've been a big reason we tied and lost our last two games."

"Well, don't feel like the Lone Ranger," Loren rebutted forcefully. "I feel badly about some of my mistakes too. So does Middy."

"I doubt if Middy feels as strongly about the loss as we do."

"I think he does."

I analyzed that thought as I drove in silence. I knew Middy was a competitor and no real competitor likes to lose. For any reason! Finally I said "You're probably right. I'll give him the benefit of the doubt. Thanks."

Lake Forest looked good against Woodstock. They took the opening kickoff and moved the ball steadily to the eight yard line. Woodstock took a time out to discuss their defense. I was particularly interested to see what plays Lake Forest would use to score from that close to the goal line.

When play started up, they lined up in a balanced Tee formation. The first play went off tackle right and was stopped for no gain. Then they tried a sweep around right end and gained a few yards. Next the quarterback dropped back and threw a short pass right over the middle to the left end. He ended up just short of the goal.

On the fourth down the entire backfield started to its right. The play looked like another end sweep. At the last minute, the left halfback handed the ball off to the right end coming around back to the left. Woodstock was so faked out that the end just strolled into the end zone. After that it wasn't much of a contest. Loren and I left by the end of the third quarter.

"They looked pretty good to me. We're going to have to be at our best to beat them," I lamented to Loren.

"C'mon, we can do it," he exhorted confidently.

I hope you're right, I thought privately. Or this season is over!

## Lake Forest Scouts – At Last

After the Warren game in the locker room Coach Ellis may have showed some compassion and sympathy towards us as a result of our effort on the previous Friday, but come Monday on our practice field, he was a wild man once again.

"Leon, hit like you mean it! Philibuck, slam that shoulder into the runner when you tackle him! Move your butts! Moose, at least try to get out in front on end sweeps. Linemen, you're dogging it! Do you think Lake Forest is going to lie down for us? They've kicked your butts ever since you were freshmen. Aren't you tired of getting kicked around by a bunch of spoiled rich kids? Well, act like you are trying to do something about it," he shouted unmercifully.

In a way it was somewhat comforting to see him acting normal again. He bullied, pushed, yelled, snapped, chastised and criticized. I think we all became more immune to his carrying on, but it still had an impact on us. How could it not? Nobody wanted to lose another game. We came so close in the first two conference games and had nothing to show for it. After the first two weeks of the season, we had the fewest points scored against us in the North Suburban Conference and had a 0-1-1 conference record.

The emotions were building up in me. I needed to get them out in the open. Paul was a great Captain on the field, but we really needed pick up before the Lake Forest game. I cornered him one day after practice.

"Whatta ya say we get the team together for a pep talk... by the Captain?" I asked.

Paul looked at me with a concerned face.

"I'm not any good at that kind thing, Moose," said Paul. "I can lead... but I don't do it by talking."

"Okay... I thought you might want to do it."

"You're the guy who can talk," said Paul. "I'll set it up... you talk."

"That's the way you want it?"

"Yep."

Ellis made us run check plays until we knew our check offs forward and backwards. While he didn't personally single out Middy for throwing down the ball prematurely, he emphasized several times during the week the need to run through the end zone to insure a touchdown had been scored no matter what the ref signaled.

We hadn't thrown a single pass against Warren, so we sharpened up that part of our game as well. Daily we had our blocking and tackling drills. We all tried our best to keep our spirits up, but it was tough to do at that point. We needed a victory! Badly!! Now!!

## A Well Timed Prank

The team was slowly winding its way back to the locker room after a particularly tough and long practice. We were mumbling to each other as we approached the front of the high school.

"We need to do something to perk the team up," Phil said as we slogged along. "Anybody got any ideas?"

No sooner than he said that, we came upon Betty Rae's little Austin Healy sitting in the street in front of the school. She apparently was staying late for a meeting in one of her many activities.

"Hey," Leon laughed. "How's about us picking this thing up and putting it in the rotunda next to Cueball Pearce's office? When he comes out, he'll have a fit."

"What do you think, Loren? She's your girlfriend." I felt he should have the chance to nix it if he didn't think it was a good idea.

"Let's do it. She'll think it's funny!"

Eight of us gathered around Betty Rae's car and with a heave picked it up and headed toward the school. The rest of the team stopped and watched the proceedings with great glee. The rotunda was the main entranceway to the high school. It had the photos of the school board and the school administration on the wall and a giant ZBTHS logo directly in the middle of the floor. So we placed her car over the logo and yelled "Go Zee Bees! Sting'em!" Immediately we hightailed out of there before we got caught.

When Mr. Pearce walked out of his office a little later to go home, he saw this car blocking his way out the front door. He knew exactly to whom the car belonged. He stalked back inside and sent for Betty Rae.

"Betty Rae," grumbled Mr. Pearce, "your car is in the rotunda."

Betty Rae looked at Mr. Pearce as though he'd lost his mind. "Are you sure, Sir?"

"Go see for yourself," said Mr. Pearce with a sly smile.

They walked together to the rotunda, and there, sure enough, was Betty Rae's car.

"Strange place to park, young lady," said Mr. Pearce, the humor of the situation growing on him.

Betty Rae shook her head, guessing precisely how the car might have ended up in the rotunda.

"I'll call my Dad...we'll get it removed," Betty Rae said sweetly.

"You got any idea who might've done this?" asked Mr. Pearce in a very official voice.

"Oh, no, Mr. Pearce. I have no idea!"

Betty Rae's Father and Brother arrived and the car was dragged down to the street once again.

The next day first thing in the morning the loud speaker system in the school came on with a loud crackle. Mr. Pearce's voice was loud and clear. "There will be no more... uhm.. parking cars in the rotunda of the school. That is all."

There was a moment of silence. Then everyone in school cracked up. There was much talk about who might have done it. It didn't take long for the word to get around. It was a kick in the pants for the football team... the humor of it made the practices for the rest of the week a little more bearable.

The excitement began to build as the days passed. The bitter memory of the loss to Warren began to fade and the intensity of desire to beat Lake Forest grew. Finally the week was over. Friday evening we were in the locker room getting ready for this final test against Lake Forest. The atmosphere was one of grim determination.

"We have to win this one, Loren," I said with urgency in my voice.

"We've been getting closer every year," he replied confidently. "This year is ours."

"I hope you're right," Phil added. "And we need to pray that the referee's calls go our way for a change."

Coach Ellis got us all together before going out on the field which was an unusual thing for him to do. "Boys, we've had some tough breaks in our first two games. I'm sure there are folks who are counting us out of the race already... but I don't think we're out... and I don't believe any of you think so either. Let's keep our heads together tonight!"

I looked at Paul. He nodded. "Coach... we're gonna do well," he said determinedly. "I've asked Moose to put how he and I feel in words...okay?"

Coach looked at Paul and then at me. He hesitated just a moment, and then stepped aside and allowed me to move to the front of the locker room. "Okay, Paul. Moose, the time is yours."

"Guys, I never said anything before a game during the four years I have played for the Zee Bees, but Paul asked me to put how he and I feel into a few words, so I'll try. While this is for all of you, it's especially for those seven teammates who have played together since we were freshmen."

Everyone looked at me somewhat surprisingly. This was something new for Moose to stand up and have something to say before a game.

"Do you all remember how Lake Forest crushed us when we were freshmen... twice?" I asked emotionally. "Do you remember how they crushed us again as sophomores? Last year we almost got'em, but things went bad for us at the end. We have a chance to make up for all that tonight."

"Yeah!" shouted Paul. There were more shouts.

"Those guys think we're losers," I continued. "Because they have had all the advantages in life, they think they can beat old Zion any time they want. I want to cram the ball down their golden throats!" I screamed as my emotions kicked into overgear.

The team answered with a roar. "Cram it down their throats."

"Tonight's the night," I shouted. "It's time to show those rich kids that Zion is just not dog meat any time they play us... let's go out and kick their butts," I yelled at the top of my voice with far more emotion that I ever thought I had in me.

We all raced onto the field in our maroon jerseys and white pants ready to do battle...to seek revenge for three lopsided losses that were thorns in our sides.

"Good job, Moose," said Paul as we ran. "That was exactly the right thing to say."

We all wanted to beat Lake Forest so badly we could taste it. There was no better time to do it than in front of our home crowd.

No one expected us to win. Lake Forest was undefeated. They rolled over all their opponents played to date. The series since we were freshmen was a classic match up between a rich school and a poor school, and the poor school always came out on the short end of the stick. Tonight was the time to even the score. When it really counted.

The game didn't start well. We fumbled on the kickoff and had to kick deep in our territory. The Scouts moved the ball quickly downfield to our four yard line. It looked dire for the Zee Bees. Lake Forest ran the first play off right tackle. Paul and I stopped them cold. Suddenly something jangled in my brain! I couldn't quite connect the dots, but my mind was on alert. The next play was a sweep around their right end. Lugan threw off his blocker and dropped the runner for a loss. Ding!! Ding!! Ding!!

I've got it! Those were the same two plays they used last week against Woodstock. Could it be that they were going to run the same sequence again?

Normally in a situation like this Ellis always told me to go into a six man line defense with Loren in the line and the two remaining linebackers snubbed up close. But this time I had the intuition that I knew they were going to pass. Even if Ellis were to yell at me for it later, I was determined not to regret my indecision again. I called a timeout on my own for the first time in four years.

My stomach was doing roller coasters as I looked over to the sidelines where Coach was standing. In a way I hoped he would send in the defense so I wouldn't have to make this critical decision. We had been through so much together I was in turmoil. He knew me: I knew him. Make the right decision here and Coach will never say a word. It would be what he expects me to do. But make the wrong decision and I knew what life would be like next week. But he didn't send in a defense. The decision was all mine.

## 5-3 Defense 1954

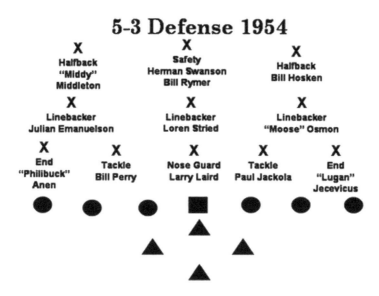

| X | X | X |
| Halfback "Middy" Middleton | Safety Herman Swanson Bill Rymer | Halfback Bill Hosken |

| X | X | X |
| Linebacker Julian Emanuelson | Linebacker Loren Stried | Linebacker "Moose" Osmon |

| X | X | X | X | X |
| End "Philibuck" Anen | Tackle Bill Perry | Nose Guard Larry Laird | Tackle Paul Jackola | End "Lugan" Jecevicus |

I huddled my defensive team around me. "Loren," I said excitedly. "I think they're going to try to throw a pass right over the middle to their left end. Remember they did this last week against Woodstock? Hold your ground and keep your hands up."

To the team I barked, "5-3 Defense! 5-3 Defense! Watch for the pass!"

Loren looked at me skeptically and said "Do you know what you're doing? If we use a 5-3 and they score on us up the middle, Ellis'll have you skinned alive."

"Trust me. I feel it!" I pleaded. Then I almost panicked. If I'm wrong on this and Lake Forest scores, I'll be vilified by Ellis for the rest of the season. God, help me be right!

Loren knew me well enough to know I seldom went off half cocked. And he trusted me. He took his spot as the middle linebacker about three yards deep instead of up tight in the line as we always did near the goal line.

Just as he did the week before, the Lake Forest quarterback dropped back to pass. He looked right over the middle for his left end coming across. But there stood Loren with his hands up ready to intercept the ball if it were thrown. Since his left end was covered, the quarterback suddenly panicked and started to run to his left. Bill and Larry broke through the line and dropped him for a three yard loss. Now I was absolutely sure I was right.

I huddled my defense once again. "Julian. Phil. I'm sure they're going to try to run the reverse your way. Phil, hold your ground so they can't go wide around you. Julian, after the snap come across the line, stay low, and stand tight in the hole so you force the runner wide. But most of all don't chase the play."

They did exactly as I told them. The entire backfield started right with the left halfback carrying the ball. Just before they went head to head with Lugan, the halfback handed the ball to the right end coming back to his left. When the end saw Julian standing right in the hole to which he was headed, he tried to flare wide around Phil. But Phil was far too good a tackler to let that happen to him. He dropped the Lake Forest player with another loss! They lost ten yards in four plays. Zion ball on the 14 yard line!

I looked over at the sidelines again. Coach was clapping his hands and giving me thumbs up. Maybe this is what he has wanted from me all along, I wondered briefly. We took over on offense.

There are times when the breaks are with you and times when they are not. This time the breaks were with us.

On the very first play from scrimmage after we got the ball back, Loren called the 409 sweep. We practiced this play so many times we could do it in our sleep. Loren and I headed for the left end. Loren took him out with a solid block and I headed up field. Just as I did with Tucker Howard the previous week, I threw a perfect cross body block into the defensive halfback. Herm made a clean block into the safety so the field was wide open. Middy took off like a rabbit. He ran untouched 86 yards to pay dirt. There was one major difference this time. After he arrived at the goal line, he continued to run through the end zone, turned around, and came back up through the goal posts before he gave up the football to the refs. No throwing the ball down before crossing the goal line this time. Herm kicked the extra point. We had the lead against Lake Forest 7-0. For the first time! Ever!

I ran to Middy and clapped him on the back. "Way to go, Middy!"

Middy looked at me in a way I'll never forget. The old arrogance faded and he looked grateful that I ran over to him to congratulate him.

"Pieca cake," he yelled. "As long as you keep throwing those blocks!"

In the second quarter Middy returned a punt to the 26 yard line and we worked it down to the three yard line with fourth down coming up. Loren called "Moose up the Gut", but when he got to the line of scrimmage, he saw the defense packed into the 5 hole. Their coaches had obviously watched the Crystal Lake game. So he checked off at the line. This time I had no doubt that Middy caught the check off. He ran the ball as if he were going into the line and then stopped short. He jumped in the air and lofted an easy pass behind the crashing linebackers into the waiting arms of Herm. Beautiful. Touchdown!

Just the way it is supposed to work. Herm kicked another extra point. 14-0.

In the third quarter potential disaster struck. On an end sweep, Middy took a pretty serious blow and went down hard. We all stood in silence as the trainers ran out with the stretcher. The doc thought his leg was broken. He was slowly lifted into the stretcher and carried off the field.

"Middy," I said as he was carried past us, "this one isn't going to slip away. You got us the lead...we'll keep it."

Middy acknowledged with a nod of his head. "Stick it to'em, Moose."

Fortunately Julian proved to be a very capable replacement. Back and forth, first him, then me, we moved the ball steadily down the field controlling both the ball and the time. It was into the fourth period when we finally got to the Lake Forest one yard line.

Loren called my play. "Okay, Moose. I know how much this game means to you. Ram it down their throats. 'Moose up the Gut'! On one. Break!"

I bulled into the end zone behind great blocks by Paul and Bill. Those "Moose up the Gut" drills paid off in a big way as I hit the line with power and determination. How satisfying it was to finally score a touchdown against Lake Forest after all these years. I was so happy I almost wanted to cry.

I could hardly express my emotions at that moment. It was as if all was well again and no matter what would happen for the rest of the season, we beat Lake Forest. Final score: Zion 20 Lake Forest 0. We shut out the highest scoring team in the conference. Furthermore I scored a TD against them which made it even more delicious. Redemption! Finally!

I could not help but recall Jackie Gleason's famous trademark line, "How sweet it is." Victory can only be truly savored by those who know the sting of defeat. During our four years together our team experienced more than its share of stings. But not tonight.

Our defense shut the Scouts down for the rest of the game. We gained 174 yards and scored three TDs against one of the two teams picked to win the conference. Further, they were undefeated coming into the game without even experiencing a close game against them. We only attempted four passes, but one was for a TD. Herm did a great job of punting, keeping the Scouts deep in their territory throughout the game.

The defense once again was like a rock. With the exception of the opening drive, the Scouts offense went nowhere. Our line was impenetrable. Our defensive backfield kept their receivers under close wraps. Loren, Julian and I had our share of tackles at linebacker. Another shutout. Still only eight points scored against us.

Good news awaited us in the locker room. It turned out Middy's leg wasn't broken after all. He took a hard hit which numbed his leg, but he was walking around by the time the game was over. He'd be with us for next week's game.

Coach Ellis wanted just one small word with us before we hit the showers. "Boys, more than any other team in our conference, I've wanted to stick it to Lake Forest since all of you were freshmen. Tonight you brought me that victory. Thank you all." He smiled broadly, turned around and went into his office.

"Hmm!" I said to Loren as we were dressing. "This marks two weeks in a row Coach said something good to us. I know it doesn't mean he's dramatically changed, but it's nice to hear some good things for a change."

"You analyze him too much," said Loren. "Just take the compliment as sincere."

"You're right."

"By now we all know he doesn't say anything good about any of us unless he really means it," said Loren with a note of appreciation in his voice.

"I'll take it that way," I replied with a firm nod.

Betty Rae and Barb met Loren and me in the parking lot with enthusiastic hugs and kisses.

"You guys were great tonight!" screamed Barb, her arms around my neck.

"What an exciting game!" squealed Betty Rae. "I guess I'll have to forgive you all for the car thing."

Rooks that Friday night was bedlam. Every one on the team showed up with their girlfriends and the atmosphere was as festive as I had ever seen it. Cheers, songs and good natured ribbings flew fast and furious. It was an evening I never wanted to end. The Zion Benton Zee Bees finally beat the Lake Forest Scouts. Hooray and hallelujah!! Hurrah for Zion! Bring on the Blue Streaks!

## The Dream Rekindled

The following day Loren and I drove out to Lynn's home in the afternoon. It was early October and the leaves were beginning to turn color. The timing and mood were perfect for Lynn to hold her last pool party of the season.

"Maybe the change of season will coincide with the change of fortunes for our team," I said hopefully to Loren as we walked up the steps to Lynn's home after we parked the car. "Our dream is still alive."

We could clearly hear the Crew Cuts crooning out the latest hit song as we neared the house.

*"Hey, nonny ding dong, alang, alang, alang,*
*Boom bad oh, ba doo, ba doodle day.*
*Oh, life could be a dream (Sh-Boom)*
*If I could take you up to paradise above (Sh-Boom)*
*If you would tell me I'm the only one you love,*
*Life could be a dream, sweetheart.*
*(Hello, Hello, again. Sh-Boom, hoping we'll meet*
*again)"*

"How sweet it is to have beaten Lake Forest. And the way we did it was no fluke. We crushed the number one team in the conference. The Crew Cuts have it right. Life is just a dream," I exulted.

"How in the world did you remember the plays that Lake Forest ran against Woodstock?" asked Loren. "That amazes me. How'd you do that?"

241

"Betty Rae and Lynn have accused me of having an eclectic mind since we were freshmen," I laughed with great pleasure.

"What the heck does that mean?"

"I store a lot of unrelated information in my brain," I mused. I never really thought much about what it meant. "It just jumps out when something triggers it."

"I guess this was one time when your eclectic mind was actually useful," teased Loren.

"Thanks a lot," I said sarcastically. Then I lightly punched him in the shoulder.

"Those two defensive plays you called when they were down on our goal line... that was the turning point of the entire game," Loren said appreciatively.

"For the last three years and for the first three games of this year, Ellis had me so intimidated that I was afraid to change his game plan at all," I admitted openly.

I paused for a moment to gather my thoughts. "But I realize now that by not going with my gut feeling in both the Crystal Lake and Warren game, it cost us badly. By going with my gut in the Lake Forest game, it made a huge difference and we won the game."

"It sure did."

"From now on, I'm gonna do what's right for this team. After all, this team belongs to you and me as much as it does to Coach. Right?"

"Make your calls as you see them on the field... but listen to the Coach, too. We both know he's a brilliant man when it comes to football."

"Thanks, Loren. I will from now on. I promise."

As we entered Lynn's home everyone was in great spirits.

"Congratulations, you two," Lynn crooned as we walked in. "That game yesterday was so... so wonderful. We wanted to beat Lake Forest just as badly as you!"

Joyce chimed in. "Cheering at that game was one of the most exciting nights I ever had. I was so happy for your team. I can't wait for the next games... I know you can beat everyone else in the conference!"

"Whoa, Joyce. Let us savor this one first. I can't even begin to think about the next games yet," I replied quickly.

"You know, I love all you guys dearly," Betty Rae started with her hands on her hips. She showed a hint of amusement on her face. "But which of you clowns put my Austin Healy in the school rotunda last week?"

We all looked at each other, feigning innocence.

"Leon and Phil, you two are the most likely culprits!" accused Betty Rae. "You should've seen the principal's face when he called me out of a meeting to come and get my car."

"I guess that little car had wings," said Leon with a sly smile on his face.

"At first I was shocked," said Betty Rae. "Then... I thought it was really funny."

"How could you ever accuse Leon and me of doing something like that to you?" Phil harrumphed indignantly. "You know what straight arrows we are!"

"Yeah! Yeah!" Betty Rae retorted. "You two'll be straight arrows when the Cubs win the World Series!"

Everyone laughed. Even in 1954 the Cubs were the butt of many jokes. The rest of the party was relaxed and enjoyable. We reveled in our victory and enjoyed it even more knowing the girls in our class were happy for us as well. They too could feel the joy we experienced from beating our most reviled opponents.

## Woodstock Blue Streaks – DeJa Vu All Over Again

Spirits were much improved all week long. We finally beat our biggest nemesis and that monkey was off our back. Woodstock was next on our schedule. We all remembered how we beat them soundly as freshmen. Thus we all felt a win would be a fairly sure thing. Not overconfident, but as a team we anticipated a big win.

We were scheduled to play them again on their home field, the site of our single biggest victory as freshmen. They had a big tackle whom none of us remembered from our freshman year, but he was a force to be reckoned with. At least according to the newspapers. Coach didn't seem too concerned. He knew Paul, Bill, and Lugan could handle any tackle Woodstock might throw at us.

There was yet another thing that was a coincidence for this game. As we boarded the bus on a Friday afternoon to head out to Woodstock for a night game, Coach Rushforth made an announcement to us.

"Today Coach Ellis' wife gave birth to another little girl… Laurel Jean Ellis. He is with his wife and daughter now, so he won't be going with us. I'll serve as the head coach and Coach John Timmerman, the JV coach, will serve as my assistant."

"How about that?" I exclaimed to Loren as we shared a seat together on the ride out of town. "Three girls. I can't even imagine what that would be like. Hope I have at least one boy when I become a father. And why does his wife always have them during the football season? Can't she plan any better than that?"

Loren nodded. "Must be tough on a football coach to have all girls. Maybe they'll calm him down someday."

"For their sake, I hope so," I noted sarcastically.

I sat quietly for about 15 minutes pondering the possible effect that not having Ellis with us at this game might have on the team. For those of us who played under him for the previous three years, we knew his football knowledge and ability to adjust in a game was uncanny. And while he continued to bluster at us non stop, by now most of us had grown from fearing him to respecting him… a major difference in the minds of young men playing football. So my mind was a little ill at ease as the school bus headed out Route 173 to Woodstock.

Woodstock was a good two hour ride away, so after about an hour I couldn't sit still any longer. I decided to talk to all my defensive players on the trip out just to be sure they understood what my different defensive calls meant. Everyone had a good grasp of the defensive alignments and what their responsibilities were. Until I came to John Jecevicus.

"Hey Lugan," I said as I sat down next to him on the bus. "I'm just reviewing defensive alignments with everyone to make sure we are all on track. Do you have any questions about the differences in your assignment when we go from the 5-3 to a 6 man line? Remember you have to hold your ground and cover the end sweep for me when I crash. I'm just double checking to be sure we're all in synch."

Lugan looked at me rather oddly. "I never pay any attention to what defenses you call. Coach Ellis told me to knock down any player with a different color jersey on and that would suit him fine. So that's what I do."

Well, I thought indignantly. So much for the importance of my calling defensive signals. But then, Lugan never allowed anyone around his end for any gains, so why change a system that works? From then on I realized my defensive calls were for the other ten players.

Joe Rushforth gave us more incentive just before we left the locker room.

"Boys, Coach Ellis hates to miss this game, but wants you to know he is very proud of the way you fought back from a disheartening defeat and knocked off Lake Forest last week," he said with great sincerity. "Now he wants you to keep the ball rolling. He expects nothing but the best out of you tonight."

The impact of these words was felt by us all. This one was for Coach Ellis.

The game went well for us. Even though Coach's physical presence was absent, everything he drilled into us was coming to fruition. His impact on our team was evident even though he was two hours away back in Zion.

We dominated Woodstock in every department. We moved the ball up and down the field at will, although we did have trouble scoring when we got near the goal line. Once in the first quarter and once in the third quarter we were knocking on the door when errant handoffs between Middy and Bill on reverses resulted in fumbles that Woodstock recovered. I believe we would have scored on both plays had the handoffs been clean.

In the second and fourth quarters, Middy scored touchdowns on end sweeps. The final score was 12-0. The game wasn't nearly as close as the score indicated. Middy gained 150 yards rushing and I had 50 in short plunges.

The defense was brutal. Lugan, Paul, Larry, Bill, and Phil nailed the Woodstock runners every time they made a move. They had only a few first downs and little yardage. Loren and I both intercepted passes and made excellent tackles throughout the game. Maybe now some one would begin to notice who Osmon and Stried were.

We now had two shutouts in a row and still only eight points scored against us. More importantly, I felt we were continuing to gel as a team. The offense was showing signs of life. The defense continued to dominate every team we played. Everything was looking up.

One of the fun things about going to Woodstock was their swimming pool, something Zion never had. After the game we were all allowed a quick swim. With a win under our belt, it really felt good to splash around for a while. John Timmerman later told me that the Woodstock coach came up to talk to him while we were swimming.

He asked John half mockingly, "What's with this guy Moose Osmon? First of all he beats us up on the football field, running through our line, making tackles, intercepting passes, and now it looks like you'll never get him out of the pool. Doesn't he ever get tired?"

John laughed and said, "We train them to be tough in Zion."

Another good thing about Woodstock was that they filmed their games...one of the few schools in our conference that did so. Most of the schools didn't have the money for it. Many years later I drove to Woodstock and specifically asked the Athletic Director if I could have the film from the 1954 game. He was happy to oblige me as no one ran the Single Wing anymore, so they had no need to review the game film. It is the only film I have that shows our team in action. The film is in black and white, and very grainy, but it holds live action shots of our team. I had it transcribed onto video tape and gave everyone on the team a copy. I still watch that scratchy, dark, poorly made movie film from time to time and feel the thrill of competition as if it happened yesterday.

We arrived in Zion much too late that night to enjoy a celebration at Rooks. It closed hours earlier. We all simply bid goodbye to each other in the parking lot knowing we had another victory under our belts that was well deserved. We looked forward to the next game against McHenry and Homecoming.

## The Veer

As practice started on Monday after the Woodstock game, Coach Ellis gathered us around and started off in his usual serious tone. "Boys, Coach Rushforth and Coach Timmerman told me you all played an excellent game on Friday night. I'm very proud of you... but we do need work... two fumbles on our reverse are not acceptable. I also have some changes I want to incorporate this week in our offense. We have some tough games coming up and this may help us move the ball better."

Hmm, I wondered. What changes might that be? I wonder if this is going to affect me. I never doubted Coach's brilliance when it came to football, so I knew whatever it was going to be, it had to be good for us.

"But first of all I need to ask you all a deep down, soul searching question and I need some good answers," Coach intoned dramatically drawing us all into his facade of seriousness. "Now, boys, every one of your fathers has at least one son. So I want you to go home tonight and find out what your Fathers did to have a boy. Did they keep one foot on the floor? Did they wait for a full moon? Did any of them eat steak and eggs for dinner that night? When you get an answer from them, please pass it on to me. I now have three girls and obviously I am doing something wrong." With that he broke into one of his patented guffaws and we all couldn't help but laugh. It was great to see him in a good mood.

After we completed our calisthenics, Coach called us together again. "Boys, McHenry is not going to be any pushover. We've got three tough games in front of us and I know we are being scouted. I'm very satisfied by the way our defense is performing, but I'm going to throw a few wrinkles into our offense. Maybe we can keep their defense off balance and move the ball a little better."

He turned to me, and what he had to say earned my respect for him for the rest of my life. "Moose, do you remember the first practice after the Crystal Lake game, when we had our little heated discussion over running 'Moose up the Gut' so many times against the first team defense?"

Of course I remembered I wanted to shout. How in hell could I forget? But instead I nodded my head.

"At that time you asked me why we didn't have a play that would start with you headed up the gut to draw the linebackers to the middle, but hit another hole. I talked this idea over with Coach Rushforth and Coach Timmerman, and they think it would be a good idea to install a play like that. So I have designed a new play that I think will work for us. It'll stop the other team from keying on you in short yardage situations. I'm going to call it 'The Veer' and we can run it left or right, depending on our offensive alignment."

I was absolutely flabbergasted! I quickly ran this new development through my mind. Coach Ellis actually admitted he was wrong and I came up with something right? It was beyond my comprehension! I was speechless! I understood the concept immediately because I was the one who often had to face the overloaded line exactly where I was supposed to run. This just might be great!!

He lined us up and we ran through it a few times. It was so simple I wonder why he hadn't put it in the play book before. After taking the snap from Bogie, I headed straight into the gut as normal as if I were going to plow right behind Paul and Bill over tackle. Then, after a good fake into the line, I planted my right foot and suddenly veered to the left. Hence the name. The right guard, Larry Laird, pulled and took out the defensive right end while Herm blocked in on the linebacker. Leon took the man over him or over the center by himself. The fake set up the key block because the linebacker ran to the middle to tackle me. No one was assigned to the defensive halfback as it was designed to be used in short yardage situations only. I had to deal with him on my own. But I didn't care about that at the time. To me this single play meant no more embarrassments like the ones that occurred against Crystal Lake.

After we ran it a dozen times, I knew it would work. As we tromped back to the locker room that night, I said to Loren, "Man, I can't wait to try the veer in the game. You'll know when to call it."

"I'll use it the first chance I get," Loren replied confidently with a smile. He knew it would work also.

Neither of us could envision just how well this single new play really would work. It brought our offense to life for the rest for the season.

## Homecoming - 1954

There is one thing I miss about no longer living in Illinois. It is the breathtaking, beautiful, crisp fall days of autumn. The maples are ablaze with their bright crimson colors. The oaks have a beautiful golden hue. The mugginess and mosquitoes are gone from the summer and the cold winds of winter haven't blown in yet. Everyone's energy levels are at a peak. This period starts about the middle of September and sometimes goes into early November. Some people call it "Indian Summer". I remember it as the State of Illinois football season. What a wonderful time of the year it was.

To play football and be part of the annual high school homecoming was a very moving experience. I remember being so filled with such emotion that it is difficult to describe. So it was for my teammates and me as the Zion Benton Homecoming approached in October 1954.

Each class and several of the clubs built floats representing their organizations. In a small town like Zion there wasn't a lot of money and most of the work was done by the students. But the end result was as glamorous to us as the Rose Parade was to Pasadena. A total of 24 floats were in the 1954 parade.

A big hay rack was used to haul the football team down Sheridan Road. The sign on each side was brightly emblazoned in big maroon letters, "The Zion Benton Zee Bees, Football 1954." To me, it was part of an experience I can vividly recall 50 years later.

Starting at the school, the parade snaked its way through town down 23rd Street to Sheridan Road, then right through the middle of town turning right again at the water tower diagonal, and headed back to the school along Emmaus Avenue.

More than 2000 Zionites turned out for the parade. My Mom was there waving enthusiastically as we passed by her. Even more people showed up for the game. Not bad for a town of only 4000. One advantage of growing up in a small Midwestern town in the 50s is that everyone in town supported the high school football team.

As part of the Homecoming pageantry, each class elected two girls to serve on the Homecoming Queen's Court. In addition the football team was honored with selecting the senior who would become the Homecoming Queen. Kay Suttie and Pat Friend, two very pretty and popular girls, were elected as the senior class representatives. Throughout the school there was a buzz as to who the Homecoming Queen would be. There were so many excellent candidates that everyone knew it was a tough choice to make.

Lynn, Joyce, Betty Rae, and several others were all good choices. Finally the football team met and cast its votes. I was delighted to learn that Kay Kern was selected. It felt right that someone who was dating one of our players became our Homecoming Queen. Bogie was beside himself and walked around with a beaming face all week.

There was no doubt among our teammates that Kay represented our school well. She was as lovely on the inside as she was on the outside. We all thought she was just perfect as our Queen.

At a pep rally held the day before the game, the Queen and her court were introduced. On a sunny, beautiful fall day, two long columns of students were formed outside the main entrance to the high school and stretched across 23rd Street to the football field. The nine senior lettermen escorted the Queen and her court through the cheering columns receiving words of encouragement and shouts all along the way.

Homecoming Queen - Kay Kern
Left to right: Phil Anen, Pat Friend, Bobby Middleton, Janice Baumgartner, Herman Swanson, Myra Ballegooyen, Leon Hallgren, Judy Holley, Kay Kern, Paul Jackola, Myra Parker, Bob Osmon, Marlene Cook, Loren Stried, Laura Hodge, Bill Hosken, Kay Suttie, Dick Bogue

I can still envision that event in my mind as clear as a bell. Leon and I led the procession escorting the two freshmen girls, Myra Parker and Judy Holley. Loren and Herm were next with the two sophomore girls, Marlene Cook and Myra Ballegooyen. Bill and Middy escorted the two junior girls, Janice Baumgartner and Laura Hodge. Philibuck was with Pat Friend, but since Kay Kern was the Queen, Bogie escorted Kay Suttie. Paul, as Captain, was given the honor of escorting Kay.

The cheerleaders worked everyone up with cheers and the school song resounded from the stands. Our Principal,

Hubert Pearce, and our three coaches, Ellis, Rushforth, and Timmerman came out in front of the student body and led their own special cheer. It netted a lot of laughs, but I thought it wasn't bad for a bunch of old guys. Paul gave a warm speech thanking everyone for their wonderful support, Coach Ellis talked about the dedication of the team, and Mr. Pearce reminded students not to get too rowdy during the Homecoming Parade the next evening. As if that were really needed. This was, after all, Zion.

Too soon it was over and everyone got the rest of the afternoon off. It created a nostalgic moment which has never been duplicated in my life. Rather than regret that it never happened again, I am grateful to God that I experienced it once in my life.

## McHenry Warriors - A 48 Yard Ramble

On Friday evening after the parade brought us back to the school, we were all in the locker room and fired up and ready to go! We put on our uniforms proudly, had our pre game talk by the Coach, and went out to the field for our calisthenics. After a good warm-up doing our normal pregame drills, Ellis called us over for last minute directions before the start of the game. Just as he started to talk, the lights went out on the field and over the announcing system came the word that in celebration of the 1954 homecoming, there would be a special fireworks display.

Coach absolutely lost it and went berserk. "Who in hell authorized fireworks to be lit off? I didn't authorize it! Did McGrew do this? Get those damn fireworks off my field! It's time for the game to start," he shouted loudly to the refs, but to no avail.

Even though his voice was strong and forceful, it was no match for the noise generated as the fireworks began to erupt. It was a beautiful display and there was nothing to be done but for us to lie on the field on our backs looking up into the sky and enjoy it all. The fireworks lit

252

up the sky for about 15 minutes. Coach was livid for the entire time.

For a dedicated football coach, there is nothing worse than having your team fully ready to go on the field and then have your players sit on their butts for fifteen minutes cooling down. If he could have strangled Coach McGrew at that very moment, he would have. We all knew there would be strong words between them again on Monday morning.

Finally the game started. We received the kickoff and moved quickly to their 48 yard line. In a third and two situation, Loren called "Moose up the Gut" and we broke out of the huddle. McHenry was in a normal defensive lineup, so I didn't have much doubt I could make the first down. I took the snap from Bogie and started my drive straight ahead. Bill, Leon, and Paul opened a huge hole for me and I plunged through.

After I ran several yards down field, I expected to be hit by somebody. I quickly glanced left and then right... there was no one in sight. Incredible!! So I took off for the goal line as fast as my "All Slow" legs could go! The crowd was going wild... probably because they had never seen me run farther than five yards before! But the field was wide open. I put on what for me was my utmost burst of speed and headed for the end zone. Just as I got to the goal line, one of the McHenry players caught me from behind, grabbed me at the ankles and tripped me hard as I flew into the end zone.

All I could think of was for God's sake, Osmon. Don't fumble the ball.

I tucked both arms around the ball tightly. As I hit the grass in the end zone, I saw the ref signal a touchdown. I just scored the longest TD of my four year career and I did it at homecoming! In front of more than 2000 people! It was beyond my wildest dreams. My teammates ran up to me and started pounding me on my back and shoulder pads. What a great sense of elation!

We huddled up as Loren called for the extra point. Leon grinned and said, "Moose, I never knew you could run that far." Everyone had a good laugh at that comment.

As a team we hit our stride in the McHenry game. On offense we rolled up 312 yards rushing. Bill had several 20+ yard runs, Middy gained more than 135 yards, and I netted 86 yards total rushing. Herm caught another 25 yard pass and Middy scored two of our touchdowns on the end sweep. After I intercepted a pass deep in the Warriors territory, I scored my second touchdown of the evening on a veer left.

Several times Loren called for the veer just to see how it would work. It worked to perfection. He waited until it was a short yardage situation. McHenry was expecting me to come straight up the middle as they had seen me do many times in the past. I took two steps right toward the five hole and then veered to the left. Larry, Herm, and Leon cleared out a big hole for me each time. I garnered about eight yards every time we ran it. I don't think they ever figured out what hit them. We added a new play to our arsenal and it was to pay even bigger dividends in the future.

Our defense was once again brutal. McHenry never got inside our 30 yard line all night and only crossed the 50 one time. We gave up a total of only 60 yards and five first downs. Lugan, Philibuck, Larry, Bill, and Paul were devastating on the defensive line. Loren, Julian, and I backed them up aggressively with some solid tackles. Our defensive backs, Bill, Herm, and Middy allowed only one complete pass all night. We won the game 26-0. Another shutout! Still only eight points scored against us! We were on a roll.

There was one dark cloud on our celebration however. Herm intercepted a McHenry desperation pass late in the game and started up field with it. I was several steps ahead of him with only one man between us and the goal line. I was doing my best to block the tackler, but Herm was so much faster than I that he zipped right past me. As the McHenry player came up for the tackle, Herm tried to hurdle him. But the tackler rose up and caught him in the groin with his helmet. Ouch!

The injury Herm sustained not only put him out of action for the rest of the season, but also badly hampered him in both basketball and track. He was a big loss to our team. Not only were his superb pass catching skills gone, but also his punting ability. In particular I was saddened to lose him because I felt it was my fault that I didn't get to the tackler first. I wished that he remembered that I had been selected for the "All Slow" team. There was a good reason why Ellis dubbed me with that honor.

After the game in the locker room, Coach walked up to me with a big grin on his face. "Moose, I never thought I'd see the day when you would score a 48 yard TD on a 'Moose up the Gut'. I think that is the fastest I ever saw you run. Ho! Ho! Ho!"

"Thanks, Coach. I was so surprised to see a wide open field I almost didn't know what to do."

"Well, I'll tell you one thing. This team is full of surprises. I never know what the hell you guys are going to do next!"

"As long as we keep winning, Coach, that's what counts."

"You're right, Moose. That's what counts."

That night was the formal Homecoming Dance and once again the nine of us were honored to escort the Queen and her court to the throne erected for just this event. All the girls wore off the shoulder, long gowns and each of them was absolutely elegant. Kay was a beautiful queen and her court just as attractive. I was proud that Zion Benton High School produced such lovely ladies.

After the ceremony, Barb threw her arms around my neck and kissed me. "That touchdown run was great! In the stands we all went wild," she exulted in her special way. "I'm so proud of you."

"Barb, I'm proud of you too. You look absolutely lovely tonight," I told her in complete honesty. "I've got the best looking date here."

"Thank you," she said demurely. Her eyes told me there would be more kisses tonight.

We joined Loren and Betty Rae at the table reserved for the football team. Betty Rae looked terrific as well. I thought to myself, she certainly is a striking redhead! We danced the hours away without ever getting tired. I had such a great time I silently wished it would never end. Life was good at ZBTHS.

**********

# Chapter 10
# The Excitement Grows

"It's Showdown Time in the North Suburban Loop"
screamed the headlines of the News Sun as I quickly
flipped to the sports page.

*"The North Suburban Conference gridiron pot, which
has been sputtering through the first five weeks of a topsy
turvy campaign, is expected to come to a boil this Friday
when the Libertyville Wildcats and the Zion Benton Zee
Bees meet."*

Dan Loblaw was building excitement in the conference
with his dynamic writing. And with good reason. The
race for the championship was still wide open.

One of the things I absolutely love about football is
that it is almost impossible to pick a winner in many of
the games. Logic doesn't hold forth in many cases. For
example, if Team A beats Team B by 20 points and team
B beats Team C by 20 points, then logic would tell you
that when team A plays team C, Team A will beat Team
C by 40 points. But that is almost never true. In fact,
many times, more than one would expect, Team C
actually beats Team A.

The reasons for this can be multi fold. A star player
could be hurt for any given game, the refs could make
some bad calls as in the Warren game, the field conditions
could be different, or a fumble or interception at the
wrong time could completely change the complexion of the
game. And so it was in the fall of 1954 in the North
Suburban Conference.

A case in point. We tied Crystal Lake 6 -6. We then
beat Lake Forest 20-0. So logically one could assume that
Crystal Lake would beat Lake Forest quite handily. Not
so! Actually Lake Forest beat Crystal Lake that weekend
13-6. That was good for us.

Another case in point. Libertyville beat Crystal Lake
33-13, and Crystal Lake won over Barrington, so it was a

good bet that Libertyville would beat Barrington. Not so! Barrington actually shut out Libertyville 12-0.

As I read the newspapers on Saturday morning after the McHenry game, I quickly came to a rather startling realization. Because of these series of events, Lake Forest and Crystal Lake both had two defeats. The only team in front of us with one loss was Libertyville, and they were our opponent for Friday night. At home!!

I immediately got on the phone to Loren.

"Hey, read Waukegan News Sun sports page. Lake Forest beat Crystal Lake this weekend. That means they both are behind us with two defeats and only Libertyville with the one loss to Barrington is in front of us. Do you realize what that means?"

"If we beat Libertyville Friday night," said Loren excitedly, "we'll be in first place by ourselves with only Barrington to go."

"We've waited for this for a long time," I said with a bit of edginess. "Do you think the Wildcats are that good?"

"We took 'em last year. We can do it again."

"You're right! We're on a roll. Plus we'll be playing at home in front of a huge crowd! We'll kick their butts," I replied confidently.

## The Johns Manville Open House

On Wednesday of that week Johns Manville, my Mother's employer, was scheduled to hold its first ever open house. It was to be held after work, 3:30 PM, and was primarily for the employees who worked there to bring their families in to see their workplace. My Mother worked there for more than 14 years and wanted very much for me to attend, as much to show me off as for me to see where she worked. Mothers are like that!

Because of all the publicity that the Zion Benton football team was now getting in the newspapers, most of the folks working around my Mom knew she had a son who played football for the Zee Bees. If they didn't know, my Mom was sure to tell them all, including her boss. Moms are like that too.

My Mother understood how important it was to me to play football and other sports when she easily could have insisted I go to work after school to help earn money to defray expenses. Because I realized that, I sincerely wanted to give back to her what little I could. Visiting her place of work was a small payback for all her sacrifices.

Norman Perry, Bill's Dad, also worked at Johns Manville. Bill wanted to attend this event as much as I. We both knew that asking Ellis for a night off with Libertyville coming up would go over like a lead balloon. We both knew we were going to get hammered.

"I'll ask him first and see what the result will be," I told Bill. "I don't think he'll throw me off the team at this point."

"Okay," he agreed. "Let me know the results."

I sucked up a big breath, let it out slowly, and knocked on the door to Coaches' office just off the locker room. "Come in," Ellis snapped.

Hmm, not in a good mood, I sensed. Maybe I ought to back out while I have the chance. But it was too late.

"Coach, my Mother works at Johns Manville. There's gonna be an open house on Wednesday and she'd really like me to attend. May I please have permission to miss practice that one evening?" I asked tremulously.

As expected, he exploded. "What?" he shouted at me. "We have the biggest game of the season coming up this Friday and you want to take the day off?"

"Yes Sir... you see..."

"What the hell is wrong with you, Moose? Don't you want to win this conference?"

After all the effort and hard work I put into trying to be a better football player, for him as well as for myself, this attitude was absurd and really ticked me off. In previous years I would have turned tail and told my Mom I couldn't make it. But I knew how much it meant to her. I wasn't going to accept his answer this time.

"My Mother worked at Manville for almost fifteen years. She never complained about my playing football while she worked to support me. This means a lot to her and she really wants me to attend this event."

"Come to practice, Moose," said Coach, glaring at me.

"I never missed one single practice in the almost four years I played for you," I continued trying to control my temper, "and whether you like it or not, I'm going!"

As I stormed out I thought, Osmon, you've really done it now. This is going to be one miserable week of football.

I'll never know exactly what went on in that coaches' office. Whether Coach had a change of heart independently, or whether Joe Rushforth and John Timmerman were the voices of reason, is one of those mysteries of life I'll probably never solve. But just as I finished putting on my equipment and was ready to head out to the field, Coach Ellis came up to me and asked me to step into his office.

"I do appreciate the fact that you never missed a practice in four years. So I am giving you my blessing to miss practice...for just that one night." He paused for a moment to reflect on his words and continued softly. "Please tell your Mom how much I appreciate her allowing you to play on our team. Her sacrifice has helped this team immensely."

I fought back the tears as I absorbed what he had just said. The Coach is actually backing off one of his hard core positions and giving me his blessing to attend. This is incredible!

"Thanks, Coach," I managed to mumble.

I quickly retreated before he changed his mind. I immediately told Bill what had happened.

"Guess I had better strike while the iron is hot," he said hopefully.

He immediately went in and asked the same permission. He told me that Coach Ellis didn't look happy, but did agree to allow Bill to attend as well. I'm sure Coach Ellis hoped there weren't any more parents of players who worked at Johns Manville.

Bill and I both attended and our parents were deeply appreciative. As we met our parent's co workers, they all remarked how proud our parents were of us. Many of them added that they were following the fortunes of our football team as well and wished us success against

Libertyville. It was a wonderful moment. This was the one and only time in my life I ever visited my Mother's place of work. My Mother never looked prouder. Thank God Coach Ellis gave me his blessing to attend.

## A New Wrinkle

With Herm out, Philibuck now became the new starting offensive left end. Phil started at this position for the three prior years, so I had no doubts about his knowing the plays. I also knew he was a rugged blocker, so he would take good care of clearing out the linebacker for me on the veer.

To fill Herm's role as defensive safety, Bill Rymer, a junior, was moved up to the starting position. I knew Bill had excellent speed and was an aggressive pass defender, but this would be his first start. And it was in a big game, so he had to be nervous.

Bill came to Zion from Lane Tech High School in Chicago. He was not very happy about leaving a big school for a dinky one like ours. His Dad took over the Sears television factory in town as general manager, so his family moved with him to Zion the year before. Bill decided to make the best of it by joining both the track and football teams. Soon he found out that he lived right next door to Coach Ellis and his family.

While his parents became very close friends with the Ellis family, Bill soon learned that every time Coach Ellis saw him, he was harangued unmercifully about sports, grades, or anything else that came to Coach's mind. So he devised a scheme to avoid Coach Ellis altogether. Even though the direct route to school was directly past Coach's front door, Bill rode his bicycle the other way around the block just to avoid him. I understood exactly why he did that.

Would the pressure of a big game get to Bill and cause him to make a big mistake at a bad time? I wondered. I knew he had the speed we needed in that position. Coach Ellis picked him as our new safety, so he must have the skills. So I put my concerns aside. Coach knew his players. If Coach had confidence in Bill, then so did I.

As we walked to the practice field on the Monday after the McHenry game, I told Loren and Paul about Coach's decision to allow me to go to my Mom's open house at work.

"You know, he is really starting to treat us all with a little more respect and concern than he ever has in the past," I observed.

"He's only human," replied Paul. "Look how far he's brought us since freshmen year."

"Part of it, I'm sure," said Loren "is his pride in seeing us play so well now."

"I'm sure that's a big factor," I said. "I know I'm enjoying football now more than I ever have."

Coach started practice with an inspirational talk.

"Boys, I am very proud of the way all of you played last Friday. We looked like a team to be reckoned with. Coaches Rushforth and Timmerman agree. I'm sure I don't have to tell you, but right now we are in second place with only Libertyville in front of us. Beat these guys this Friday and we'll be in first place all by ourselves. Are you ready for 'em?" he shouted, his voice showing more emotion that we were accustomed to hearing.

We all bellowed in response, "Yes, sir!"

It wasn't Coach's way to be particularly rah rah or to dwell on team spirit, but I think we all sensed a renewed enthusiasm in his attitude toward us and football. We were back in the running for the championship and he could smell success in the air. But there was a lot to be done.

The Coach went on. "We had good fortune with the veer on Friday. Frankly, it appears I should have put this in long ago. But since it clicked so well, I want to try to add a wrinkle. We'll work on it this week and if it seems feasible, we'll try it out in the Libertyville game. They'll never expect Moose to do this!" he said cryptically leaving us all hanging with anticipation as to this new development.

We lined up in our normal offense for the Single Wing. I received the ball as in "Moose up the Gut". Then after two steps toward the line to bring in the defensive linebackers, I veered left as before. But in this new play Coach Ellis told Middy to start right and then flare back to the left as a trailer about five yards behind me.

## Veer With Lateral 1954

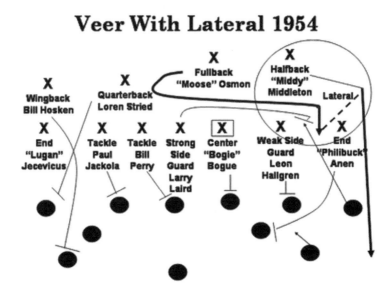

"Moose, as you approach the defensive halfback, you will have to make a decision. If he reacts slowly to make the tackle, then run as far downfield as you can. But if he comes up quickly to tackle you, I want you to pitch the ball back to Middy. His tackle on you will be as good as a block. It'll take him out of the play. Lugan will come from the right side to block the safety. If it works we just may get some good yardage against these guys. Let's run through it," he barked as he clapped his hands.

We ran the play about a dozen times. I didn't seem to have much trouble with it. I knew running it in the game would be different, but I thought it was a great idea. I wished he designed this play when we were freshmen.

## My Left Knee Gives Out

The next day I was coming down the stairs from the second floor of the school. I finished up my physics lab and had one more class to attend before practice. As I came around the bend in the stairs, I saw Coach standing at the bottom talking with another student. When I was about halfway down the second tier he looked up at me.

At that very moment a most unusual and frightening thing happened. My left knee totally gave away and I fell face forward the last four or five steps. Coach caught me and broke my fall just as I hit the bottom. But it jarred me badly.

"Are you okay? What happened?" he asked concernedly.

"I don't know, Coach. My left knee gave way. I had no control over it at all," I replied feverishly.

Good Lord, I thought. I don't want my high school career to end this way. Not after what we have gone through. Especially with two games to go. I worried that the rheumatic fever finally caught up to me. I remembered what Dr. Kalem said about "possible nerve damage to my legs".

Coach sent for a stretcher. I was lifted into it and taken to the nurse's office. We had no doctors there, but the nurse ran me through a series of tests. For almost an hour I had no feeling in that leg and knee at all, but slowly I began to move it again. Coach Ellis stayed with me the entire time.

Gosh, I thought to myself. A guy has to get injured before he gets any sympathy around here. Maybe I should have thought of this sooner.

In retrospect I don't know whether this was a psychosomatic reaction to seeing the Coach at the bottom of the stairs or a latent reaction to the rheumatic fever attack. I do know it scared me to death. Surely God wouldn't allow this to happen to me at this time. As feeling gradually came back to my leg, I slowly limped around on it. It only hurt a little.

Ellis immediately wanted the nurse to clear me to play. "Is he okay? Can he practice tonight? Can he play Friday?" he peppered at her.

I was terrified that they might call my Mom... or worse, make me go back to see Dr. Kalem.

"Coach, I can't really find anything wrong," said the nurse. "I'd go slowly tonight, but if it doesn't recur, I'd let him play."

If I thought I was going to get any respite because of this injury once I arrived at practice, I was sadly mistaken. In Coach Ellis' eyes I was already moving slowly enough. He did give me the accommodation of excusing me from wind sprints at the end of the practice, but that was about it. Otherwise I continued to run plays as if it never happened. I think he knew what he was doing. Had I babied my knee, I would never have been ready for Libertyville. It's the same reasoning that cowboys get back on a horse immediately after they have been thrown off.

I never told my Mom about the knee incident. In ensuing years, my left knee has always been the weak point in my body. There seems to be no real physical reason for it. I have had it x-rayed and examined by numerous doctors with no prognosis forthcoming. It continues to be my one area of concern today when I play tennis. I often wear a knee brace just to be cautious. I have always wondered if it had anything to do with the nerve damage suffered by the rheumatic fever I had. I'll never know, but fortunately it has never created any worse symptoms than occasional weakness.

**The Excitement Grows**

Everyone in Zion Benton High School knew what the stakes were on Friday night. All week long classmates, underclassmen, teachers and coaches came up to me to wish me good luck. They all were planning on attending the game and were hoping for a victory. None of them wanted it any more than I did.

Friday afternoon the entire school was let out of the last class period for a pep rally in the boy's gym. It was thunderous!! Our cheerleaders had everyone worked up to a screaming mass of students. Speeches were given by Principal Pearce, Coach Ellis, Coach Rushforth, and Captain Paul. I sat high in the bleachers in the area roped off for the football team next to Phil and Loren.

The spirit was incredible! The school had not experienced excitement like this in its history. There was lots of talk about our winning the North Suburban Championship if we could knock off Libertyville.

What a turn of events, I thought to myself. Used to be only Loren and I talked much about a championship and now the entire school is talking about the possibility. Are we living in a dream?

Everyone stood up for the singing of the school song. "Hurrah for Zion, we know you're trying!" The words rang from the rafters. As the school was dismissed for the rest of the afternoon, the team lingered together on the gym floor to breathe in the spirit. The excitement still permeated the now empty gym. None of us wanted to lose the emotion. What a great time to be alive!

I didn't have to be back to the school until almost 6:30 for the game, so as I did routinely, I drove downtown Zion to meet my Mother to buy groceries for the following week. The town populace was as excited as the students about our chances to win a championship. Signs were up all over downtown Zion saying "Go Zee Bees! We are proud of you!" and "Beat the Cats!" Another proclaimed "Win this one for Zion."

Even my minister, Reverend Clarence Ploch, who normally didn't follow sports much, said he was coming to the game. In fact, the newspaper was predicting a sell out crowd of over four thousand for this event. It was a key game and Libertyville was only about 20 miles away.

I walked into Bickett's Pharmacy which was now refurbished after the fire and was back into service. I needed a few minutes to kill time before my Mother arrived from work. Immediately I spotted someone wearing a Libertyville letter jacket. Something told me I should go talk to this person. So I went over and said "Hey. Do you play for the Libertyville football team?"

He answered, "Yeah I do. But I got hurt last week and won't be playing in tonight's game. So I came over early with my family to see us kick Zion's butt."

I bit my tongue. "What makes you think you're gonna beat Zion tonight?" I asked with a sincere curiosity.

He replied much too cockily, "Cause all week long we've been planning a defense to stop this Moose Osmon guy. We're going to load the middle of the right side of Zion's line and stop him cold. We have a big, mean tackle that's going to clean up on Zion's Single Wing tonight."

I wisely kept my mouth shut and walked away. I really wasn't too worried about one guy stopping our offense, not with Lugan, Paul, and Bill to take care of him. However if they're going to load up the middle, I needed to let Coach Ellis know about that.

As I walked out, he yelled, "Too bad we're gonna beat you guys tonight."

"Over my dead body," I mumbled to myself.

I met my Mom, helped buy our groceries and headed for home. I couldn't wait to get through dinner and head over to the locker room. As I left, my Mom who normally didn't have much to say about football said, "Robert, good luck tonight. Play well." She too understood the stakes for which we were playing.

"Thanks, Mom. I'll do my best," I promised and gave her a big hug.

## A Last Minute Wrinkle.

As soon as I arrived at the team locker room, I knocked on Coach Ellis' door. As I entered I could see the coaches were in a huddle discussing the game.

"Whatcha got Moose?" asked Coach Ellis.

I related the story concerning the Libertyville player I met in Bickett's. Coach Ellis was quite interested to hear this news.

"If they load the right side of the line to stop you, the veer and lateral should work just fine. That's good information. Thanks. I'll watch for it."

"Okay, Coach."

"Now we have something for you. We believe we can stop their running game without too much trouble. But they have an end by the name of Larry Ray who's fast and has good hands. We suspect they're gonna throw to him a lot tonight. We want you to take him man to man in the short yardage area. If he goes deep, Bill Hosken will pick him up. How do you feel about this?"

I wanted to tell the Coach, "You've got to be kidding!" Larry Ray was about 6' 4", fast as the wind, a hurdler in track, an excellent basketball player, and you want me to guard him one on one? Hey Coach, remember I'm the guy you put on the All Slow All Conference team. He'll run circles around me.

But instead of expressing how I really felt, I muttered, "Yeah, sure, Coach. Whatever you want me to do. I'll do my best."

"What we want you to do is to hold him up as much as possible on the line," explained Ellis. "Wherever he lines up, we want you to line up right over his head. When the ball is snapped, give him a forearm shiver. If you can break his stride or make him go around you, we think our defensive secondary can cover him from then on."

Oh, great, I thought again sarcastically. Libertyville will be loading the line against me, I have to try a new play using a lateral, my knee is questionable, and now they want me to guard Larry Ray man to man! Just what I need to learn 30 minutes before the game.

I told Loren what Ellis wanted me to do as we jogged out to the field. "Why does Coach pile this stuff on me? I've got enough to worry about. He needles me about being so slow and then puts me one on one with Ray? Sometimes I think Coach is nuts."

"Ellis picked you to guard Ray because he knows you can do it," said Loren. "Figure out a way. Lugan can stop their sweeps. Paul will stop anything off tackle. I'll cover the inside for you as much as possible."

"I'll give it my best shot," I said determinedly. "But I don't like this responsibility hanging on my head."

Loren slapped me on the back and said with encouragement, "You can handle it, Moose. I know you can."

Good old Loren. How could I have made it this far without him?

## Dad's Night

The night of the Libertyville game was also Dad's Night. This was a special night when the fathers of all the senior players were honored. My Dad was not a big advocate of my playing football, so I doubted that he'd come. His philosophy was that my time could be better spent learning a trade to become an electrician or brick layer so I could make a living for my family when I graduated. Also I could get hurt and be crippled for life which would be even worse.

Dad also carried a grudge because the school wouldn't pay for a tooth replacement when my brother Carl got his knocked out 12 years before. My Dad carried grudges for a long time. During my four seasons to date he never saw one game. But I thought what the heck do I have to lose? I may as well ask him to attend this one.

"Dad, this Friday is Dad's Night at the high school. All the senior players and their dads will be honored on the field before the game starts. It would mean a lot to me if you'd attend," I said with a bit of trepidation.

"Sonny Boy, I watched your brother get beat up for two years and the high school never helped out with any of the expenses when I patched him back up. Why should I come to your game?" he asked in a skeptical voice.

"For no other reason than I want you there," I responded forcefully. "All my teammates' Dads will be there. I'm proud of you, so I want you to be there too. These are guys I played with for four years and it would mean a lot to me."

"Well, let me think about it," he replied quietly and that was the end of the discussion.

Norman Perry, Bill's Dad, came to all of our games, and often came out to many of our practices as well. So one evening that week I walked over to him after practice and asked, "Norm, you know how my Dad is about football. I asked him to attend Friday night, but he hasn't said one way or another yet. Would you talk to him about coming to this particular game? After all, it is my last home game and it is Dad's Night. I would really like him to be here."

"I know how your Dad feels about football," Norm said candidly. "He didn't like it when your brother Carl played. I'm not sure I can do any good, but I'll try. I'll call him tonight."

Norm was even better than that. He told me that he would tell my Dad that he would drive to his house, pick him up and they would go to the game together. How great to have good relatives in a small town! I wanted to kiss him for doing that, but football players don't do those things.

So I thanked him profusely as I pumped his arm. "Norm, you're great! Thanks!"

So my Dad gave in and came to the game with Norm. I believe he actually had a good time. Before the game started the seniors took their positions in the middle of the field. When the announcer called the name of each senior, our Dads walked out from the sidelines to stand next to their sons. It was an extremely proud moment for me when my Dad took his place alongside me. I looked around at the other seniors out there... guys with whom I had played football for almost four years and knew their families almost as well as I knew my own. I was sure that all of them were as proud to have their Dads there as I was to have mine. It was a poignant moment.

## Libertyville Wildcats – The Battle for First Place

Libertyville won the toss and elected to receive. I suspected I was going to be tested immediately. They broke the huddle and Larry Ray lined up right in front of me. My intuition told me they were going to throw to him on the first play. I was panicked that I couldn't handle him. Suddenly, in that moment of desperation, inspiration came to me.

Ellis told me that my responsibility was to hold him up at the line. I quickly wondered if it was legal to hit him on his side of the line. I didn't have much time to ponder this question as the quarterback started the count. So I said to myself, what the hell. If it isn't legal, the refs will flag me and then I'll know. But even so at least I can get his attention.

As soon as the ball was snapped, I lunged across the line and slammed into Ray as hard as I possibly could. He did not expect it at all and fell straight over backwards on the turf. He looked up at me in disbelief. The quarterback took the snap, dropped back in a passing position, and immediately looked our way.

I was right, I quickly analyzed. They were going to throw to him. After one quick look and seeing his end lying on the ground, the quarterback began to run. By that time, Lugan and Paul had him. I looked around. No yellow flags. Hmm, I may try this again.

On the next play, Ray's assignment was to block me on a running play. But again I beat him to the punch. I bolted across the line and hit him hard. The run was stopped cold. The third play was another pass to Ray, and this time it went to the left flat area. As he turned his left side to me to sprint toward the sideline, I hit him solidly and knocked him down again. The quarterback threw the ball a split second later and the ball sailed well over Ray's head. No flag. This just might work.

When he got up, he looked at me with an angry expression. He turned to the nearby ref and shouted, "He can't hit me like that. That's pass interference."

The ref replied, "Not until the ball is in the air. Before that he can hit you all he wants."

Well, how about that, I gloated! My game plan for defending against Ray had just been validated by the referee. As he headed back to the huddle, I observed Ray had a noticeable limp. Must have nailed him in a vulnerable spot, I thought. Now I need to keep pounding away.

I met Larry briefly at one of our track meets, but he was a super star in track and I was a lowly discus thrower. Seemed like a nice enough guy, but he was definitely in a class over my head. He may have known Bill Hosken and Philibuck from running hurdles and sprints, but he really didn't know me from Adam. I said to myself, Mr. Ray, before this night is over, you will know me well.

The Cats punted and we took over on our own 27 yard line. Evan told Loren to test the middle of the Libertyville line early on, so it was "Moose up the Gut" to open our series. I saw that they were loading the right side of the line, but I also knew we wanted to set them up for the veer. So I hit the line as hard as I could and gained about four yards. Somewhere in the pileup, someone punched me in the nose. I came back to the huddle with blood running down my nose and was mad as hell.

"Those guys are dirty players. Loren, give me that damn ball again. Let's shove it down their throats."

Loren knew when I was mad it was a good time to let me keep running the ball.

Again I hit the line as hard as I could and gained another four yards. Again someone punched me and this time the hurt brought tears to my eyes. Now I was furious.

"Give it to me again. I want to crush these guys." For the third time I hit the line and made another four yards for a first down.

I think I would have kept that up all night, but Loren was wise enough to call another play. Middy and I slowly worked it down the field. Bill picked up 17 yards on a reverse. Then it was time.

"Okay, Moose, let's see if this will work. Veer lateral left. Veer lateral left. On three. On three," Loren barked out.

I took the snap from Bogie, took two strong steps straight into the line and the Wildcats were ready for me. I saw their right linebacker head straight into the middle of the line. They were anticipating where I was going. I veered sharply to the left. Larry pulled and took the end out of the play. Leon and Bogie took care of the guy over center. Philibuck perfectly blocked out the linebacker who now was trying to recover.

There was a huge hole for me to run through. The defensive halfback met me about ten yards downfield. I waited until the last moment just before he tackled me and lateraled the ball to Middy. It caught Libertyville totally by surprise. He took off on a 25 yard run, finally being shoved out of bounds on the eight yard line.

Everyone was elated. The first time we ever ran the veer lateral and we gained 25 yards. I know everyone thought the same thing. We should have had this play years ago.

Middy scored on the next play on an end sweep and we were up 7-0.

Throughout the first half I continued to beat on Larry Ray as much and as often as I could. Our defensive line was doing a terrific job containing the running game, so they didn't need me concentrating on the run. Libertyville again tried a number of throws to Ray, but I never allowed him to get free of me. I really didn't do anything special except consistently bang into him to break his stride and tangle him up. I saw his frustration growing and his limp becoming more pronounced as the game went along. When he dropped two passes in the left flat that he should have caught, I knew I was getting the best of him in this man to man match up.

In the second quarter we took a punt on our own 25 and started off again. Middy, Bill, and I continued to pound their line and move the ball steadily down field.

In a third and two situation Loren said "Okay, gang. Let's try it again. Veer lateral left on two."

Again I headed into the line where I could see they were piled up waiting for me. Larry made another great block on the end and Philibuck nailed the linebacker good. I ran about ten yards up field until the halfback came up to tackle me as before and again lateraled to Middy. He took off for another 25 yard gain before being run out of bounds on the seven. A few plays later I took it over from the one yard line. We were up 14-0 going into halftime.

The veer lateral was working and working to perfection. My Dad saw me score a touchdown on Dad's Night. This was my last home game. Now there was just one thing left to do to make the night perfect. Win this game!

At halftime Ellis and Rushforth both complimented me on the way I was handling Larry Ray.

"This is exactly what we wanted from you. He concentrates more on what you're going to do to him than he does on catching the ball. Keep up the good work," Ellis exhorted.

"Now this is a welcome change for halftime," I told Loren excitedly. "I must be doing something right."

We received the kickoff to start the second half and were stopped after several first downs. We punted back to the Cats.

"Okay, Mr. Ray. I'm coming after you again. Let's see what you have for me this half," I said to myself as I positioned at my left linebacker spot.

Obviously the Libertyville coaches were concerned about me too. Much to my surprise, Larry Ray flanked a good 15 yards off to my left, well beyond my normal assigned area. My first reaction was to let my ego get into the picture.

"You wimp! Are you afraid to take me on this half? Am I too tough for you?" I yelled at him.

He ignored me. Then I panicked. If I follow him out to the far left flat I completely gave up the run. Also he has a lot more open space to maneuver around me. Now how do I play him?

I turned to Coach Ellis on the sideline. I gave him the old palms up and shrug meaning "Now what the hell do I do?" Much to my relief they didn't throw to him on the first play and Ellis sent in the guidance. Now it was time to switch. I went back to my normal position on defense and Bill Hosken took over covering him.

I knew Bill had the speed to keep up with Ray and was a tough tackler. In the first half I held him to only two completions and they were both for very short yardage. More importantly he now limped heavily. I did my job. I was glad to be relieved of that responsibility and eagerly let Bill take him.

Libertyville tried a number of times to throw to Ray in the second half, but with the exception of two late fourth quarter meaningless catches, Bill shut him down. He also intercepted one of the passes the quarterback tried to throw to Ray. So we effectively took their star out of the game and he did not hurt us one bit. Another brilliant move by Evan Ellis.

In the third quarter we tried the veer lateral for the third time. Once again it worked to perfection. After I lateraled the ball to Middy, he flew down the left sidelines for a 37 yard touchdown. Nobody caught him this time. We won the game 20-0.

We out gained the Wildcats 292 yards to 54 in rushing. They did gain 50 yards passing, but they were due to desperation throws at the end of the game. Middy gained 179 yards, I gained 60, and Bill had 49. Our line, both on offense and defense was incredible. Lugan, Paul, Leon, Bogie, Philibuck, Larry, and Bill were all superb that night.

Loren played his usual strong game at defensive linebacker and called a great offensive game. Julian was solid as the right linebacker. Bill Rymer performed well in his first test at safety. Another win for the Zee Bees! Another shutout! Still only eight points scored against us! But the most exciting stat of the evening was that we were now in first place with one game to go!!

The locker room was bedlam. My brother Orval brought my two young nephews, Dave and Steve, out from Chicago for this game. They sat in the stands with my Dad and Norman. Everyone came to the locker room after the game and told me how much they enjoyed watching us crush Libertyville.

"You played very well tonight, son. Congratulations on your victory and your touchdown. I'm very proud of you," my Dad said softly as he patted me on the shoulder. My chest swelled up to twice its normal size and tears came to my eyes.

"Dad, I really appreciate your coming tonight. Thank you so much," I told him sincerely.

Orv told me that my Dad actually got excited watching the game and jumped up yelling when I scored my touchdown. This was big as my Dad never got excited about anything.

Orval also told me that he read an article in the Chicago Tribune about the Zee Bees earlier in the week about how we were coming on strong at the end of the season. It particularly highlighted our amazing defense. He said we were described as an impenetrable wall. Everyone where he worked asked if he was related to the Moose Osmon in the sports page of the Trib. He told me that he proudly told them he was. So we were picking up publicity and fans from all over Northern Illinois.

One humorous thing happened to Loren and me after the game. Because there was some problem with the showers in the visiting team's locker room, the Libertyville players had to shower in our shower room.

The Wildcats defensive left end came up to the two of us and said, "You guys aren't that tough. My coach told me that my responsibility was not to let you around me ever. And I didn't. You never got around me once the entire night."

Loren and I looked at each other and laughed. On the end sweeps Middy made good yardage all night long. Loren and I went at the defensive end together shoulder to shoulder. If Loren thought he could handle him alone, I broke behind him and headed downfield to block for Middy.

After the second time we ran in it, Loren said to me, "Moose, the defensive end is running backwards so fast I can't even catch up to him. I don't need to block him. He takes himself out on every play."

So the entire game I cut up inside as a leading blocker for Middy and the play clicked for us all night. But that defensive end didn't think we were very tough. I often wondered if after the game his coach told him he did a great job of stopping us from going around him.

Betty Rae and Barb met us in the parking lot outside the boy's locker room.

"Congratulations on a great win!" squealed Barb.

"Now you're in first place!" said Betty Rae excitedly. "You've got a chance to win the championship."

What a great feeling to have our girlfriends share the joy of winning with us. Rooks was wild that night! More cheers! More songs! "Hurrah for Zion" was sung about a dozen times. We replayed the game among ourselves over and over! Nobody wanted to go home. We waited four long years for this to happen and none of us wanted it to end. It was a memorable and exciting evening. How wonderful that these few dedicated, but long suffering Zee Bees had the chance to experience the feeling of finally winning a big game. It beat the hell out of losing.

Zion was in first place with one game to go! Destiny was now in our hands. The smell of victory was in the air. Bring on the Barrington Broncos!

## The Radio Replay

Before we left the locker room, Coach Ellis came to speak to us. "Boys, I can't begin to tell you how proud I am of you tonight. This was the biggest game we won in the four years since I've been coaching you. You all played superbly tonight. We are now in first place in the North Suburban Conference."

With that we all roared with a deafening sound that rocked the locker room.

"Furthermore I learned that WKRS out of Waukegan broadcast this game live tonight all over Northern Illinois. They recorded the game play on tape and are going to re-air the game tomorrow morning at 11 AM. My wife Dru and I would like to invite all of you to our home for breakfast tomorrow morning to listen to the game. Hope you all can make it."

In the four years I played for this man, I never came to his home. I wasn't even sure I knew where he lived.

Had I known I would have avoided it like the plague anyhow. Now we were all being invited into his home? Another sign of respect for us.

"This has been an odd year, Loren," I said after Coach left the locker room. "Did you ever dream we'd see the day when Coach would invite us to his home for breakfast?"

"We've been his team for four years and now we're making good on all the things he taught us. Maybe he wants to show us some of his appreciation," Loren responded thoughtfully.

The only response I could conjure up was "Well, this ain't' the same coach I've known for four years. I like this new one a whole lot better."

"Well, maybe he's different now."

I thought about that for sometime afterwards. Loren was right again. Coach Ellis was different now.

## Breakfast at the Coach's Home

I picked up Loren that Saturday morning about 9 AM and we headed over to the Coach's house.

"Loren, do you realize how little we know of Coach Ellis' life? I know he has had three little girls since he became our coach, but I don't know how many children he has altogether."

"I've never even met his wife."

To this point he was a coach only and that is the only way either of us could think of him.

"This is going to be odd," I predicted.

"He seems to be reaching out to us. Maybe he sees something we don't," Loren replied.

"Let's see what happens."

When we arrived, Coach was at the front door to greet us. "Moose. Stride. Come on in. Been looking forward to having you. There are juices and sweet rolls and doughnuts on the table. Help yourself. We'll be serving eggs a little later," he said enthusiastically.

Loren and I looked at each other quizzically as if to say "Who is this guy?"

He took us into the back of the house to the kitchen and introduced us to his wife. "Boys, I'd like you to meet my wife Drusilla. I call her Dru."

Dru was as sweet as can be. "Hello, Moose and Loren. I have heard so much about both of you I feel I know you personally."

"Thank you, Ma'am," managed Loren.

"These are our daughters, Betsy, Mary Beth, and Laurie."

"Glad to meet you," I said with a small bow to her three cute little girls. They all giggled and smiled sweetly.

"Help yourself to some food and be comfortable," Dru softly crooned.

I was stunned! How in the world did this tyrant marry such a good looking, sweet natured lady like this? What was I missing? And what a nice little family. And why was he talking about us to his wife? Somehow it didn't all add up, at least not in the image I had of Coach.

"Do you believe this?" whispered Middy as he walked up beside me.

"I'm not sure," I replied.

"The Coach is human after all," said Middy in disbelief. "I'm glad I came back to the team."

"So are we, Middy. So are we!"

"By the way, Moose... you didn't fool me... getting the girls to tell me how wonderful I was... and all that stuff."

"Shucks," I said jokingly. "I thought we had you fooled for sure."

Middy grinned at me and poked me in the ribs. I poked him back. "But I do appreciate you guys wanting me back... really!"

"I know it, Middy... and it's paying off! We wouldn't be where we are now if you weren't part of this team."

I still didn't hang around with Middy. But we were teammates... and that eventually formed a strong bond between us. Being a "teammate" is, after all, something very special. I respected him for his contribution to the team.

Soon everyone arrived including Joe Rushforth and John Timmerman. A lot of yakking went on about last night's game. Our stories got better each time we told them. Coach was right in the middle of everything cracking us up with his jokes and observations on some of the funny things that happened during the game. Soon the bacon and eggs were served. It was a pleasant experience to gather in our Coach's home and revel in the turn of events that put us into first place in the race for conference championship.

Then at 11 AM the radio broadcast came on. It was the first time any of us ever heard our names mentioned on the radio and it was quite a thrill for us all. In retrospect I wish I had the wherewithal at the time to realize the value of that tape in future years. I should have asked Coach get a copy of it for each of us, but I wasn't prescient enough in those days.

The game got underway. We cheered when the starting lineup was announced, when it was mentioned that someone made a tackle or a good block, and when anyone made a gain in yardage.

The first time we ran the veer left, the announcer said in an excited voice, "My gosh. There was a hole so big on the left side of Zion's line that the Zee Bees could have driven the Libertyville fire truck through it. Anen, Hallgren, and Bogue did a terrific job of blocking."

Of course, this received great howls of laughter, none more than Coach himself who roared his famous "Ho! Ho! Ho!"

When the announcer saw us run the veer lateral for the first time, he had no idea what actually happened. He analyzed the play by saying, "Osmon over the left side. Again there's a huge hole. He's tackled by the defensive halfback. No, wait! Osmon fumbles the ball! But Middleton cleverly scoops it up and runs for a 25 yard gain. Lucky for the Zee Bees that Middleton was backing up Osmon."

Of course, Ellis thought this was hilarious and broke into one of his huge guffaws. "Moose, if you can't hold on to the ball any better than that, we'll have to stop running it. You can't count on Middy always being there to help you out. Ho! Ho! Ho!"

The second time we ran the veer lateral, the announcer's words were almost a repeat of his first misanalysis. "Big hole! Osmon gains eight yards. Oh no! Osmon fumbles again. But wait! Again Middleton is there to scoop up the fumble and he goes for another 25 yard gain. The Zee Bees are fortunate that Middleton is so alert."

The final time we ran the veer lateral, the announcer started off the same way. "Osmon goes to the left. There is a huge hole. He is tackled, but fumbles for the third time!!! Again Middleton....." He then stopped short in the middle of his sentence and paused as Middy ran the final 37 yards for the touchdown. After a brief silence he said rather sheepishly, "You know folks, I think that's a planned play. When I thought Osmon was fumbling, he was actually lateraling the ball to Middleton. Sorry about that. I think the Zee Bees have been faking out not only the Wildcats, but me as well."

This brought down the house. We all were laughing so hard we couldn't hear the radio. Tears were rolling down Coach's face from laughing so hard. "Sorry, Moose. Guess I should have briefed him before the game. The first time you're mentioned on the radio and you were credited with three fumbles."

When the game was over, no one wanted to leave. We all were having a great time. It was such a treat to see Coach Ellis in his role as father and husband. It was good to know that he had another side. It took four years to get to this point and I guess we all wanted to savor it. But finally it was time to leave and as we all piled out of the house, Coach thanked us all for coming and left us with just one thought. "One more! One more!"

**********

The 1954 Zee Bee Championship Team

Front Row, Left to Right: King Woodward,
Larry Laird, Dick Bogue, Leon Hallgren, Ron Stanton,
Gene Robinson, Bill Delaney.

Second Row, Left to Right: Phil Anen, Bill Perry,
Bob Schmidt, Paul Jackola, Jerry Koskinen,
John Jecevicus, Wesley Hosken.

Third Row, Left to Right: Joel Swanson (Manager),
Bob Middleton, Julian Emanuelson,
Coach Evan Ellis, Herman Swanson, Bill Hosken,
Assistant Coach Joe Rushforth,
Bob Osmon, Loren Stried, Bill Rymer,
Loren Leech (Manager)

# Chapter 11
# One Last Game

Often we are so involved in our daily lives that we don't see the imperceptible changes that occur right in front of our noses. A good example is the coming of fall. Each day becomes a little cooler and a little shorter. But because we are wrapped up in our own daily concerns we don't perceive this happening. One day the leaves on the tree turn into beautiful reds and yellows, and we often say to ourselves, "When did this happen? It was just summer a few weeks ago and I was playing on the beach."

In retrospect, so it was with Coach Evan Ellis and his football team, most of whom he had personally coached for four years. While it seemed to most of us that we were still the same old gang of guys who stumbled around the football field as inexperienced freshmen, in fact subtle changes took place all along in everybody.

The obvious changes, of course, were the facts that we were now three years older and we were all bigger and stronger. But then so were the teams we played against as freshmen. It was the subtle changes that made the difference. During each season Coach spent hours and hours training us to run his designed plays in a specific way, or how to intimidate the opposing team on defense. We ran the Single Wing so many times since we were freshmen that it was now second nature to us. But even more of a factor was the team attitude of pride and determination. We had these characteristics as a team from our early freshmen days, but then lacked the skills to be effective. Now after four years together, our pride, spirit and determination in conjunction with the skills and discipline driven into us by the Coach were all coming together at a most propitious moment in time.

The difference between confidence and over confidence is a thin one indeed. I believe confidence is knowing you have the ability to accomplish a specific feat, but are aware enough of the consequences of defeat to realize that you must prepare for that event as if you are fighting for your life. Over confidence is when you know you can accomplish a feat, but you don't prepare yourself properly. There was no doubt in my mind that this small band of 16 Zee Bees finally attained the confident category and it showed. We walked differently, talked differently, and acted as if we knew we were going to be the champions. We just had to prove it one more time.

Subtle changes took place in Coach Ellis as well. There were signs all along, but I was never receptive enough to organize them as a pattern in my mind: the way he talked to us after the Warren game telling us we were finally a team when we expected the usual screaming; his softening on his position when he allowed Bill Perry and me to go to our parent's open house; his admission to me that he should have designed a play like the veer earlier in the season; his invitation to the team to have breakfast at his home. All of these were clues that he was changing even as we were changing. The synergetic effect of these two sets of confluent growth resulted in the Coach and his team moving slowly toward each other in both thought and respect. We were now doing the things the way he demanded we do for four years and he was giving us the credit for the development of our skills as individuals and as a team. The scorecard to date was a 5-1-1 record with only eight points scored against us. One more game to go! Could this be a team of destiny? One more! One more!

**The Hype**

Suddenly it seemed everyone was on the Zion Benton bandwagon. Not only did the Zion Benton News, the local paper, and the Waukegan News Sun, primarily a Lake County paper, give us excellent reviews, but we also got another very good write up in the Chicago Tribune. The Trib rated us among the top 20 in the Chicago area. These were heady times indeed, especially considering how we started the season. In particular the newspapers extolled the fact that our defense was overpowering. All the articles pointed out that none of the teams we played against gained many yards against us. Even more importantly, only eight points were scored against us with one game to go.

"A major accomplishment in these times of high powered scoring," the headlines stated. "The present defensive record of only 13 points is held by the 1951 Lake Forest Scouts. Zion could break that record this weekend."

But Dan Loblaw of the News Sun threw in a bit of skepticism.

*"Stats show that the Zee Bees have yielded only 420 yards and 20 first downs in their first seven games. However, all of this was accomplished against orthodox opposition. The Zee Bees may have a bit more difficulty against the Broncos razzle-dazzle, lateral-forward, hit and run style of play, which has netted better than 200 yards a game and a total of 92 points, tops in the conference. Key figure in the Barrington offense is John Walbaum, talented sophomore quarterback."*

*"Further Barrington has lost but one home game in the last seven years. Although Zion Benton beat Barrington in its very first game in 1940 when Joe Rushforth, presently the assistant coach, led his team to a 7-6 victory, over the past two years since Barrington joined the North Suburban Conference, the Broncos have beaten the Zee Bees by a combined score of 47-0. In short, you may be on a roll, Zee Bees, but you've got your hands full with Barrington."*

"Mr. Loblaw, you're wrong!" I said to myself emphatically as I finished reading the article in the Sunday paper's sports page. "As they say in the old cowboy movies, 'Them's fighting words'." I knew Dan Loblaw was a born and bred Zion boy. I was sure that in his heart he had to be pulling for us, even if he didn't show any favoritism in this article. The thought occurred to me that he might be writing in this manner to fire us up to have us on a fine edge when we took the field against Barrington. Whatever his motivation may have been at the time, it worked. We were all upset about the article as we took the field for practice on Monday.

# A New Defensive Wrinkle

We were having Indian summer this last week of our football season. The leaves were still in full color, but it was unusually warm. The temperature of the air had no effect on the mind set of any of us as we strode out to the practice field on Monday full of confidence. With enthusiasm we crowded around Coach Ellis after calisthenics.

"Boys," Coach started solemnly, "I guess you all read that article in the News Sun written by Dan Loblaw. It seems that he thinks this razzle-dazzle offense of Barrington might be too much for us to handle. Well, Dan is entitled to his opinion, but that's not my opinion. I think if we continue to play just as we have since the Lake Forest game, we can take them down."

We all roared our approval.

"Furthermore, I have a little surprise for them which may slow their razzle dazzle offense down a bit," he said animatedly as he waved his arms about.

During the four years that we played for Coach Ellis, we used only two basic defenses. The standard was the 5-3 which meant we set up in a five man line with three line backers, two halfbacks and a safety. The alternate was a 6-2 in which moved Loren up into the guard position to beef up the line in short yardage situations. The only other defense we ever used was an eight man line on the goal line. Fortunately we needed to use this goal line defense only once so far this season. Thus it came as a shock to us when he started to explain a new defense to us.

"Barrington likes to use the quarterback option with Walbaum coming down the line either left or right. He runs with the ball if he sees an opening or pitches to the trailing halfback much like we now have Moose pitching to Middy. The key to stopping this style of offense is to jam up the holes where he likes to run. To do this, we're going to move our defensive tackles from over their offensive tackles to head on their offensive ends. We'll move our two linebackers over the tackles and move

Loren up into the line as a guard. I'm going to call this defense the 'Wide Six'. Additionally, I'm going to give Moose authority to call crashes by the linebackers whenever he sees fit, without my direction. With luck, we can upset their entire pattern of offense."

"Whoa! He has changed," I mumbled to myself. "Not only is he putting in a new defense for the first time in four years, he actually is going to allow me to call the linebacker crashes." While I was somewhat bewildered by his newly expressed confidence toward me, I was ready to take on the responsibility. I realized this was simply one more indicator of his change in attitude toward all of us.

We worked all week long on the "Wide Six" defense. Several nights our JV ran the option against us. We stopped them cold on every play. We knew Barrington ran the option a lot better than our JV, but at least we had an idea what the Bronco's offense would look like and what to expect. I started to get the rhythm of when to call linebacker crashes as well.

I couldn't wait to try out this new defense against Barrington. "Razzle-dazzle, my butt," I told Paul and Loren as we walked back to the locker room. "We're going to show the Broncos and Dan Loblaw that we can handle anything they throw against us on Saturday. They'll be stunned to see our new defense."

Paul and Loren enthusiastically agreed "Wait until their end sees me lined up over his head," Paul laughed. "He's probably never faced a defensive tackle before."

**Pep Rallies and Practice**

Because the Barrington game was going to be played on a Saturday afternoon at Barrington, it gave us one extra day for practice that we normally didn't have playing Friday night games at home. We put it to good use as we honed our offense and learned our new defense. Coach Ellis was in the best mood I ever saw in four years. It was as if he knew this was a once in a lifetime opportunity and he was going to savor every bit of the moment. There was no yelling, no needling, and no sarcasm. He treated us all like respected adults rather than as incompetent ninnies as we were accustomed.

One evening he brought over a very tall, red headed man and introduced him to us. "Boys, this is Johnny Kerr from the University of Illinois. He is my brother-in-law. He is married to my wife's sister, Betty. He wanted to watch our practice and will attend the game on Saturday," he said casually.

No one had to tell us who Johnny Kerr was. He was the All American center for the U of I basketball team. His name was in the paper daily. We all were in awe of him.

He told us, "Good luck, Zee Bees. I'll be watching and so will a lot of folks in the Chicago area. You've captured the hearts of a lot of fans with your Single Wing offense and crushing defense. Play well." (Johnny Kerr was a three time All Star with the Syracuse Nationals. He later became the first coach for the Chicago Bulls. He is now the color commentator for the Bulls on WGN TV and COMCAST Sports.)

One night one of our former alumni, L. T. Bonner, who gained fame as an excellent running back at the U of I, came out to our practice. He too told us how people all over Illinois were reading about us and were pulling for us to win our first championship.

Coach Ellis put him in a pair of football pants and told him to run the option play against us. For the first few plays it was like trying to catch a rabbit. He was so quick and so shifty that we could barely touch him. We chased him all over the field while Coach was giving us his old "Ho! Ho! Ho!" the entire time. Finally we realized that by gang tackling we could bring him down. It was a fun thing to do at practice and good preparation for Walbaum. I could see that Coach was just trying to keep us all loose.

On Friday evening, our last night of ZB football practice ever, Coach Ellis made an announcement with great ceremony. "Boys, I have been wearing these same pair of socks every day without washing them since we started our winning streak with Lake Forest. Some of the teachers in the teacher's lounge are beginning to leave the room when I walk in, but because they are all pulling for us, no one has yet complained."

He sat down and took off his cleats to show us his now raunchy socks. We all proclaimed that they stunk something terrible and held our noses. He thought this was real funny and laughed his big guffaw.

"After we beat Barrington tomorrow, I intend to leave these on the Broncos 50 yard line. They deserve them, don't you think?" he yelled with a big grin on his face.

This brought out a huge cheer from us all. None of us ever saw this side of the Coach before. It was the most fun and relaxed week of practice in our four years at Zion Benton High School.

It is hard to imagine that there could be a better pep rally than the one we had the week before, but the Barrington pep rally topped them all. The boy's gym rocked. The cheers, the songs, the speeches. Each one seemed to carry special meaning to the team. The senior lettermen were asked to come down on the gym floor and give a cheer for the crowd. I came up with the harshest words I could muster, which by today's standards are laughable. This was Zion, after all. Philibuck, Paul, Loren, Leon, Bogie, Lugan, Herm, Middy, Bill, and I got out in front of everyone and let loose.

*"Potato Chips! Potato Chips!*
*Crunch! Crunch! Crunch!*
*Barrington. Barrington. Here's your lunch."*

A simplistic cheer, I know, but it got a good laugh and a big cheer from the stands.

Coach Ellis told the student body how proud he was of all of us. "These boys had several very bad breaks early in the season. Many teams would have quit after those setbacks. But your team fought back from adversity and now is on the brink of a championship. The first football championship for Zion Benton High School. Thank you for all the support from the student body. I can assure you that the coaches and everyone on the team are appreciative."

How we all reveled in the mood of the moment! It brought tears to my eyes to realize that this was the last pep rally we would ever experience at ZBTHS. I wanted it to never end. I wondered if all the other seniors had the same feeling. As my eyes gazed over the seven of us who had been together since we were freshmen, I had no doubt they did. They all knew how far we had come since those days of incompetence and frustration.

## Barrington Broncos – The Final Test

The Saturday bus ride to Barrington was quiet and subdued. It was more than two hours by our old yellow school bus, but it gave us all time to think. We all knew what was at stake. We knew we had a job to do and we all were ready to have at it. Paul interrupted the silence.

"Hey, Coach, we need Moose to talk again," shouted Paul from the seat ahead of me.

Coach got up from his seat in the front of the bus. He looked back at Paul and then at me. "Okay, Moose… whatcha got?"

I stood up, clinging to the seat as the bus bounced along. "Guys, when we lost so many games as freshmen and sophomores, almost everyone thought we were losers. Everyone except us! This season, after we tied Crystal Lake and lost to Warren, almost everyone thought we were losers. Everyone except us! This afternoon, with a win against Barrington, we can wipe off that loser label forever!"

"Tell it like it is, Moose!" shouted Leon.

"No one will remember our freshmen and sophomore years and certainly not how this season started. Win this one and we can go out as winners. Big winners! Conference champs!" I shouted, the intensity of my voice growing with each sentence. "Can we do it?"

The roar that came back to me answered the question with no doubts. Paul gave me a thumbs up.

"Couldn't have said it better!" exclaimed Paul.

In the Barrington locker room Coach had a few emotional words for all of us. "Boys, I coached most of you since the day you were freshmen. Those were bleak days that we struggled through. I saw you grow and mature over the years. I saw you play your hearts out against Warren under terribly adverse conditions and lose because of a biased referee. Yet you never quit. You never quit as freshmen. You never quit as seniors. Now you have the opportunity to do something no other Zion team has ever been in a position to do. Win a North Suburban Conference championship. I feel confident we will. But I want you to know, win or lose, I'm extremely proud of each and every one of you. Play your best!"

With a loud roar and a sense of mission, we headed out of the locker room to face the Broncos.

It was an unusually warm day for early November as we raced onto the field. It was as if summer was doing its best to hold on for a few more days. The colors of the trees had started to fade and leaves were falling off the trees in batches. Fall was coming to an end. To the seniors on our team, it had an even bigger significance. It meant the end of our high school football careers.

About 2000 fans from Zion drove out to the game and were already in the stands cheering for us long before we took the field. My stomach was in knots. Barrington's stadium was much bigger than ours, yet it was packed. The newspapers predicted that fans from all over Northern Illinois would attend this game to see what could be a history making game in the annals of Illinois High School football.

As I warmed up I prayed softly. "Dear God! Of all the games in which I have worn this uniform, this is by far the single most important one for me. Please don't allow me to let down my teammates. Help us all to play to the best of our abilities. Help us to win this one for Coach Ellis."

Coach walked among us as we stretched and ran our drills. No sarcasm, no yelling. He offered encouragement to everyone in a calm supportive voice. "Larry, drive your shoulder into that defensive end when we run the veer. Phil and Lugan... don't let Walbaum get outside you. Push him inside to the tackles. Julian, when you crash, come across aggressively and look for the quarterback. Stride, mix those plays up well today. Use the veer when it is appropriate. Bill and Paul, keep the ends tied up and watch for the quarterback coming down the line. Stay alert for the pitchout. Leon, keep the defensive nose guard off Bogie as much as possible today."

When the Coach came to me, he started to say something, but remained silent. He put his hand on my shoulder with a soft pat. Our eyes met. Without a word being spoken, I knew exactly what he was saying to me. It was the unspoken gesture between two people who were adversaries for years, yet now had a mutual respect for each other. That pat meant more to me than any words he could have ever spoken at that time.

The Captains met in the middle of the field and Paul won the toss. Coach wanted to try out our Wide Six right away against their razzle dazzle offense, so he told us to kickoff. It was a propitious decision.

Barrington fumbled the ball on the opening kick and Philibuck started the most notable day of his playing career with a recovery to get us off to a great start. Zion ball. We broke the huddle to see that Barrington was in a seven man line. Three of their defensive linemen and a linebacker were positioned strong right and three linemen and a linebacker were positioned strong left. The nose guard was over Larry and behind him were two of their defensive backs no more than three yards deep.

It was clear they had a wrinkle of their own. It was immediately obvious that they were willing to give us yardage up the middle, but were determined to stop the wide sweeps and reverses. Basically the Barrington coaches designed their defense to stop Middleton and Hosken. They decided not to be that concerned about Osmon.

"Well," I mumbled indignantly as I jacked up my emotions, "we'll soon find out whether or not you should worry about Osmon."

On the first play we tried to sweep right with Middy carrying the ball. Their linemen and linebackers over shifted to the outside and stopped him with a short gain.

Then we came out in left formation and tried to sweep the left end. Again they stopped us with little gain. In the huddle our linemen told Loren about the over shift of their linemen to the outside leaving the center of the line vulnerable.

"Well, Moose, looks like we need you. 'Moose up the Gut'. On three," Loren barked.

I took the snap from Bogie and headed into the line. There was only one defensive player on either side of the hole where I was going. Larry and Bill double teamed the defensive guard to the left and Paul blocked the defensive tackle to the right. I boomed up the middle for eight yards and a first down. Loren immediately spotted the weakness in their defense and had no qualms about banging away at it.

"Let's do it again, gang! Let's drive it down their throats. 'Moose up the Gut.' On One!" Loren snapped with complete confidence.

Again Larry, Bill and Paul opened a gaping hole and again I made good yardage. Four straight times Loren called the same play and four straight times I burst up the middle. I gained 30 yards in four plays and gave us two first downs. We were moving deep into Bronco territory.

"They want to leave the middle open? We'll show'em!" I yelled to my teammates. "Let's keep sticking it down their throat."

A 15 yard penalty took us back to the 27 yard line. Phil wasn't about to let this game turn into another Warren game. He boldly walked up to the ref who made the call and stated, "You make any more lousy calls like that one and you'll end up being blackballed, just like the last ref who pulled this crap on us!"

The ref looked at Phil with unbelieving eyes and a slack jaw, mouth wide open. It was obvious he had never heard a player talk to him like that ever in his life.

I shook my head and smiled. "Good move, Phil. That should endear him to us."

"Just want to keep him honest, Moose. We don't want another Warren ref screwing us."

Loren then called for a seldom used play. It was a left formation run or pass. Middy started as if he was going to run the end sweep. But after several steps he pulled up quickly and threw the ball to Bill who was all by himself downfield. The pass was high and wobbly. Under normal circumstances it probably would have been intercepted. But because their linebackers and safety were so up tight to stop the run, Bill had all the time in the world to catch it. He stopped, waited for the ball, caught it, turned and sprinted into the end zone for the first score. We were up 6-0 just a few minutes into the game. A great start!

We kicked off again. This time Barrington held onto the ball. They broke out of the huddle for their first play. We lined up in our wide six with our tackles over their ends and the two linebackers between the guards and tackles. Their first play went to our left and Paul and Lugan smeared them for a loss. On the next play I decided to try out the crashes early.

"Crash Right! Crash Right! Julian, you're on! Focus on the quarterback. Don't let him pitch the ball," I yelled excitedly.

The timing was absolutely perfect. As John Walbaum, the Barrington quarterback headed to his left, Julian broke through the line and nailed him dead after two steps... never had a chance to pitch the ball. Next they tried a quick pitch to their halfback running left and Philibuck nailed the runner cold. Three downs and nothing. No gain.

In a state of exultation I yelled to my teammates. "This is the razzle dazzle offense? Don't look so tough to me! Our 'Wide Six' is going to eat them up!"

We got the ball back after their punt and Loren started attacking their weak point once again. I carried the ball five out of the next six plays straight up the middle. The upfront blocking was superb. I gained 30 more yards and three more first downs. I hoped they stayed in this defense the entire game.

On one of these plays as our linemen got down in their offensive stance, I heard Leon needle the man over him in a boastful and condescending manner. "Okay, Ace. Here we come again. Right over the top of you!"

I gained another six yards on the play, but when we got back in the huddle, I barked "Leon, what in hell are you doing? Are you telling Barrington where our plays are going?"

Leon, with the supreme confidence which marked his style of play, answered calmly, "Don't sweat it, Moose. I can handle this guy!"

Everyone laughed except me. It was hard enough to get yardage without his giving the play away. But his man never tackled me, so I couldn't complain too much.

The ball was on the Barrington 23 yard line when Loren called for the veer lateral. It couldn't have worked more to perfection. I took the snap from Bogie, headed straight into the line, where by now they were starting to expect me, cut suddenly to my left, and broke free in a huge hole that Larry, Leon, Phil, and Bogie opened up for me. I headed downfield waiting for the defensive halfback to come up to tackle me. Just before he hit me, I pitched the football back to Middy. He sprinted the remaining 15 yards untouched for a touchdown... through the end zone and back up through the goal posts. 12-0. The game was only in the first quarter.

The Broncos took over the ball and once again we set up our "Wide Six". I'll never know exactly what my intuition was in calling defensive plays that day, but I had incredible success guessing correctly where they were going to run. Maybe it was simply preparation. Every time I called Julian to crash, they ran left and he stopped them cold. When I called my own crash, I came across the line untouched and Walbaum ran right into my arms.

Barrington seldom ran to their right as they clearly knew from scouting reports that running at Jackola and Jecevicus was not a high percentage thing to do. But when they did come right and Walbaum got the pitch off, the three of us smeared the halfback. We seemed to do everything just right on defense that afternoon.

It was obvious that Coach Ellis made another brilliant adjustment moving our tackles over their ends. Ends weren't used to taking on tackles, thus Barrington's blocking wasn't as effective as it was against other teams. Further, we were shifted one full man farther outside the Broncos than they ever saw before so their wide sweeps and pitchouts were being stopped cold. The only potential weak spot in this alignment was in the middle. Our two smallest players on the defensive line with no linebacker behind them had to look vulnerable to the Barrington quarterback. However, every time Barrington tried to run straight into the middle of the line, Larry and Loren shed their blockers and nailed the runner at the line of scrimmage. The Broncos were stymied in every attempt to penetrate our defense.

On one play, however, Loren took their big fullback head on. Even though he was outweighed by about 50 pounds, he dropped him to the ground with a low, clean tackle. But when he got up, blood was streaming down his chin. Loren bit clean through his lower lip when the runner's helmet hit him.

I was shaken. I never saw my old buddy hurt before. "Loren, are you all right? You're bleeding badly from your lip."

Loren looked at me with a goofy grin and shouted, "Hey, Moose. Did you see me nail that fullback? No knocking me on my can like last year!"

I couldn't help but laugh. As long as he made a great tackle, Loren could care less about his lip. We called time out as Coach came out to look at him.

After most of the blood was wiped away, Coach Ellis asked, "Well, Stride, do you want to come out? You need some stitches, but I can't do it here."

"Are you kidding me, Coach? I'm not coming out of this game unless I'm dead. I've been waiting for this for four years. I'm ready to go," he yelled with conviction.

Ellis looked at him with admiration, the same way he did when Loren stood up to him as a freshman. "Okay, Stride. Go get 'em. I'll take care of you at halftime."

Bill made a 27 yard run on a reverse that got us deep in Bronco territory, but several penalties killed us and prevented us from scoring. I prayed Phil wouldn't unload on the ref again.

I continued to make good yardage up the middle as we controlled the ball, but we couldn't seem to take it in for a TD in the second quarter. At halftime the score was still 12-0. I gained almost 80 yards in the first half. I was pooped!

It grew hotter as the game went on. I carried the ball more times in the first half than I usually did the entire game. We exploited their weakness to our gain, no doubt, but the heat and unusually high number of times I ran was taking a toll on my stamina. As I flopped down in the grass in the end zone during the halftime I said to Coach Rushforth, "Coach, I'm whipped. I don't know if I can go like this for another half." Boy, was that one big mistake!

Joe looked at me as if he was ready to rip my head off. He grabbed me by my shoulder pad and lifted me up off the ground with one hand. He screamed loud enough for the folks in the stands to hear him. "Whipped! You can't be whipped! You've got another whole half to go. You let down your teammates now and we lose this game. You'll get back out there and play as tough in the second half as you did in the first. Do you understand me?" With that he threw me back on the ground.

Right then and there I decided I wasn't that whipped after all. Coach Rushforth had a way of doing that to players. He made injuries and fatigue disappear magically just by walking among us. I guess we should have nicknamed him St. Joseph. But thank God for those 15 minutes of rest. I felt much better after several big cups of water and sitting down for a while. When the whistle blew for the second half, I was ready to go.

## The Second Half

We received the ball on the kickoff. Immediately it was obvious that the Barrington coaches made a major change in their defense for the second half. There were now two defensive linemen where I was hitting the hole the entire first half and a linebacker was snubbed up right behind them.

"Goodbye to big gains up the middle with 'Moose up the Gut'," I said to myself. "It was great while it lasted. But this means the sweeps and reverses should start becoming effective."

They did. With the linebackers now inside and the defense concentrated in the center looking for me, Middy and Bill began to tear it up. We controlled the ball on offense and kept Barrington back on their heels. But we just couldn't get in the end zone.

On defense our "Wide Six" dominated the Broncos. They were stymied at every attempt to run or pass.

We did have one tense moment however. Walbaum intercepted one of Middy's few passes and returned it for 27 yards. Then a 15 yard penalty against us took it to our 12 yard line and it looked like they could score against us. But as we did against Lake Forest, our defense reared up and slapped them down. On fourth down with one yard to go, Walbaum chose to carry the ball himself on a sweep to his left. Philibuck, adding to his already sterling performance for the day, nailed him for a 10 yard loss on the Barrington 26 yard line. The third quarter ended 12-0.

Early in the fourth quarter, Middy and one of the Broncos got into some fisticuffs. Both were ejected. Personally I believe the Barrington coach sent this guy in just to taunt Middy. Julian came in at tailback and performed admirably. Between the two of us, we moved the ball down field steadily. Julian picked up 30 yards in five running plays. Frankly, I was happy to have fresh legs running the ball. We moved the ball down to the Barrington 12 when a fumble stopped us short of the goal line again.

Finally the Barrington coaches realized that their running game was going nowhere. Walbaum turned exclusively to passing to try to move the ball downfield. He completed several passes which got them out of the hole, but then came the play that will live in my mind forever.

The quarterback went for broke and heaved a Hail Mary pass as far down field as possible. Bill Rymer was at the safety position and covered his man like a wet blanket. He timed his leap perfectly, intercepted the ball, and headed back up field. As soon as I saw his interception I picked out the closest Barrington player and took him down with a cross body block as Bill sped past me. As I lay there on the ground, I watched Bill zig right, zig left, zig right, and zig left one more time as he picked his way through the entire Barrington team. When he finally broke into the clear and sprinted 30 more yards into the end zone, my heart experienced a sense of exultation. Bill Rymer's runback of that pass interception ranks as the finest example of broken field running I have ever seen in my entire life. Bill will always hold a hero's position in my heart for that one single play.

Furthermore, I now knew that we were going to win. Somehow, someway, we pulled it off. We were the new North Suburban Champions! I jumped and screamed all the way down the field to join my teammates who were now pummeling Bill on the back at the goal line.

When we finally calmed down and went into the huddle to call the extra point, everyone was talking at once. "Loren, let Paul attempt the extra point," I said. "We never make it anyhow. He deserves it as Captain."

"Okay, Paul," Loren said with a big grin on his face. "Every Captain should have the chance to score once in his career, even if he is a tackle. Let's see you put that ball through the uprights."

Paul took my position as fullback as he lined up for the kick. I moved into the tackle position next to Leon to block for Paul for this one play. Actually, I felt quite comfortable being back in the line again. I had my glory for the day. Now I was pleased to give Paul the chance for his.

Just before the ball was snapped, Leon looked at the man lined up against him and said loudly, "OK, Ace. I'm coming after you again."

Then he turned to me. With supreme confidence he directed, "Now, Moose, watch me and take a lesson."

This time I could only chuckle at his bravado. "Get him, Leon," I encouraged gleefully. "You've done a great job for me all day."

Leon was excited about having his long time friend beside him for this one play and was determined to show his fullback exactly how he handled big, bad opposing linemen. He charged across the line like a wild rhino. The Barrington defensive player was bowled over and flat on his back on the goal line.

"If you are going to be a lineman, Moose, that's the way to handle your opponent," he exclaimed with a big grin.

All I could do was laugh.

Paul's kick was about 20 feet wide of the goal post, but frankly none of us cared. We were all glad he had the chance to score once in his four years.

There were but a few minutes left in the fourth quarter when one of the referees came into our huddle. He said, "Boys, you obviously are going to win this game, so how about taking it a little easier on the Barrington players. They seem to be getting very banged up!"

"What?" I snorted to our team. "After the way Barrington stomped us last year, he wants us to take it easy on them now? I don't think so. In fact, let's hit 'em even harder."

Phil cracked us all up. He said, "If that damn ref sticks his nose in our huddle again, I'm going to let him have it with my elbow. I'll make his snout look like Loren's lip. That'll show him how much we're gonna ease up."

The final score was 18-0, but it really didn't indicate the total domination Zion had over Barrington. For starters, it was the first time that Barrington was shut out in seven years. Secondly we held them to a total of minus two yards rushing for the entire game. While they did have 30 yards passing, most of it was meaningless yardage at the end of the game. Offensively, we gained a total of 198 yards rushing and held the ball throughout much of the game. Only penalties and a fumble stopped the score from being much higher.

Our fans surged down on the field to congratulate everyone on the team. The sense of elation and jubilation was so ecstatic I felt as if I were in another world. Classmates, parents, family, and friends all descended on us in a show of support and congratulations. It was a wonderful, breathtaking moment.

Joyce was the first one to reach me. "Bob. Congratulations on a great victory! You guys are now the Conference Champs." With that, she reached up, threw her arms around me, and gave me a big kiss right on the lips.

My first reaction was, "Well, it's about time! I've waited four years for that kiss. Let's do it again!" But before I could say anything she was off to congratulate the rest of the team. I wondered if she was going to kiss everyone.

Barb soon made her way down onto the field as well. "Conference Champs! Conference Champs! You guys did it," she screamed. Her kiss couldn't have been sweeter.

Betty Rae slapped me on the back as she was headed toward Loren. She was about to give Loren a big congratulatory kiss when suddenly she stopped and gaped. By now Loren's lip was all puffed up, black and blue, and still bleeding.

"Oh, no, Loren! What happened?" she exclaimed. "Your lip looks terrible."

"It hurts, but it's worth it," Loren yelled back. "We're the Champs!" With that he took her in his arms and twirled her around.

After 20 minutes of backslapping and hugs, players, coaches, and fans accompanied Coach Ellis as he went to the center of the field. With great flourish and ceremony, he sat down on the 50 yard line and pulled off both of his now stinking, raunchy socks.

"Boys, this will help them fertilize their field for next year." And with that he broke into one of the best guffaws, "Ho! Ho! Ho!" any of us had ever heard. We all roared our approval. It was a joyous moment.

We picked him up and carried him off the field, the one and only time we ever did so in four years of football. We

carried Coach Rushforth off also. Laughing and
barefooted, Coach Ellis was savoring the moment, as was
Coach Rushforth. It was a feeling of elation I'm sure
neither of them wanted to end.

Carrying Coach Ellis off the field after he removed his
socks. Left to right: Paul Jackola, Bill Hosken, Dick
Bogue, Evan Ellis, Bob Osmon

**The Aftermath**

Surprisingly, the locker room was not nearly as
raucous as anyone expected it to be. It was as if we all
recognized the import of what we just accomplished and
were absolutely relieved that it was over. For the seven of
us who suffered through all those discouraging losses as
freshmen and sophomores, it was true vindication. A
glorious reward for all the toil and struggle through those
losing, difficult seasons.

I for one was absolutely worn out. I carried the ball
more times in this game than I had in any game in my
entire high school career. I couldn't complain to Loren
that he never gave me the ball. I was content to sit on a
bench and soak it all in.

My Dad, my Brother Orval and my twin nephews,
Dave and Steve, came in and exuberantly wished me
congratulations.

"Dad, I'm so pleased you came to the game. Thank you!" I almost sobbed. As tears came to my eyes, I got up and hugged my Dad. All I could say was, "Thank you, Dad. Thank you."

"Well," he said smilingly. "It's not everyday that a father gets to see his son win a Conference Championship. Congratulations, son. Orval and I are very proud of you. I know your brother Carl will be also."

Carrying Coach Rushforth off the field. Left to right: Phil Anen, Loren Stried, Joe Rushforth, Bill Perry

Other parents filed in one by one expressing their well wishes to us all. All the coaches came around and told each of us how proud they were of us.

Probably by far the best compliment I received came from the Coach himself. "Moose, you did an excellent job calling defensive plays today. I should have had you calling crashes all season long."

Again tears came to my eyes. All the insults, snide remarks, and harassment over the last four years were forgiven at that very moment. I could tell from the sincerity in his voice that he had paid me the supreme compliment. My season couldn't have ended on a more satisfying note.

Dan Loblaw came into the locker room for a few minutes and yelled out congratulations to all of us. I couldn't resist putting in the needle.

"Hey, Mr. Loblaw," I yelled. "What do you think of Barrington's razzle-dazzle offense now?"

He laughed heartily. "Moose, I wanted to be sure you all were up for the game, so I tried to give you some incentive. I guess it worked!"

"It sure did," I answered enthusiastically.

The bus ride home was subdued and calm. We were all whipped, physically and emotionally. It was the last game of our lives for the seniors and to end on such a glorious note was awesome! It was hard to take it all in. The sack lunch that my Mother prepared for me to eat on the way home never tasted so good.

Because the game was so far away from Zion, most of the spectators and ZB fans went their own way after the game. Since they were all dispersed, Rooks was not in its normal full celebratory status. A few of the players met their dates there. But most of us just ate together in a subdued and low key manner. We enjoyed each other's company immensely, reliving the game in a personal and intimate manner, as only young men who have experienced and shared an incredible achievement can do.

Finally everything began to wind down and most people left the restaurant. None of the football players wanted to go home. We lingered and lingered knowing that when we left Rooks this time it would mark the end of all football celebrations involving any of us. It marked the end of cheers, the end of singing the school song, the end of our days as football players for Zion Benton Township High School. It was.....the end.

Finally, reluctantly and sadly, but being exhausted both physically and mentally, we gave each other one last slap on the back and straggled home for the night.

When I walked in the door, my Mom asked anxiously, "Robert, how did your game go?"

I replied wearily. "Great, Mom. We won the championship."

My Mom shrieked excitedly. "Oh, Robert! How wonderful! I know how important this has been to you all year long. I'm so happy you accomplished your goal."

"Thank you, Mom. I appreciate your telling me that."

Then she added, "Now remember, we're going to church early tomorrow. It is our turn to set up chairs for Sunday School, so don't sleep late."

With that quick return to reality, I dropped into bed and was fast asleep in seconds. I had one of the deepest and most contented sleeps of my life.

## Basking in the Glory

In the ensuing weeks and months, the Zee Bees received many accolades and honors from many sources. We set several new defensive records which pleased us almost as much as being champions. The All Conference selections were still in the offing.

First of all it turned out that the Zee Bees were not only the champions of the North Suburban Conference, but also we had the best winning record in Lake County. Thus we were the Lake County Champions also. A 6-1-1 record was good enough to rank us 20th in the final Chicago Tribune polls. This marked the first time the Zee Bees were in the Top Twenty high schools in the Chicago area ever.

Secondly, holding our opposition to only eight points for the season set new defensive records for both the North Suburban Conference and Lake County. It was pointed out by all the newspapers that we came within a TD and a safety of having a perfect unbeaten, untied, and unscored upon season. I was content to take the championship and not dwell on the "Could Have Beens".

When the North Suburban All Conference selections came out from the Chicago Tribune, the Zee Bees dominated both the first and second team. On the first team were Lugan at end, Paul at tackle, Middy at halfback, and me at the fullback spot. All four of us later appeared on the Illinois All State selections as Honorable Mentions.

On the second team was Bogie at center, Philibuck at end, and in a selection that pleased me tremendously, Loren was selected as an All Conference defensive guard. In the Single Wing the quarterback doesn't get the attention he does in the Magic Tee, so on offense Loren was an unsung hero. But on defense he excelled and was always in the middle of the action.

Although I have not personally researched this detail, I would suspect strongly that Loren is the only offensive quarterback in the history of the North Suburban Conference to be selected as All Conference at the defensive guard position.

My only disappointment was that somehow we all couldn't have made it. Certainly Bill Perry was a major force at tackle. Julian was a standout at the linebacker position and filled in beautifully for Middy when needed. Larry and Leon were both tough, gritty players who often went up against opponents much bigger than they were and handled them very well on traps and cross blocks. If Herman was not hurt near the end of the season, he too would have been a strong candidate to be selected as All Conference as an offensive end. Early in the season, he was the one who kept us in many of the games with his pass catching and punting. And Bill Hosken, always a standout on defense, gained more than 150 yards in our last three games when it really counted. In my mind, all of these teammates were deserving and their selection to the All Conference team would have been appropriate.

The student council put on one last event to honor the team. We had a party one night in the boy's gym and reveled in the fruits of our success. There were more speeches by the coaches, Mr. Pearce, and several of the players. More cheers. "Hurrah for Zion" had never held such meaning for me. That was true for all my teammates I'm sure. Philibuck made the recommendation that the school put up life sized portraits of us all in the boy's gym, but that didn't seem to go over so well with Mr. Pearce.

Actually I thought it was a great idea then and still think it was a great idea.

The Zion Exchange Club held a big dinner celebration for us one evening. All the players and their Dads were invited. This time my Dad came without Uncle Norman's persistence. The festive mood was exhilarating. Even my Dad seemed a little animated and excited about his son's accomplishments. The main speaker was a football coach from Northwestern. He told us how the Wildcats almost beat Ohio State. This was big time. After all we lived in the heart of Big Ten country.

When Coach Ellis stood up to talk, initially he entertained everyone with his crazy jokes but then turned serious. "By improving through the season to win the North Suburban Championship, the team was a pleasant surprise to me and the other coaches. We realized the season might be full of upsets and surprises, and after the Warren game, we wouldn't have been surprised if someone took the ball, skinned it and ate it like a banana. (Ho! Ho! Ho!). After the Barrington game, the locker room was like a morgue. I guess it was because the boys had given everything they had. There was nothing left for the yelling and hollering which often culminates a successful season."

One last Monday night I came to the Stried's for dinner and to watch TV. As Loren and I took in the highlights of the final Bears home game, a melancholy fell over both of us.

"Three years ago you and I sat right here in this living room and made a pledge to each other that we would do everything in our power to win the North Suburban Championship for Zion when we were seniors," I reminisced thinking back to our days as freshmen.

"No one would have ever given us a chance then to win it all. It was just you and me at first."

"Now three years later, somehow we've done it. Isn't that incredible?" I observed shaking my head in amazement.

"And we set a new defensive record which could last a long, long time," Loren added enthusiastically. "Only eight points in eight games. It was more fun to play defense this year than offense. We stopped everyone cold."

We both reflected on that thought for a moment. "And we both were selected as All Conference players. Do you remember when we set those as goals for ourselves?" he asked me knowing of course that I remembered.

"I sure do. We came a long way from those stumblebum freshmen who didn't even know how to put on our pads when we started. This team and this championship will be part of lives from now on," I stated with conviction. "It never can be taken away."

There was definitely an air of emptiness that hung over this glorious experience in our lives. The excitement of planning and discussing strategy to the finest detail for the next game was no longer needed. Our discussions on how the Single Wing was superior to other offenses were over. There would be no more Evan Ellis yelling at any of us again. No more calling us "Stride" and "Moose". No more games. No more pep rallies. No more celebrations at Rooks. No more next season. No more "Moose up the Gut!" No more veers! No more crashes! No more! ......No more!! ......No more!!

**\*\*\*\*\*\*\*\*\*\***

# Chapter 12
# The Fourth Quarter

I sat in the hospital room for about four hours before I was shaken out of my reverie by Evan grousing about food and the temperature.

"For God's sake," he said irritably. "Can't they turn some heat on around this dump? And when the hell is dinner being served? A guy could die of hunger before they feed him anything in this place. Nurse! Nurse! Turn up the damn heat and bring some food."

Well, obviously he was still in good spirits. The cancer hadn't calmed his temper down at all. This was a good sign in my mind. The nurses fussed around him for a bit and turned up the heat. He slept through dinner hour, but wisely one of the nurses saved one tray for him. Probably because she didn't want to catch any crap from him.

When he finished eating, I knew I had better ask him what was on my mind while I had the chance. For years I wondered why he acted the way he did toward both the team and me, but I never had the guts to ask. I had been sitting at his bedside for two days, but could only stay one more since I had to get back to my wife and family in Wisconsin. So I took a deep breath and plunged ahead.

"Evan, I need to ask you several personal questions. First of all, I know you were tough on everyone out there on the field, but honestly I know you singled me out more than a few times."

He smiled and nodded his head. "Go on. I think I know where you're headed."

"Like the 'Moose up the Gut' night. It wasn't just my responsibility to score, so why did you hammer me so hard? You were always on my butt for everything I did wrong. I always gave you my best ... so why did you honor me with all this special attention?"

Evan gave me a look of understanding that came from his heart and hesitated before answering. He knew exactly what was bothering me.

"Moose, before I answer that directly, let me show you something. Please get my wallet from over there on the table," he requested quietly.

I retrieved his wallet and gave it to him. He took out an old, faded, well used piece of paper.

"All my life I have tried to live with one guiding principle. When I needed inspiration or guidance or comforting regarding the life's work I have chosen, I looked at this piece of paper and it always got me right back into focus."

He handed the paper to me.

"Read it," he ordered.

I took the paper gently as if it were a valuable document. I unfolded it carefully and read out loud,

*"I would consider myself a great success in life as long as wherever I may have trod on this earth, I have left the grass a little greener behind me."*

Evan looked at me with a small smile. "From the time you were a freshman, I knew you had the ability to be a leader... but you never seemed to want that role. I tried everything I knew to fire you up. It wasn't until the night I made you run all the 'Moose up the Gut' plays that you ever stood up to me. It was the first time I saw fire in your eyes. And it wasn't until the Lake Forest game that you really started being a leader on the field."

Coach paused a moment, gathered his thoughts and went on. "I saw a change in you after the Warren game... you kept taking on more responsibility. I never had anything against you personally. But I did want you to be a better leader and a better football player."

This revelation absolutely stunned me. All these years I thought Evan personally didn't like me or had a prejudice against me that I couldn't comprehend in my teenage mind. All along he simply was trying to make me a better person. I thought of all the hours I wasted agonizing over this perceived slight when if I only knew better, I would have been honored to realize this man truly cared about me.

My mind raced with new thoughts. How many of us go through life thinking that a teacher didn't like us or a coach had a grudge against us because they pushed us to do things we didn't want to do, even though what they pushed us to do bettered our lives in someway? I'm sure I am not the only one. No doubt many of my fellow teammates or classmates felt this same emotion towards a coach or teacher who really pushed them hard to strive higher, learn more and achieve greater things in life. Finally the truth was known. Thank God it hadn't been too late. Finally I could release all the pent up antagonisms I had inside me all those years. As Aristotle quoted for history, yet needs to be learned by every individual on this earth in his own place and time, "The truth shall make you free."

With that nagging discomfort out of the way, I felt more confident to move on to my next inquiry.

"The second question has to do with a cryptic message you wrote in my yearbook." With that I pulled out my 1955 Nor'easter (The name was due to Zion Benton High School being located in the most northeastern corner in the State of Illinois) and turned to Coach's photo.

There in his hand writing were words which were a mystery to me for years.

*"Good luck, Moose. I wish all my fullbacks could drive like you. You helped make a coach out of me. Evan Ellis. "Moose up the Gut"! 48 yards?"*

"What did you mean by my helping make a coach out of you?"

Evan took a deep breath as I saw him reach back in his mind 15 years earlier. "When someone is a head coach, we think we know all the answers. We set up our offense and we expect all our players to fit our mold. At Zion, I tried to coach like that. It took time for me to learn I could not be successful in that mode. I needed to learn what the skills of my players were and adapt our offense to their ability. It was necessary to learn your personalities, what your home lives were like, and what kind of grades you earned. I had to get down in the dirt to teach you specifically how to block and tackle."

Evan stopped for a moment as he caught his breath. I could see this was a struggle for him to keep going, but since this was something I had wanted to know all my life, I didn't ask him stop. He went on thoughtfully.

"You all were more like sons to me than just players. Once I finally realized what each player's individual skills were, I adapted the offense to the player, not vice versa. For example, I stopped trying to make you into a speedy fullback and changed our plays to use your drive and strength. That's why I finally accepted that you were right about designing a play that would have you appear to go into the line, but then veer off right or left. Had I not been so stubborn, I would have incorporated it earlier in the season. It probably could have won the game against Crystal Lake and Warren. But please realize coaches are human too and we learn from our mistakes as well," he explained in an apologetic voice.

The hospital room was absolutely quiet as I listened to what Coach had to say. I always knew that I could never be the kind of fullback he wanted me to be, but I also knew I always tried to give him my best. And I never doubted his coaching skills. I simply accepted that I never performed up to his standards. To hear him admit he had to change his coaching style to fit our team was a major revelation to me.

"When I served in the Marine Corps during WWII, I learned the way to save men's lives was to scream and yell at your men until they did exactly what you wanted them to do. Out of fear, if necessary. That works well in a war where lives are at stake, but in other areas of life this may not be the best approach," he said philosophically. "Humans are all different."

I could see in his eyes that he must have been thinking about some occurrence back in WWII that may have caused him to bring this coaching technique to his teams. I would never ask about the horrors he must have witnessed during those amphibious landings on those far off Pacific islands. In the ten years I spent in the Navy I came to understand that WWII veterans kept all those stories locked within themselves.

"I learned from my five daughters that each one was motivated by a slightly different approach. Sometimes I barked at them. Sometimes I gently urged them. They all responded differently. In retrospect, I probably should have given you more encouragement rather than come down on your head so often. But I was very hardheaded in those days, and until you all became seniors, it was the only way I knew how to coach. So, now that I have explained myself, will you forgive me?" he implored. His eyes slowly misted.

I slowly realized the impact of what he had just said to me. Tears came streaming to my eyes as well. Although I wanted to know exactly why he berated me so much and what he meant by the comments in my yearbook, I was not looking for an apology. I thought to myself, here he is on his death bed, with only days to live, and he is asking for my forgiveness! It was just too much to comprehend at that time.

"Coach," I responded, my voice choking with emotion. "I wasn't looking for an apology. I just wanted to know what you meant by your inscription. There's nothing to forgive. You've been a big influence making me into the person I am today. Your guidance and friendship since my graduation from Zion has been a blessing to me. I'm honored to call you my friend!"

"As you know, Moose, I never had a son. But if I had one son, I would have liked him to grow up just like you," he whispered.

I saw tears come into his eyes and through the unspoken word between us, we both knew we had said enough. The air was clear. We could move ahead in peace.

We spent the rest of the evening going through my yearbook, laughing at photos, events, characters, reliving the entire season, and talking about the what ifs. One touchdown, one safety. The difference between an undefeated and unscored upon season. So close. We both mused how long our defensive record would stand.

"With all these high powered Magic Tee offenses that all the high schools are running now, everything is offense, offense, offense," he chortled. "That defensive record of only eight points scored against us will be in the books a long, long time."

He never knew how absolutely accurate he was with that prediction. Finally he had enough talk for the evening and slowly sunk down into the bed covers.

"Good night," I said, "and sleep well Coach."

He replied softly "Moose up the Gut!" He quietly guffawed and drifted off to sleep.

I sat there at his bedside for about another hour, just looking at his features and silently wishing this time could never come to an end. Dru came in and shook me a little to get me back into the moment.

"I think Evan is gone for the evening, Bob. Why don't you go back to your motel and get some rest. You've been with him all day. I'll take over now."

"Thanks," I answered. "I'll be back tomorrow morning, but I need to leave about noon to get back home. I'm sure you understand."

"Bob," she replied softly. "You've done more for Evan than you could ever imagine. I do understand and so will he. Goodnight."

**********

# Chapter 13
# Farewell

The next morning I was back at the Highland Park Hospital bright and early as usual. But as I walked up the steps and looked around the big lobby, I had a sinking feeling. It was like being kicked in the gut by a mule. Coach was not there.

Maybe he started without me was my first thought. I scurried up and down the halls, but did not see him. Maybe he's in the bathroom was my second thought. Not there either. I couldn't and didn't want to accept the obvious. Finally I dragged myself to his room... dreading what I might find. My heart leapt with joy when I saw him lying in his bed.

"He's still with us," I moaned happily.

Dru walked up behind me.

"He slipped into a coma late last night," she said glumly. "He hasn't awakened."

I took her hands. "I'm so sorry, Dru."

Tears came to her eyes as she tried bravely to hold back her emotions. "Stay awhile, Bob. He may come around."

Dru walked away and went into a nearby waiting room. It was only about 7 AM, so I began to pray that I could talk to him one more time.

"Dear God, it's a small favor. I deserve this. Bring him back if just for a moment."

With that I leaned back and left it in God's hands. As I sat there, I began to think about the series of events that occurred after the football season and graduation which brought Coach Ellis and me together at this place at this particular time.

**Time Marches On!!**

Soon after the New Year I received some disappointing news. Barb and I were chatting in the girl's gym when gravely she told me what was on her mind.

"Bob, I…I really hate to tell you this, but over the Christmas vacation I got back together with my old grade school boy friend from the Harbor," Barb stammered.

"What… do you … mean?" I choked out, a great gulp of emotion lodging in my throat.

"You're a wonderful guy," said Barb, "and I've had many good times with you. But… well, you're going to college next fall… and I'll be left alone. I'd like to date someone in my own class."

I too thought about the fact that I soon would be off to college and that romances with high school sweethearts seldom last. Suddenly I remembered the scene with Lynn two years before when she explained to us what it was like to lose Tom Douglas. Now I understood how she felt… only the shoe was on the other foot. Barb must have observed these breakups happening and knew she had to take the initiative. I wasn't happy about it, but at least I could understand.

Thus the disappointment wasn't as severe as it may otherwise have been. But it still stung more than I would have liked.

"Gosh, Barb. I would have liked to finish out the school year together," I lamented. "Remember the great time we had at the prom last year? I was hoping we could do it again."

"I'm sorry, Bob. Please don't hate me for doing this," she implored with a small tear in her eye.

"Come on. I could never hate you. You were my first ever girl friend and I'll always think of you that way."

"Thank you," Barb sighed. She gave me a quick kiss on the cheek and walked slowly out of the gym.

I observed a number of the upper class boys leave several of the girls in my class behind when they went off to college. Some of the girls in my class dated the upper classmen while we were freshmen and sophomores and a few even as juniors. But when the boys graduated and went off to college the relationships waned and the girls left behind suffered through it. So I really couldn't blame Barb for moving on before I did so. But it didn't feel good.

As some great philosopher once said, "It all depends on whether you are the dumper or the dumpee."

Interestingly enough, most of my friends on the football team didn't date the younger girls. Loren went with Betty Rae all four years, a rock solid relationship. Philibuck dated Pat Friend, Paul dated Betty Kastamo, Bill went with Marcheta Neely, and Dick Bogue was with Kay Kern. Herm's girlfriend Nancy was a senior at Kenosha High School. That really left Leon and me as the only two who pursued the underclass girls.

As soon as the word was out that Barbara and I were no longer an item, several of the senior girls approached me about dating Lynn. She and I were always the best of friends during our years in school together. I looked forward to talking to her at our gang's parties and at our church functions. She was delightful in many ways. But she had one overwhelming, disqualifying flaw: my Mother thought she was wonderful.

One night I made the mistake of mentioning to my Mother that the other senior girls thought I should start dating her. From that evening on almost every night when I came home my Mom asked, "Robert, did you see Lynn Reinier today?"

"Yes, Mom. I saw her".

"Did you talk to her?"

"Yes, Mom, I talked to her."

"What did you talk about?"

"School stuff, Mom."

"Well, I can't see why you don't go out with her more often. She is the sweetest and nicest young lady I have ever met. If you don't ask her out soon, somebody else will," my Mom observed candidly. My Mom always ended our conversation with this particular observation.

On Sundays we always arrived early at church. Lynn's Father, Glenn Reinier, was a wonderful man and very active in church activities. I thought the world of him as did everyone else in our church. He served as an elder and his efforts on behalf of the church were highly appreciated by everyone. His family also always arrived early on Sunday mornings.

As soon as my Mom spotted Lynn, she started in. "Robert, there is Lynn Reinier. Why don't you go talk to her?"

"Mom, cool it. I'll see her tonight at our MYF meeting," I'd reply in an evasive attempt to get off the subject.

Allow me to make a modern day observation. There is not a single teenage boy, not one who grew up in the 50s, not one who grew up in the 80s, nor one who grew up in the 2000s, and every one in between who wouldn't tell you that having a mother trying to push her son into a relationship is the kiss of death for that particular girl. As teenage boys, we all are just starting to stand on our own two feet and getting guidance from one's mother on dating isn't something any of us want to hear. From dads, okay. But from moms, no way!

Jerry Seinfeld is a modern TV comedy show that I absolutely love. In one episode Jerry met a beautiful, charming, intelligent, loving, sweet young lady who was perfect in every area of her life. He loved the way she dressed, kissed and thought. So he called his parents in Florida and they flew up to check her out. After they spent a full day with this young lady, he asked his parents what they thought. His Mom answered, "Jerry, we think she is absolutely wonderful. I wouldn't let this one slip away."

Jerry said, "That's it. I made up my mind."

His Mom asked, "What? Are you going to ask her to marry you?"

Jerry replied emphatically, "No! I'm going to dump her! If you two like her that much, there must be some deep seated flaw she has that I haven't seen yet!"

Unfortunately, I think it was this mentality that prevented Lynn and me from having a long term dating relationship in our senior year. It was too hard and too difficult to admit my Mom was right. We did date a few times and each time I had a wonderful evening with her. When she kissed me it was like being enveloped in warm honey. But in the end, I let my golden chances pass me by.

In later, much more mature years of our lives, I apologized to Lynn about a dozen times for not making our senior year one that could have produced terrific dating memories. She forgave me every time, but we both admitted this was an opportunity lost. Ahh, the ignorance and ego problems of teenage boys. What was that saying again? About youth being wasted on the young?

## The Big Blast at Birky's

Because there was no post Barrington game celebration at Rook's, Betty Rae and her Mother were determined that there would be one in their barn's second story party room. The place was decorated in ZB pennants and a big "Congratulations, Zee Bees. Conference Champs" banner was hanging between the rafters. There was food in plentiful supply and the music was blaring as Loren and I walked in.

*"One, two, three o'clock, four o'clock rock.*
*Five, six, seven o'clock. eight o'clock rock,*
*Nine, ten, eleven o'clock, twelve o'clock rock.*
*We're going to rock around the clock tonight.*
*When the clock strikes two, three, and four,*
*If the band slows down we'll yell for more."*

"We're going to rock tonight," I enthused loudly. "I'm so ready for a party. I bet we play the new Bill Haley and the Comets record a dozen times tonight."

Rock and roll recently made its debut on the American scene and all teenagers were ready to embrace it. My classmates from Zion were no different than the ones we watched on American Bandstand broadcast on TV from Philadelphia. The girls were always the first ones to pick up the steps and they taught them to the boys. I was ready to learn the new rocks steps from anyone who would teach me.

"Rock Around the Clock" hit the big time as the theme song for "Blackboard Jungle", a story of an inner city high school. The movie was considered far too risqué to be shown in Zion, but we all knew about it.

"Loren! Bob! How good to see you. You all deserve this celebration after what you accomplished," exulted Betty Rae in her new flowery party dress.

It is one thing to be feted by parents and adults who sing your praises for your deeds, but it is far more meaningful to be congratulated by one's peers. Especially when those peers are long time friends. Joyce, Lynn, Kay, and others were there. They were all there. A warm and comfortable atmosphere set the tone for the evening! It couldn't have been any better.

Phil was still pushing his plan to make sure we got our proper recognition. "I told Mr. Pearce the school should put life sized photographs in the gym with spotlights shining on each of us," he chuckled with a big smile on his face.

Leon wasn't about to be outdone. "How about all the cheerleaders kissing everybody on the team? If we're going to be honored, I want some making out," he said half seriously.

Of course, he was hooted down by all the girls in the room.

Lynn stepped up and said "Well, we think you should get some reward. You are the first Zion team to ever win the North Suburban Conference Championship."

"Thanks," I replied. "This party is all the reward we really need." All my teammates nodded in agreement

And with that, the discussion was over and the rest of the evening was spent dancing to the rocking beat of Bill Haley and the Comets.

When we finally dragged out about midnight, we all said goodbye to each other using the lines from Bill Haley's latest smash record.

"See ya later, Alligator."

"After while, Crocodile."

We were so cool!

## Second Semester

In the midst of all the merry making in the aftermath of our Championship, there was one disturbing revelation, however. Somewhere along the line Coach Ellis learned that the Exchange Club wanted to give us a small memento of our championship. They offered to buy each of the football players a small gold football with engraving on it to commemorate our achievement. But Coach McGrew, in his capacity as Athletic Director, vetoed the idea saying it wouldn't be appropriate for athletes to receive any gifts.

This led to additional shouting matches between McGrew and Ellis in the halls of ZBTHS.

Coach Ellis was absolutely furious about the decision. "These boys accomplished something no other team has ever done and you won't let them have a little gold football to serve as a reminder of their success? I think your decision stinks."

"Well, I think you're out of line and if you don't like it, that's tough!" With that McGrew stormed away and that was the end of the discussion.

The news of the face off raced through the school and no one was happy with the decision. It put a damper on the celebration for the entire school.

I could not help but wonder how this would affect Coach's future. When the Athletic Director and the Head Football Coach hate each other, it can't bode well for the school. Obviously the team would have enjoyed receiving gold footballs as a lasting memoir, but it was more disturbing to us to see Coach Ellis so frustrated that he could not reverse the decision. We knew something had to give.

## The Coach's Decision

In the late spring, a Navy recruiter came to the high school to talk about the possibilities of serving in the Navy. I planned to go to Lake Forest College the following fall, but he outlined a program in which I could join the

Navy Reserve, go to officer training camp during the summer, attend drills in Waukegan during the school year and at the end of four years of college be commissioned as an officer in the U. S. Navy. The best part was that I got paid for doing this. This sounded very good to me because I knew money would be at a premium throughout my four college years. So I signed up to attend boot camp at Great Lakes that summer. It was the start of a 32 year career for me in the United States Navy.

Near the end of our senior year at Zion, Coach Ellis made a shocking announcement to all of us. He accepted a teaching and coaching position at New Trier High School in Winnetka, Illinois, a suburb of Chicago. New Trier was a very wealthy school unlike Zion and his teacher's salary almost doubled. Additionally, New Trier ran the Single Wing and won the Suburban League title the previous fall, so he was a perfect fit as an assistant coach.

Even though Coach more than once told us that the main reason he was leaving was to take better care of his family, we all knew in our hearts that the main reason he was leaving was the bad blood between the Athletic Director and him. His situation had become untenable at Zion and none of us blamed him one bit for making that decision. It was a sad state of affairs, but, alas, one of the realities of life.

## Graduation

Phil, Loren, Leon, Paul, and I were all at Rook's one bright sunny day in late May. We were discussing our plans for summer and the following year.

"I'm headed to North Central College in Naperville, Illinois," Phil said. "Guess I'll try out for football, but don't know for sure yet."

"I'm probably going to enlist in the Marine Corps," Leon stated firmly. "Chicks love that Marine dress uniform."

"I'll probably work a while or join the Army," Loren offered. "Guess I should see something of the world before I settle down here in Zion."

Paul stated that he eventually would like to open a body shop of his own, specializing in foreign cars. "I think the European cars are really going to catch on in the United States," he predicted firmly, "and I want to cash in on that trend. Also the Japanese are just beginning to export their cars to this country. Who knows how successful they will be?"

Coming to the end of my senior year was clearly a bittersweet experience. I was excited about moving on to Lake Forest College and my Navy experience, but at the same time I knew I would miss my friends and teammates something terrible when we finally said goodbye.

"Guys, I'm going to miss all of you. We've had a fun and rewarding four years here at Zion. It isn't going to be easy to say goodbye. Let's agree to get together as often as we can during vacations and reunions. We want to keep the spirit of our old football team alive."

"You got that right, Moose," responded Leon.

Graduation Night came too soon. As I sat on the platform of the Zion Auditorium, I watched as one by one all my friends, guys and gals, walked across the stage to receive their diplomas. Each one held a special place in my heart and my mind. It appeared to me that each one of my teammates received a little more applause than normal. That pleased me to no end. It was very satisfying to me to realize how much our accomplishment was appreciated.

As the "Almighty Crowd" girls walked up to receive their diplomas, I reflected on how supportive they were during our four years together and how much of a role they played in keeping our spirits up when things weren't going well. My teammates and I were blessed to have friends like these ladies.

When my turn came to walk across the stage, tears came to my eyes. This is it, I said to myself. This is it. The end of the road. I received my diploma and returned to my seat in a numb state. Goodbye to Zion Benton Township High School. But I knew that even though I would be gone physically, the memories would never leave my mind. That was my refuge.

## Summer and Beyond

I reported to boot camp at Great Lakes, Illinois soon after graduation. Because I was in such good physical shape, I didn't find it to be that much of a challenge. So as an extra responsibility, I volunteered to be on the Recruit Drill Team. During the course of the summer I was selected to be the Commander of the team.

We performed at the graduation of the recruits every Saturday morning and participated in numerous parades in the local area. When it was time for my graduation, my Mother attended accompanied by Lynn. It was an honor to have them there and see me perform. That summer was the beginning of a 32 year career in the U.S. Navy.

I was awarded a $500 scholarship by the Zion Exchange Club which could be used toward my college tuition. Mr Reinier helped me get accepted into Lake Forest College (he was on the Board of Trustees). I played football that fall, but needed to work in the cafeteria for my meals and cleaned the dorm to pay for my room.

I didn't do a lot of studying, but I got through the year with passing grades. Herm was my roommate and close friend during that first year. Pat Friend and Lynn also attended Lake Forest College. I was happy having good friends from Zion with me in these new surroundings.

At the end of the summer Coach went off to New Trier High School and I went off to Lake Forest College. When I could get free, I attended some of the Zion and New Trier football games. John Timmerman took over as Head Coach at Zion and almost pulled off another championship.

The team, led by Bill Perry, Larry Laird, Bill Rymer, Jerry Koskinen, Bob Schmidt, and Julian Emanuelson, went into the last game of the season with a chance to bring home another title. With Bill Perry hurt and sitting on the bench, the Zee Bees lost their final game to Crystal Lake, our old nemesis, 14-7. But the Zee Bees were knocking on the door at the end of the game. There is no doubt if Bill had been healthy, a second championship trophy would now be sitting in the showcase of the school lobby.

Coach told me it was much, much easier coaching at New Trier than at Zion, but frankly he missed the close relationship with his players. While we had a total of 16 players on our team and almost everyone played both offense and defense, New Trier had 100 players forming two complete teams, both offense and defense, with two complete teams as backups. He told me that it was hard just learning everyone's name. There were too many players to give nicknames to everyone. So while he was pleased with his new job, he did miss the give and take of the personal contact with the players as he had at Zion. But he also didn't have to fight with the Athletic Director.

During my second semester at college, the Navy Reserve unit gave me the opportunity to compete for an appointment to the Naval Academy. Most candidates enter through appointments by their Senators or Congressmen. But the Navy selects 80 enlisted sailors a year for appointments to get fleet experience at the Academy.

I didn't say much about this opportunity to anyone as I figured my chances of obtaining this appointment were slim to none. Besides, I was enjoying myself at Lake Forest. I joined the Kappa Sigma fraternity and was starting to savor the frat life. But much to my surprise, I did very well on the exam and late in the spring received a telegram telling me I earned an appointment to the U.S. Naval Academy at Annapolis, Maryland. Up until then, I really hadn't given it much thought. Now I had to make a major decision.

The very first person I went to see was Coach Ellis. Although he was teaching in Winnetka, he remained living in Zion for quite a number of years before moving closer to his new school. I caught him at home one weekend.

"Coach, what do you think about my going to the Naval Academy?" I knew he understood the opportunity well based on his Marine Corps experience.

Coach looked at me with a surprised look. "You've got a chance to go to Annapolis?"

"Yes Sir. It seems like the right thing to do …but I'm doing well in football at Lake Forest and could possibly start as a sophomore."

"Heck, Moose… it's a one in a million opportunity!"

"Navy has nationally ranked teams…I don't think I'll ever make it as a football player at the Naval Academy."

"Playing football is a wonderful experience," said Coach slowly and thoughtfully. "But no matter what, it's just a game. It can't be your life."

"Yes Sir… but I'm doing well," I said, unwilling to give up the thrill of competitive football.

"The Academy will offer you a life's experience that you might never obtain after graduating from Lake Forest."

"Yes sir… I've thought about that…it's just that…"

I was afraid of the unknown offered by Annapolis. I was too comfortable. Coach shocked me out of that.

"Hell, Moose…you could break an ankle and your playing days could be over at either place. Forget about football and go to Annapolis!"

Frankly, I was surprised to hear him say these words. Once again, only in retrospect can I really understand that he only had my welfare in mind. After hearing him talk, breathe, and espouse football for four years, I was a little stunned to hear him say it was only a game. But I took his recommendation to heart and it helped me to make the right decision.

I also talked to my minister, Reverend Clarence Ploch, of the Memorial Methodist Church and to the Mayor of our town, Lee Fleming, who once served on Macarthur's staff in Japan after WWII. They both strongly urged me to take advantage of this opportunity.

After long talks with my Mom and Dad, they too encouraged me to accept this offer and challenge. They both realized their son had an opportunity that could change his life and they wanted me to take full advantage of it.

So later that summer, with my telegram in hand, I headed to Annapolis, Maryland to enroll in what was to become the greatest adventure of my life.

I went out for Plebe (Freshman) football that fall and I made the cut to be on the team. But after several weeks of banging heads with some of my Navy teammates, I realized I was much too slow for not only the backfield, but also to play even guard. I wasn't nearly big enough to play tackle. If college ball had allowed the two platoon system as it does now, I think I could have been competitive at the linebacker position, but alas that rule wasn't changed until years later. Reluctantly, but with the Coach's words embedded in my mind, I gave up big time football.

There was one particular achievement I accomplished at the Academy, however, which was the result from my playing high school football. Each year the junior class at the Academy played the sophomore class in a tackle football game on the morning of Thanksgiving. It was called the Turkey Bowl and was a way of developing spirit for the upcoming Army/Navy game which occurred a few days later in Philadelphia. In my sophomore year, several members of my class came to me and asked me to coach the Class of 60 team.

I agreed to do so only if we could run the Single Wing. They all agreed and I found myself in my first coaching position. I emulated everything Coach Ellis and Coach Rushforth taught us at Zion… ran the same plays and the same defenses. I played my old fullback position, but had to select players for the other spots. I taught everyone the basics how to line up and run from Single Wing.

Fortunately many of my classmates played in high school, so it was just a matter of my coordinating their efforts. The end result was that we upset the highly favored Class of 59 by a score of 7-6. I scored the winning touchdown and extra point. "Moose up the Gut" was still an effective play.

The following year I once again served as coach for the Class of 1960 and once again we won. This time we beat the Class of 61 by a score of 26-0.

It was with great pride that I came home at the Christmas break to tell Coach about my coaching victories. For the first time I understood how being a coach makes you aware of the performance of the entire team, not just yourself as an individual. No wonder he was as tough on us as freshmen and sophomores. There wasn't much there of which to be proud in those early years, except for the way we kept trying. Maybe that was why he never gave up on us.

Two more babies came into the Ellis family and two more times Coach had girls. Alta Jo Ellis (Jodie, named after Bill Rymer's mother) was born on June 29, 1957 and Drusilla Ann Ellis (At first Drucie and now Dru) was born November 16, 1959. He never got his son, but I guess to some degree I became a surrogate son over the years. At my Christmas break during my last year at the Academy, I played Santa Claus to the Ellis family.

As I sat there with my Santa suit on making fun talk with the girls, Coach said to me with his usual snicker, "Santa, you're the first Santa Claus I have ever seen who wears a Naval Academy ring!" With that he broke into a big "Ho! Ho! Ho!"

I told him, "Coach, Naval Academy graduates are found in all parts of the globe. It's the US Navy and US Marine Corps that makes our families safe at Christmas and clears the way for Santa to make his rounds."

Coach liked that... brought back his Marine pride!

During my Christmas and summer breaks from the Academy we became closer and closer. I spent quite a bit of time at Coach's home during those periods. Each year my Mom hosted a reunion of our football team as we kept the spirit and stories alive even though we were slowly going our own ways. The camaraderie between us was wonderful and Coach reveled in very minute of it. It was a different experience being treated like an equal with Coach, but one I relished.

During our time together he often opened up and told me stories about his military experiences. One in particular was his favorite. He told me with great glee how on the beaches of Guadalcanal he was told by his commanding officer to fall back and bring up more ammo.

"Moose, I crawled through the sand and over dead bodies trying to find some ammo cases so I could haul them back to our platoon. When I finally found several boxes marked 'Ammunition' I opened them up and guess what? I found two lawn mowers. Can you believe that? Lawnmowers on a tropical island!!! During a war!" Of course, a huge guffaw followed that story.

He also told me about being scared to death as his landing craft was headed into the beach at Tinian. His grizzled old gunny sergeant got his troops together and said in a gruff voice, "Now boys, the enemy will not be happy when we land on their little beaches... so they will try to kill us. Our job is to shoot back and kill them first. Any questions?"

Coach told me that became his modus operandi on how to talk to his men in dire situations. As I learned more about him, I understood better the way he thought and acted. None of us become what we are by accident. Our lives are a compendium of every event that happened to us along life's journey and the effects these events had on us.

Eventually Coach Ellis moved his family from Zion to Northbrook, and I completed my four years at the Naval Academy. Slowly our paths began to diverge.

I was graduated from the Naval Academy in June 1960. I was commissioned as an Ensign in the Supply Corps, the logistics branch of the Navy. Much like all young men who are free to explore the world for the first time, I soon left behind my ties in Zion. I only returned home once in my first four years in the Navy. I was home ported in San Diego and cruised to Japan and the Philippines on the USS Buck, an old WW II destroyer. I often wrote Coach Ellis from afar and told him of some of my exploits. He occasionally wrote back, but I knew he was always with me in spirit, always coaching me to do better and be better.

Then I was assigned to Amphibious Construction Battalion One, the Sea Bees, in Coronado, California. The

Sea Bee mascot is a big bee with each leg holding a different tool used by the Sea Bees in their construction efforts. The next Christmas I had a Christmas card made with me in uniform standing next to this mascot. On the caption of the card I had printed, "First I was a Zee Bee: Now I am a Sea Bee." Coach really liked that. He sent me a card telling me he guffawed for days.

I later went to Panama for two years and then on to a nuclear submarine, the USS George Washington, home ported in Holy Loch, Scotland. During that period I married and started to raise a family of my own. The letters between Coach and me became more infrequent.

In June 1970, two events occurred in Coach's and my lives that appeared to be totally unrelated at the time, but which were actually in Divine Order. Because of some marital problems I was experiencing, I left the active Navy after ten years of service in an effort to keep my family together. I came to live in Racine, Wisconsin and attempted to start up my own manufacturer's representative business. Almost simultaneously Coach was diagnosed with cancer and had to retire from teaching and coaching.

I visited Coach as often as I could at his home and we had some great evenings together. He loved my telling him about the military experiences I had since graduation. It brought back his good memories of the Marine Corps. But the need to take care of my family and the pressure of building a business didn't allow me the time with him I would have liked. I believe that my being close by to him at that particular time wasn't just a happenstance. It was meant to be.

When Dru called to tell me that Evan's death was imminent, I knew what to do. I dropped everything to be by his side. That was how I came to be at the Highland Park Hospital at this particular confluence of time and place in our lives. Nothing is coincidental. It's all part of the Master Plan.

## The Final Play!

I was deep in thought for several hours, absorbed in my memories and the profoundness of what was happening. A movement, almost imperceptible at first, barely noticeable, caused me to stir.

"What was that?" I asked myself, suddenly becoming alert. "I don't hear anything."

I glanced around the room. At first I saw nothing unusual. In the dim light of Coach's room everything was a little hazy. But something was happening. Then I saw it. Again! Coach's index finger was slowly moving. As I watched, the movement became a little stronger. Almost a beckoning signal. I got up from my chair and walked over to the bed.

Evan's eyes were wide open and he was looking directly at me. But he didn't move. His eyes rolled up in his head as if to say "Come here." His lips moved, but I heard nothing. He continued to move his finger and roll his eyes until I figured out he was trying to tell me something. So I placed my ear down very close to his mouth as I took his hand in mine.

"Moose up the Gut," he whispered very faintly and laughed in that manner that had become so familiar to me. But this time his "Ho! Ho! Ho!" was barely audible.

Tears rolled out of my eyes. God answered my prayer. I was able to speak to him one more time. How wonderful that in his time of dire pain and I'm sure impending sense of death, he still had his sense of humor. What a great example for us all to emulate when we face a major crisis in our lives. I should be so ennobled to die with this kind of attitude.

I took this opportunity to express my deepest and most heartfelt sentiments. "Coach," I choked through my tears. "I love you. You've been a major influence in my life and I'm a better man because of you."

The Coach squeezed my hand. His head nodded slightly. He closed his eyes and a peace I will never forget came over his face. I sat as in a trance as the Coach's voice echoed in my head... the voice that drove us to become Champions… the voice that dramatically shaped my early life. I could clearly hear his words through the silence. "Moose, you've bounced back from defeat before. Now do it one more time… for your old coach."

I don't remember how long I sat there holding his hand. I vaguely remember arising and numbly walking out of the hospital room to start the rest of my life without him.

**\*\*\*\*\*\*\*\*\*\***

# Epilogue

## 50 Years Later

In September 2004, Zion Benton Township High School honored all the players who were on the 1954 Championship team. Not surprisingly, all the juniors and seniors from that team but one were present for this event. Both of our assistant coaches, Joe Rushforth and John Timmerman, were present. Dick Bogue and Herm Swanson flew in from the State of Washington. Leon Hallgren came from North Carolina and I came from Virginia. The gathering was deeply emotional for us all.

The school hosted a reception in the coaches' lounge for the team. The Superintendent, Dr. Bud Marks, the Athletic Director, Lonnie Bible, and LeRoy Cliff, now a coach emeritus, all came by and spent several minutes getting to know us and wishing us well. A big cake with "1954 Champs" emblazoned in the icing was presented to us with much fanfare. The Zion Benton News snapped photos and interviewed many present for their stories to be published. The local Zion Park District made a video tape of the entire weekend proceedings as part of its efforts to document one poignant event in time in the history of Zion. We were provided a roped off section in the bleachers to sit in during the Friday night game. Joyce and two of our former cheerleaders, Betty Rae, and many of our other classmates joined us.

During halftime we all walked on the field as each of our names were announced over the loudspeaker by the Superintendent. The young students of ZBTHS warmly greeted each of us with a loud cheer after our each of names were called. Superintendent Marks then read a commemorative plaque that detailed our accomplishment during that amazing 1954 season. He also stated that our record of allowing only eight points scored against us in a season still stood as the official defensive record for both the North Suburban Conference and the Lake County teams. He added "And it may well be never broken, ever." Coach Ellis' prediction had come to pass.

Dr. Marks also announced to the student body, "This commemorative plaque with the names of every team member engraved on it will be hung in the school in the Hall of Fame area. These players you see before you tonight are part of Zion Benton Athletic history forever."

Superintendent Marks handed the mike to me to say a few words. I told the Zee Bee students, "We were proud to be Zee Bees in 1954 and we are still proud to be Zee Bees today. Enjoy these years in high school so that you too can look back 50 years from now and have wonderful memories. God bless all of you students, God bless the faculty and staff at Zion Benton High, and last but not least, God bless America."

The resounding cheer was deafening. Patriotism and school spirit were still alive in Zion, Illinois... always have been and I'm sure always will.

The next evening we enjoyed dinner together at Stone Creek Restaurant in Windy Harbor. The stories flew unabated all evening proving the old adage, "The older we get, the better we were!"

During the previous year I made a diligent attempt to track down one of the Ellis girls so we could invite them all to this event. Finally through Johnny Kerr I was able to obtain the phone number of Dru Ellis Deering.

When I first contacted her, she didn't know me as she was born long after I graduated from Zion. But her older sisters told her, "We know Bob Osmon. He's Moose. He played Santa Claus for us one year." So between Dru and me we organized this dinner to honor Evan. She assembled photos of her Dad in college, as a young Marine, as a new coach, and his wedding photo. Personal items none of us ever saw before.

Dru and two of her sisters, Betsy and Jodie, were our guests at the dinner. Each of the players took turns telling stories about what we remembered about our days suffering under their Dad. Some stories were hilariously funny, some were very poignant. I warned Dru and her sisters that not everything we would say about their Dad would necessarily be complimentary.

She said, "Moose, whatever stories any of you can tell about our Dad, we can top it two fold." And they did. After we had our say, each of them related their remembrances of their Dad as well. It became obvious that living in the same household with Evan was no piece of cake. Their stories were as hilarious and heart rending as any of ours. But they obviously loved him dearly and they too still mourn the loss of their Dad.

The evening became a celebration of Evan Ellis, his life, his relationships with all of us, and his long lasting effect on our lives. No one left that night without recalling a vivid memory of this man. It was a deeply emotional evening for everyone who attended.

After listening to all the memorable stories about our old coach that evening I came up with the idea to try to document the story of this stormy and hilarious relationship between our team and its coach. I did it for Coach Ellis, for the Ellis family, for the team, for Zion, for me, and for anyone who may have been influenced by Coach Ellis to do bigger and better things in his/her life.

It was Coach's goal to "Leave the grass a little greener behind him wherever he trod on this earth". It is my belief that in his short time on this planet, he left many of his player's and student's lives much greener because of his drive for excellence and his sincere caring.

"Coach, on behalf of everyone who had the chance to know you and learn from you, we thank you from the bottom of our hearts."

Bob "Moose" Osmon

"Lives of great men all remind us
We can make our lives sublime,
And, departing, leave behind us
Footprints on the sand of time."

A Psalm of Life
Henry Wadsworth Longfellow

# Whatever Happened To........?

## The Coaches

**Evan Ellis** – The tragedies facing the Ellis family did not end with Evan's death. Dru died four months after Evan of a cerebral hemorrhage. For one year their maternal grandparents came to live with Laurie, Jodie, and Dru until Laurie graduated from New Trier High School. Then Jodie and Dru moved into their grandparent's home in Riverside, Illinois. After one year, the two of them went to live with their uncle, Johnny Kerr, and his family in Northbrook, Illinois. Betsy now lives in Sapiello, New Mexico and still works as a nurse. Mary Beth lived in Colorado for many years and died in December 2005. Laurie was murdered in 1975 during her college years in Grand Rapids, Michigan. Only recently has the culprit been discovered through the use of DNA. The man is now behind bars. Jodie went on to law school and now lives in Arlington Heights, Illinois as a full time housewife and mom. The baby, Dru, whom I credit with providing so much detailed information about her Father, also lives in Arlington Heights and is in her 12th year of working at the Motorola Corporation.

**Joe Rushforth** - Joe stayed on as assistant coach for several more years before leaving Zion Benton High School to become the Superintendent of the Winthrop Harbor School system. After retirement from that position, he became the Mayor of Winthrop Harbor. He was inducted into the Zion Athletic Hall of Fame as Zion's first great football player. Joe still lives in Winthrop Harbor with his lovely college sweetheart, Nan. His sons were all outstanding contributors to the Zion-Benton Athletic program. I always stay with Nan and Joe whenever I return to Zion for any of our reunions. Their warmth and kindness are only exceeded by their gracious manner.

**John Timmerman** – Because of budget cuts that were eating into the athletic programs at Zion, John left Zion in 1957 to take the head football coach position at Dundee, Illinois. He won a conference championship soon afterwards. In 1966 he became the Athletic Director at Barrington High School in Barrington, IL. John retired from full time coaching and education in 1984 from Barrington, but continued to serve as a substitute teacher and assistant football coach until 1998, a full 50 years in the field of education and coaching. He now lives in Dundee, Illinois where he serves as a golf starter and plays tons of golf. I was honored to take John to a Naval Academy football game with me in Annapolis in 2005.

# The Seniors

**Phil Anen (Philibuck)** - Initially Phil entered North Central College and went out for football, but found it uninteresting. He transferred to Lake Forest College the next year and was graduated in 1959 with a degree in business. After graduation he formed his own Manufacturer's Representative business covering Northern Illinois and Wisconsin. Phil lived for many years in Lake Geneva and Germantown, Wisconsin. He now resides in Winthrop Harbor. Philibuck has always been very active in class affairs and events. He and I have talked weekly on the phone for the last 10 years.

**Dick Bogue (Bogie)** – Dick attended Bethel College in St Paul, Minnesota and lettered in football. He later graduated from Central Washington University with a degree in Biology. Dick became a Forest Ranger for the State of Washington and served the state for 25 years in that capacity. After he retired he ran a horse ranch in Washington for many years and did many hours of volunteer work with the Boy Scouts. He also remained very active in church affairs. Bogie now lives in Sun City, Arizona with his wife Carol.

**Leon Hallgren**– Leon served in the Marine Corps for four years after high school graduation and played football on the service team. After discharge from the Marine Corps, he became a very successful computer programmer working for various corporations. Later he owned his own computer business for many years. Leon is now retired and is living in Durham, North Carolina with his wife Elizabeth.

**Bill Hosken** – Bill graduated from Antioch College in Ohio in 1960. He received a Master's Degree in Mathematics from Ohio State in 1962 and a Ph.D. from Purdue in Computer Science in 1968. He still works today in the computer field in Chicago. He also served for eight years on the Elementary School Board in Zion and then for 12 years on the ZBTHS School Board. Bill was a man who gave back to the school system which nurtured him. He is still very active in class events. He married his high school classmate, Bev McElmurry, who also received a Ph.D., hers in Education from Northern Illinois University in DeKalb. They live in Zion.

**Paul Jackola** – Paul married his high school classmate and sweetheart, Betty Kastamo. They had by far the largest number of children in our class. Their nine sons and daughters were very prominent in sports and other activities at Zion Benton. They also have 34 grandchildren with four of those graduating from ZBTHS. Paul owned and operated a foreign car repair shop on Sheridan Road and Beach Park Road for many years. His ability to foresee the huge influx of foreign cars was right on and he enjoyed great success as a result. In retirement he has become a dedicated hiker and keeps himself in great physical shape by doing long distance treks. Paul and Betty now live in Kenosha, Wisconsin.

**John Jecevicus (Lugan)** – John signed a contract to play baseball with the Phillies, but an unfortunate injury prevented him from ever having the chance to compete. He worked as a construction man for many years for the Finestra Corporation doing specialized roofing projects. He served as Foreman on two of his biggest accomplishments: building the dome for the Dane County Coliseum in Madison, Wisconsin and constructing the twin athletic domes at Notre Dame University in South Bend, Indiana. He eventually retired as maintenance man from the Kenosha High School System. Lugan now lives in Wadsworth, Illinois.

**Bobby Middleton (Middy)** – Middy attended Black
Hills State Teachers College in South Dakota for several
years and was an excellent pitcher for the baseball team.
He then returned to Zion. After trying several different
businesses, he settled on becoming a building contractor.
He became quite successful in this endeavor and built
many new homes in and around the Zion area. He now
lives in Winthrop Harbor with his wife Judith.

**Bob Osmon (Moose)** - Bob graduated from the U.S. Naval Academy in 1960. He went on to spend 27 years on active duty and was promoted to the rank of Captain. He worked in Civil Service for another 12 years for the U.S. Army training Japan's soldiers in the U.S. He retired in 2005 and lives in Williamsburg, Virginia where he has resided for 18 years.

**Loren Stried (Stride)** – Loren served in the US Army for two years and returned to Zion. He worked for Commonwealth Edison for many years retiring in the position of Foreman. I was honored to speak at his retirement luncheon when many of his close friends came to honor him. He married Mary Lynn Taylor from Zion. The two of them have been extremely active in the activities of the Christian Catholic Church and the local community. In particular, their dedicated work with the young people of the church at summer camp each year is notable. They both are loved by one and all. I believe they are shining examples of what makes small town America a great place in which to grow up. Their love of people and devotion to the church and city made them mainstays in the Zion community. Loren and I always get together each time I return home to Zion. It is as if I never left. I have always felt blessed that God guided Loren to me way back in 1951…just when I needed him most.

**Herman Swanson–** Herm was my roommate at Lake Forest College for one semester before enlisting in the Marine Corps. He married his Kenosha High School sweetheart, Nancy, in 1957. After doing his service time, he worked for several car companies and later owned several car dealerships. He received a Masters' Degree from San Jose State University in California in Marketing and did post graduate work at the University of Santa Clara in International Management. I was honored to have them both present at my retirement ceremony when I retired from the Navy in 1987. He is now retired. Herm and Nancy live in Graham, Washington.

**Julian Emanuelson** – Julian was selected as All Conference fullback in his senior year. He was awarded a scholarship to the University of Miami in Florida, but after one year did not find it to his liking. He returned to Illinois to work at Johns Manville for a while before entering the Air Force for four years. After his discharge, he earned a degree in Education at Western Illinois and received a Master's Degree from Ball State. He became a school teacher and coach at Libertyville High School. He was extremely well liked and highly respected for his coaching successes. He is now retired and lives in Libertyville with his wife Judith.

**Jerry Koskinen** – Jerry attended Stout University for several years. He then returned to Zion to work for the Westvaco Envelope Company, retiring after 40 years of service. He married his classmate Phyllis Holzman, Karl's younger sister, in 1959. Phyllis received a Master's Degree from National University in Evanston and taught in the Zion School System for 21 years. Jerry and Phyllis now live in Winthrop Harbor.

**Larry Laird** – Larry was selected as an All Conference guard in his senior year. Initially he served in the Army Reserve and then the Coast Guard for four years following graduation. After discharge he moved to Waukegan and spent 30 years with the North Shore Gas Company. He is now retired and lives in Waukegan with his wife Gloria.

**Bill Perry** – Bill was elected as Captain for the team in his senior year and was selected as an All Conference tackle. He graduated from Western Illinois University in 1960. He taught in several school systems before becoming the principal at Conant High School in Schaumberg, Illinois, a position he held for many years. He received his Master's Degree from Western Illinois and his Ph.D. from Indiana University. He married a Zion classmate, Julie Corder, in 1960. She also became a teacher and has her Ph.D. from Indiana University as well. Now both retired, they live in Barrington.

**Bill Rymer** – Bill graduated from Lake Forest College in 1961. He worked for various corporations in the Chicago area before being hired by the Zion Hospital as Director of Plant Operations. He retired after many years of dedicated service and moved to Florida, but still works as a consultant for numerous hospitals around the country. Bill married his high school classmate, Miriam Downs, in 1957. They now live in Pompano Beach, Florida, but return to Zion every summer to be with family and friends.

**Bob Schmidt** – Bob attended Northwestern University and earned a degree in mathematics. He worked for Jewel Tea and Moore Business Forms in Chicago. Eventually he retired as a Vice President of a major home improvement company in Nebraska. He now lives in Bull Head City, Arizona with his wife Judy.

**Betty Rae Birky (Kaiser)** – Betty Rae attended Whitewater State Teacher's College after graduation. Later she transferred to Carthage College in Wisconsin, receiving her degree in 1972. She taught in the Winthrop Harbor School System for 25 years and worked for Joe Rushforth when he was Superintendent of Winthrop Harbor schools. She now lives in Wadsworth, Illinois and is the Government Affairs Director of the Illinois Association of Realtors. She also served as a delegate to the Republican Convention in 2004. Betty Rae has always remained very active in class events.

**Barbara Bogue (Thompson)** – Barbara attended St. Olaf College in Minnesota graduating in 1961. She married her college sweetheart and together they ran a very successful printing business for many years. Barb now lives in New Brighton, Minnesota with her husband Lowell.

**Joyce McEwen (Therkildsen)** – Joyce obtained a Bachelor of Science Degree from Iowa State University, and a Master's Degree from Northwestern University in Education. At Iowa State she was a Varsity cheerleader. Coincidentally she was also a classmate of Tucker Howard, the former quarterback from Warren High School. She taught at Central Junior High in Zion for four years, Waukegan High School for four years, and 14 years in Arlington Heights, Illinois. Due to a back injury she suffered in a school bus accident, she was forced to retire earlier than she planned. She now lives in Inverness, Illinois with her husband Turk. Joyce is very active in class events.

**Lynn Reinier (Nolte)** – Lynn graduated from Lake Forest College in 1959 with a degree in Psychology. She became a very accomplished artist and held numerous shows around the Midwest with much acclaim. She taught art to large numbers of children and has been a Sunday School teacher for many years. She now lives in Wichita, Kansas with her husband Wink. Lynn returns to Zion for every class reunion. She still has her dazzling smile.

## Zion

**Zion Benton Township High School** – In 1974 a new high school named New Horizon was opened near 21$^{st}$ and Lewis Avenue. For 15 years classes were held at both locations. In 1989 all classes were permanently moved to the new campus. Our football team was present in a ceremony when all the old trophies from the old school were moved to a new and permanent spot in the new school.

The old school now serves as a multi purpose building, housing activities ranging from adult education to a woman's clinic. The girl's gym is used for theatrical productions and the boy's gym is used for city league intramural basketball. The old school is a little seedy in appearance, but could easily be brought back into prime condition with a little money and tender care.

The saddest moment for my teammates and me was to see our old football field in its present state. The lights and bleachers are all removed. The goal posts are gone. The scoreboard is gone. What was the playing field for our greatest glories is now being used primarily for city league soccer games. It was a bleak sight that none of us ever wanted to see.

**Zee Bee Football** – The Zee Bees did not win another North Suburban Championship until 1969. That means from1941 to 1969, a span of 29 years, the 1954 Zee Bees were the only team to win a football championship for the school. But then LeRoy Cliff took the helm as head football coach. Under his guidance and leadership the Zee Bees won numerous championships. To date only Evan Ellis and LeRoy Cliff have won a North Suburban Football Championship as a Head Coach.

Fitting was the fact that Joe Rushforth's son Dan played on LeRoy's first championship team in 1969. A full circle had taken place. Joe and my brother Carl were on Zion's first team, I played on Zion's first championship team, and Dan played on the second championship team. It kept everything even between the Rushforth and Osmon families.

**Zion, The City** – Zion had its ups and down as did many small towns in the Midwest over the years. Not long after we graduated, a low period was occasioned by the closure of the cookie factory and the Sears TV plant. Many cutbacks, including high school sports, took place. When a nuclear power plant was built on the shores of Lake Michigan on 25th Street, the revenues from that plant brought prosperity back to town. After 20 years, it too closed down and the city once again fell into a slump.

For a number of years the downtown area was boarded up as many stores went out of business. Under new leadership, Zion took an aggressive approach to bringing in new businesses and renovated the downtown area. Once again it has life and vivacity as in the days of the 50s. The population is now 22,000 and the town is thriving.

In 1987, the Illinois Chapter of the American Atheists filed suit against Zion City, citing that its city seal, which contained a cross, a dove, and the phrase "God Reigns", was unconstitutional. In 1992 the U.S. Supreme Court upheld a lower court decision that the city seal violated the principle of separation of church and state and that the Christian symbolism must be removed. The decision devastated many of the long time residents of this Beautiful City of God. Thank God my Mother was not living at the time to see it happen.

## The Osmon Family

My Father crushed several vertebrae in his back while laying a cement driveway for a friend at the age of 58. The initial operation was botched and he was flown to the Mayo Clinic as an emergency. After the operation he was told he would never walk again. To this pronouncement he replied, "Go to hell!" With the assistance of braces on his legs, he was walking one year later. He retired to Newport Richie, Florida to escape the cold of Northern Illinois. He had a stroke in 1965. I was stationed in Panama at the time and was able to fly home to spend a week with him at the hospital. God blessed me twice by allowing me to spend time with both my Dad and Evan Ellis at the end of their lives. My Dad died about a month after I went back to Panama. He is buried in North Chicago near the Great Lakes Naval Training Facility which I think is appropriate. It was the Navy which brought him to Zion in 1918. He was interred in a very moving military funeral. I still have the American flag and the shells fired from the M-1s at the ceremony.

My Mother remained a stalwart in the Zion community for her entire life. She was very active in the Memorial Methodist Church and the Senior Citizens sponsored by the Zion Park Board. She lived in the same house that was built for the Ohneth family in 1917 until her death in 1983. I was stationed in Naples, Italy at the time, but flew home for her funeral. The attendance by all her friends and the emotional words that were given to me about her impact on fellow citizens were gratifying.

One close lady friend of my Mother's told me, "Now, Robert, Beulah has her arm back in heaven."

I would like to think of her that way. She is buried in the North Shore Garden of Memories in Waukegan.

As for me, I have been truly blessed. I was selected to return to the active Navy in 1973. I ended up serving for a total 32 years. I was stationed in Panama, Scotland, Turkey, and Italy. I learned to speak fluent Turkish and excellent Spanish and Italian, with a little Japanese and Russian. I served as a Commanding Officer of a shore station in Springfield, New Jersey. It was a great honor to me to serve my country in this position. I was promoted to the rank of Captain and retired after 27 years of active duty. While I never made a lot of money, I consider the experiences I had beyond compare. As the credit card commercial says "Priceless!"

During those years I was blessed with two sons, Ted and Chris, who also had the experience of growing up in the Midwest. They both attended Tremper High School in Kenosha where they were standout athletes in football, basketball, tennis, and soccer. Both of them went on to graduate from the University of Wisconsin at Madison. Ted became a government contractor and runs a large program in Wallops Island, Virginia as the Deputy Director. After a three year stint as a successful basketball coach in Chesapeake, Virginia, Chris moved to Lakeland, Florida where he now runs a very successful real estate business. They both married intelligent, charming, and lovely ladies, Carol and Stacey. Carol teaches physics and chemistry in Arcadia High School on the Eastern Shore of Virginia. Stacey taught mathematics at Great Bridge High School in Chesapeake, Virginia before marrying Chris. She now tutors part time and helps out in the business. To date I have two lovely granddaughters, Leah and Sydney, and a handsome grandson, Vann. (My father would have loved that. His middle name was Van.)

After retirement from the Navy I worked for the Army for 12 years as a civilian at Fort Monroe, Virginia. My assignment was training the Japanese Army in the US as part of the Foreign Military Sales program. In that job I traveled extensively throughout Japan and other parts of Asia, New Zealand, Mongolia and Australia. I retired fully in June of 2005. I have now lived in Williamsburg, Virginia for eighteen years.

Eighteen years is longer than any other place I have ever lived, save for Zion. But Zion has always held and will always hold my heart. My formative years, my intense experiences, my boyhood friends, my teammates from our championship team, and the lovely ladies in my class are never far from my innermost memories. Many of my wonderful classmates from ZBTHS live there still. Returning to Zion for reunions is always an emotional trip.

I have been blessed throughout the years to receive my share of honors and awards for service to my country and I am honored to be so recognized. But I also consider my being a member of the 1954 team that won Zion's first football championship as one of the major achievements of my life. Then, now, and always, a true and loyal Zee Bee!

> Zee Bees!! Zee Bees!!
> Sting' em! Sting'em!!
> Hurrah for Zion!!!

*The old man would watch them*
*In practice each day,*
*As he dreamed and he wished*
*He could once again play.*

*In his clouded memory*
*It had all been great fun.*
*And to hear him tell it*
*His team always won.*

*But he's simply amazed*
*How these young men can fly*
*And it serves to remind him*
*Time has passed him by.*

*"Ah...but those cheers on game day,*
*His soul can still hear it*
*And he's on that field with them*
*In heart and in spirit."*

Walter J. Brodie
College of William and Mary '57
All American End